1988

IRISH WRITERS
AND
THE THEATRE

IRISH LITERARY STUDIES

IRISH WRITERS AND THE THEATRE

edited by
Masaru Sekine

Irish Literary Studies 23

IASAIL-Japan Series 2

COLIN SMYTHE
Gerrards Cross, Bucks

BARNES AND NOBLE BOOKS
Totowa, New Jersey

Copyright © 1986 by Masaru Sekine, Eugene Benson, Richard Allen Cave,
Emelie Fitzgibbon, Nicholas Grene, Heinz Kosok, Desmond Maxwell, Vivian
Mercier, Christopher Murray, Andrew Parkin, James Simmons, Sumiko
Sugiyama, Robert Welch, Katharine Worth

First published in 1986 by Colin Smythe Limited
Gerrards Cross, Buckinghamshire

British Library Cataloguing in Publication Data

Irish writers & the theatre.
— (Irish literary studies, ISSN 0140–895X; 23)
(IASAIL — Japan series, ISSN 0267–6079; 2)
1. Theatre——Ireland——History——20th century
I. Sekine, Masaru II. Series
792′ .09415   PN2601

ISBN 0-86140-234-0

First published in the United States of America in 1987 by
Barnes & Noble Books, 81 Adams Drive, Totowa, N.J. 07512

Library of Congress Cataloging in Publication Data
Main entry under title:

Irish writers and the theatre

Includes index.
1. English drama—Irish authors—History
and criticism—Addresses, essays, lectures.
2. English drama—20th century—History and criticism
Addresses, essays, lectures. I. Sekine,
Masaru, 1945 –
PR8789.17 1986   822′.009′9415   85 – 23023
ISBN 0 – 389 – 20594 – X

Typeset by Action Typesetting, Gloucester
and printed and bound by Billing & Sons Ltd., Worcester

CONTENTS

INTRODUCTION

IASAIL-JAPAN was established in 1984 and held an inaugural conference at Waseda University in Tokyo in September of that year. This conference was very successful and attended by scholars internationally known for their work on Anglo-Irish literature.

A second conference was held at Chuo University in Tokyo in April 1985 in order to consolidate the establishment of the Japanese branch of IASAIL, only six months after the inaugural conference. The conference was honoured by the presence of the Irish Ambassador, the Representative of the British Council and other distinguished guests.

This second conference was organized by Professor Kenichi Matsumura, the Secretary of IASAIL-JAPAN, and focussed on Irish drama, special guests being invited from both Northern and southern Ireland. Professor Robert Welch, the secretary of IASAIL — the International Association for the Study of Anglo-Irish Literature — represented the parent association and gave one of the opening addresses and subsequent lectures. An impressive performance of Samuel Beckett's *Rockaby* was given by Marie Kean, directed by Ben Barnes. Marie Kean and Ben Barnes then gave a most stimulating and informative joint talk on the work of actors, actresses and directors in the Irish theatre.

On the second day of the conference there was an exciting and inspiring programme entitled 'Two Voices from the Stage'. This included a very lively discussion with demonstrations given by Marie Kean, Ben Barnes, Don Kenny and Hideo Kanze, a Noh actor. Papers were also presented by members of IASAIL-JAPAN during the conference.

This book of essays has been collected to celebrate the second international conference held by IASAIL-JAPAN. It includes papers given at the conference as well as essays contributed by scholars from America, Britain, Canada, Ireland and Japan, widely known for their work on the Irish theatre.

University College
Dublin   Masaru Sekine

IASAIL-JAPAN Series
ISSN 0267-6079; v. 2

DEMYTHOLOGISING CATHLEEN NI HOULIHAN: SYNGE AND HIS SOURCES

EUGENE BENSON

It is a commonplace of Synge criticism that he is a folk dramatist who found the themes of his plays in tales he heard from Irish peasants and fishing people. The provenance of *Riders to the Sea, The Shadow of the Glen* and *The Playboy of the Western World,* for example, derives from stories told to Synge while he was on the Aran Islands. When *The Playboy* was published, Synge, stung by criticism that the play was a libel on the Irish — and especially on Irish women — insisted in the Preface that 'the wildest sayings and ideas in it' were tame compared to the fancies he was accustomed to hear from the peasants.[1] Synge's defence is disingenuous for it ignores the fact that he recasts and, in doing so, sometimes distorts the folk materials that he dramatises. An examination of his radical and characteristic transformation of this material reveals what one critic terms Synge's 'imaginative perversion of ethical ideas', seen most notably in *The Playboy.*[2] Furthermore — and this has not been remarked previously — the changes Synge introduces in his use of his sources affect most strikingly his characterisation of the leading women in his plays. Maurya, Nora Burke, Molly Byrne, Pegeen Mike and Deirdre are symbolically associated with death and are seen as exercising a malign influence on the key male characters. They also constitute Synge's composite portrait of Ireland, which has more in common with the Sheelagh na Gig figures of Celtic literature, which represent both sexuality and death, than with Mangan's romantic Dark Rosaleen or Yeats's queenly Cathleen Ni Houlihan. This aspect of Synge's art — and its influence on plot, mood and theme — has received little critical attention.[3]

Synge regarded *The Aran Islands* as his 'first serious piece of work' but there are three slight pieces among the early writings predating his first visit to the Aran Islands which are distinguished by authenticity of tone and feeling and which

1

suggest the artistic direction he was to take. The first is a poem
from *Vita Vecchia* which ends:

> Cold, joyless I will live, though clean,
> Nor, by my marriage, mould to earth
> Young lives to see what I have seen,
> To curse — as I have cursed — their birth.
>
> (*Prose*, p.19)

The other two pieces are 'On a Train to Paris' and 'Under
Ether'. All three pieces convey the typical Synge note of realism
and morbidity, and a profound sense of mortality which made
him such an outsider. He was isolated from his family because
of his atheism (or agnosticism); he was isolated from the
Catholic Gaelic-speaking peasants to whom he was drawn
because he was of the 'foreign' Ascendancy class; he was
isolated from deep commitments because of his feeling that
human relationships were so fragile — when he was drawn to
women he suffered anguish because of their rejection of him on
religious grounds (Cherrie Matheson), or pain and jealousy
because of differences in age, education and class (Molly
Allgood). His sense of isolation was not only a psychological
trait; it was rooted in a metaphysical view of the world quite
nakedly expressed in his fragmentary verse play, *Luasnad, Capa
and Laine*:

> Every beast
> Is bred with fearful torment in the womb
> And bred by fearful torments in life-blood.
> Yet by a bait of love the aimless gods
> Have made us multitudes.
>
> (*Plays*, I, p.200)

Such was the man who left Paris in 1898 for the Aran Islands
and it is hardly surprising to find that Synge projected his own
obsessively tragic — even morbid — view of life on the people
of the Aran islands. There is little feeling for their fervent
Catholicism which must have given them consolation in times
of distress or tragedy; indeed, Synge substituted a Greek and
pagan *ananke* for the scheme of salvation offered by Catholicism.
The most obvious charcteristic of Synge's Aran account is his
attraction to scenes of violence and death — the burial of an old
woman; Synge in a curragh rejoicing at the danger ('this death,
with the fresh sea saltness in one's teeth, would be better than
most deaths one is likely to meet'); a mother cradling the skull

of her daughter which has just been unearthed while the grave is being dug for her drowned son. Little wonder that Synge was attracted to the story on which *Riders to the Sea*, his first play, is based. It is told in Part Four of *The Aran Islands*:

When the horses were coming down to the slip an old woman saw her son, that was drowned a while ago, riding on one of them. She didn't say what she was after seeing, and this man caught the horse, he caught his own horse first, and then he caught this one, and after that he went out and was drowned.

An incident recorded in Part Three of *The Aran Islands* concerning a drowned man washed ashore 'with one pampooty on him, and a striped shirt with a purse in one of the pockets, and a box for tobacco' gave Synge the substance of the slight subplot relating to Michael's drowning and his identification. Synge's art in utilising such material is of the highest order and his changes anticipate his handling of themes that all the succeeding plays share. *Riders to the Sea* is not about one man drowning but about eight men drowning — the entire male members of a family — thus suggesting a more universal theme of entrapment, futility and death. A second theme — the opposition between Christianity and an older, pagan ethos — is suggested in the reference to the young priest who is characterised as powerless when faced with the strength and cruelty of the god of the Aran islands. 'It's little the likes of him knows of the sea', Maurya says of the priest, '. . . Bartley will be lost now'. As one critic observes, 'Synge, intuitively and by observation, felt the pre-Christian substratum of the Irish mind was still the most potent factor in the conduct of daily life'. [4]

The most striking feature of Synge's rehandling of his folk material is, however, the fact that he links the male with mortality; the women endure while the men die. In fact, we may go further and claim that because Synge postulates death as a 'good', [5] the women acquiesce in the men's death and preside over their burial. The three women of *Riders to the Sea* are Synge's redaction of those archetypal agents of the Greek *ananke* — the three Fates. Bartley is predestined for death, and the puzzling inability of son and mother to communicate — their enmity even — arises from the fact that he is thwarting the funeral plans for Michael and himself. It is only after Bartley's death, in which the mother collaborates and which Michael causes, that Maurya can finally give her last son her blessing. The actress Maire Ni Shiubhlaigh, who played in the original production of the play supervised by Synge, describes Maurya as 'an old woman counting the loss of her sons with a bitter satisfaction',[6] and the critic Seán O Tuama, relating Synge's first and last plays, comments: 'As Maurya has used to the full her six sons as props for her living, so also has Deirdre used to the full her ideal love for Naisi'.[7] *Riders to the Sea* may thus be seen as a counterblast to Yeats's *Cathleen Ni Houlihan*. In Yeats's play the old woman offers the young men death — and immortality. But Synge is not one of the last Romantics and his Maurya, a querulous, bitter old woman, offers only death. 'No man can be living for ever, and we must be satisfied'.

Synge's enduring antipathy towards Christianity — an antipathy shared by his contemporaries, Yeats and Joyce — was masked in *Riders to the Sea* but is evidenced unambiguously in another play he was wrestling with at the same time. *When the Moon has Set*, as Yeats quite rightly remarked, is 'interesting' only in that it shows Synge's 'preoccupation with the thought of death'. (*Plays*, I, p.155.) The central incident in which Synge exploits his favourite framing device — a wake and a wedding — concerns Colum's successful attempt to make a young nun break her vow of celibacy and marry him. Sister Eileen, in a blatantly symbolic gesture, leaves her black veil on the corpse of Colum's uncle and dons a green dress given her by Colum. The wedding — and Synge will draw on its language in the marriages of both *The Playboy* and *Deirdre of the Sorrows* — is a parody of the Christian doxology. 'In the name of the Summer, and the Sun, and the Whole World, I wed you as my wife'. (*Plays*, I, p.177.) Eileen of the green dress is an early crude sketch of Ireland liberated from the tyranny of the Christian church.

Synge first drew the ire of Irish nationalists (including that of Maud Gonne) with his one-act play, *The Shadow of the Glen*, which Arthur Griffith denounced in *The United Irishman* as a 'staging of a corrupt version of that old world libel on womankind — the "Widow of Ephesus" '.[8] Synge's defence, in a letter to Griffith, was based on the argument that his play was a 'modified form' of the story he had heard on the Aran Islands in 1898 and that it differed essentially from any version of the story of the Widow of Ephesus with which he was acquainted.[9]

What is surprising in Synge's redaction of the bare and factual account given him by Pat Dirane is his introduction of a strain of comedy. Dan Burke, the husband, is a figure of comedy (even of farce); the stage business surrounding him — his resurrection, his thirst for a drink of whisky, his presence during Michael Dara's wooing of his wife, the sneeze and the leap from the bed — is the stuff of comedy, and the very staple of the kind of play favoured by the French stage. But Synge wanted more. 'On the French stage the sex-element of life is given without the other ballancing [sic] elements', he wrote. 'I restored the sex-element to its natural place, and the people were so surprised they saw sex only'.[10] But Synge's introduction of the 'other balancing elements' is in conflict with expectations already set in motion by the play's genre. On the level of comedy the two young men, the Tramp and Michael Dara, vie for the hand of the heroine, the young widow (age was not important in the folktale). This is the plot structure of Greek New Comedy which has dominated most comedy. After the rival or blocking agent is removed, there is a comic 'discovery' (*anagnorisis*) followed by the integration of hero or heroine into a society symbolised by a wedding ceremony of some kind. Plays such as Wilde's *The Importance of Being Earnest* and Shaw's *Candida, Man and Superman* and *Major Barbara* share this pattern. But it is not the pattern governing *The Shadow of the Glen* because of Synge's decision to relate the 'balancing elements' to the *shanachie* of the original tale, now the Tramp in the play. His introduction and his central role meant that this short play now had to carry a second thematic burden which runs counter to the comedy and to the mood created by the comedy. That burden relates to the theme of loneliness, sadness and alienation mirrored so powerfully in Synge's Wicklow essays and this double theme is imaged, again, in the wake and imminent marriage of the play.

The introduction of a second theme gave rise to certain problems concerning characterisation and plot, problems which relate primarily to Nora Burke's role. Nora was intended by Synge to be the dominant character, but how is she to be played? There are many references which stress her sexuality, even her promiscuity ('... and if it's a power of men I'm after knowing they were fine men'), and both Maire Ni Shiubhlaigh and Molly Allgood (under Synge's direction) emphasised her sexuality.[11] But there are also a great many speeches that emphasise Nora's intense awareness of time and the imminence of death ('the other balancing elements' not in Pat Dirane's account) which led Yeats to characterise her as a woman 'melancholy as a curlew, driven to distraction by her own sensitiveness'.[12] It was the difficulty an actress must experience in trying to convey such disparate attitudes that caused Daniel

Corkery, an astute critic of Synge, to speak of Synge's "uncertain psychology"[13] in this play.

If we allow such uncertainty, we may also see it manifested in Synge's plot. The dynamics of the opening scene clearly suggest a mutual attraction on the part of the Tramp and Nora and this is reinforced by the jealousy Michael Dara and the Tramp show towards each other. But, inexplicably, the Tramp goes to sleep and the ensuing 'love scene' reveals that Nora is prepared to marry the spineless Michael Dara despite the fact that she is merely exchanging one loveless marriage for another without even the excuse of poverty. When she is discovered by her husband she even offers to remain with him. Her materialism, which seems to differ little from that of her husband and putative lover, is at odds with that sensitivity attributed to her by Yeats. There is a further paradox in the play which reveals uncertainty in its plotting. The play suggests that Nora leaves a repressive household for a new life but the key symbols of the play clearly associate her past and her future with death. Patch Darcy, a powerful and virile shepherd, and former lover of Nora, went 'queer in the head' and was eaten by crows. Peggy Cavanagh went on the road (as Nora will) and ends in poverty and decay. Even Dan Burke, mock corpse, is one with those powerful 'dead' figures who dominate Synge's plays — Michael in *Riders to the Sea*, Colum's uncle in *When the Moon has Set*, old Mahon in *The Playboy* and Conchubar in *Deirdre of the Sorrows* — and his 'resurrection' prefigures Nora's death:

It's lonesome roads she'll be going, and hiding herself away till the end will come, and they find her stretched like a dead sheep with the frost on her, or the big spiders, maybe, and they putting their webs on her, in the butt of a ditch.

(*Plays*, I, p.55)

Synge's handling of the close of the play reveals just how disingenuous he was when he defended his play by claiming it was based on an Irish analogue. The Irish tale he had heard from Pat Dirane ends with a vindication of the husband's rights exemplified in the beating (killing?) of the rival and the 'taming' of the wife. In his study of Synge's use of Irish folklore Seán O Súilleabháin comments that 'Synge's version also differs from the normal Irish ones in which the main episode always ends with the wife and her lover being beaten by the enraged husband ....'[14] Synge outdoes even the cynicism of Petronius' 'Widow of Ephesus' by having Nora cast out on the roads while husband and 'lover' drink together. Yeats praised the play's ending as establishing Synge 'among the men of genius'[15] and indeed it is a strikingly original touch (characteristic of the later plays) which anticipates the tendency of contemporary dramatists to recreate traditional genres and to cross tragedy and comedy.

In *Riders to the Sea* Synge had touched briefly on the opposition of the Christian ethos and older Irish folk beliefs; in *The Tinker's Wedding* that opposition becomes the central theme. The play is based on a story recounted in the essay 'At a Wicklow Fair' which tells of a tinker and his woman who agree to give a priest a half sovereign and a tin can if he will marry them. When they fail to provide the can, the priest refuses to marry them. Although no reason is given in the Wicklow story as to why the tinkers want to get married, Synge chooses to stress this point. He does so because while the original story emphasised the roguery of the tinkers and only by implication the avarice of the priest, his purpose was to demonstrate the superiority of the 'natural' religion of the tinkers to that Christianity represented by the priest.

Once again it is the women who dominate this play but again Synge seems uncertain of Sarah Casey's psychology. Sarah claims she wants to be married because it's springtime 'and it's queer thoughts maybe I do think at whiles'. Later, however, she claims that she wants to be married because it would give her that respectability she has been denied — 'and from this day there will be no one have a right to call me a dirty name . . .'. Because Sarah is a violent creature of action, unsuitable for articulating Synge's anti-clericalism, he introduced a new character into the Wicklow story, Mary Byrne, to be the sometimes too explicit mouthpiece for this anti-clerical theme. The problem is that this theme conflicts with the rollicking farce associated with Sarah's attempt to get married and threatens to drown its farcicality in didacticism. Finally, Synge even has Mary proffer a new reason for Sarah's behaviour that is totally out of character, a reason related to Synge's own extreme sense of mortality rather than to the play's dynamics:

Is it putting that ring on your finger will keep you from getting an aged woman and losing the fine face you have, or be easing your pains . . .?
(*Plays*, II, p.37)

The outcome of the clash of values represented by the Priest and the tinkers is never in doubt because Synge's sympathies are all too clearly with the tinkers and the freedom they represent. There is a further difficulty here. The play's outcome goes against the grain of comedy which usually affirms the normal and the established. Audiences at *The Tinker's Wedding* may temporarily suspend moral judgement but they expect an ultimate vindication of the 'normal'. But Synge's return to the *status quo ante* (Sarah as enlightened pagan) deflates not only a moral expectation but an esthetic expectation nourished by the play's genre. Now that we are accustomed to the theatre of the absurd, audiences might well approve of *The Tinker's Wedding*; in Synge's own time the wrenching of the genre proved too strong for what is essentially a slight farce.

The best things about it are the brilliant portraits of the two women. Sarah in her beauty and violence anticipates Pegeen Mike, and Mary anticipates the Widow Quin in her bawdiness and humanity. It is her humanity that prevents Sarah from murdering the Priest; in a letter to Elkin Mathews Synge wrote that it might be better not to publish *The Tinker's Wedding* because a character in it was 'likely to displease of a good many of our Dublin friends';[16] Synge was probably referring to the character of the Priest but it is as likely that Dublin would have seen the character of Sarah, putative priest killer, as another libel on womankind, and especially on the women of Ireland.

Synge's first full-length play, *The Well of the Saints*, fuses a number of themes that he had already explored — the outsider versus society; pagan or folk belief versus the church and the priest; the clash of reality and dream, truth and illusion. What is striking is the way in which Synge dramatises these abstract issues, investing them with a sombre and powerful theatricality. The source material, drawn from Petit de Julleville's *Histoire du théâtre en France au moyen-âge*, tells the story — which Synge summarised in Notebook 30 — of two men, one blind, one a cripple, who agree that the blind man will carry the cripple, each one thus compensating for the other's deficiency. When they are cured by a saint the cripple curses him because he has now lost the services of the blind man.

The movement and meaning of the play are reflected in the opening stage directions which indicate that the action takes place at a crossroads. There is a wall 'with gap near centre' and the ruined doorway of a church. Clearly the crossroads and the ruined church represent that opposition between the tramp and the priest that is such an enduring theme in Synge's work. But there is also throughout Acts I and II a complementary and sustained attack upon marriage. Martin and Mary Doul, husband and wife, both blind, live in a world of illusion. When their blindness is cured by the Saint, they see each other for the first time and the scene in which they do so is the most brutal Synge ever wrote. The 'discovery' here has a dual function. In formal terms Synge is parodying the conventional 'discovery' scene in comedy where hero and heroine are united in a moment that clearly implies marriage. But Synge is also using the 'discovery' to subvert 'normal' values, values associated in this case with marriage. The exchange between husband and wife in the 'discovery' scene is savage and couched in animal imagery:

I'm telling you there isn't a wisp on any grey mare on the ridge of the world isn't finer than the dirty twist on your head. There isn't two eyes in any starving sow, isn't finer than the eyes you were calling blue like the sea.

(Plays, I, p.97)

The dominant woman in the play is Molly Byrne, a beautiful young woman, and foil to Martin Doul. In Act II Martin's attempted seduction of Molly is developed in a series of speeches that represent Synge's most explicit statement on the nature and relationship of illusion and reality and on the supremacy of the imagination. Their exchanges here anticipate the love scenes between Pegeen and the Playboy where she is won, temporarily, to his vision. In this seduction scene Martin is trying to win Molly away from Timmy the Smith and, by extension, from the Saint and the Christianity he represents. 'Put your can down now, and come along with myself', Martin pleads, 'for I'm seeing you this day, seeing you, maybe, the way no man has seen you in the world'. *(Plays, I, p.117.)* One is reminded of that scene in Joyce's *A Portrait of the Artist* where Stephen rails against E.C. for preferring the priest to him. 'To him she would unveil her soul's shy nakedness, to one who was but schooled in the discharging of a formal rite rather than to him, a priest of the eternal imagination, transmuting the daily bread of experience into the radiant body of everliving life'.[17]

Synge's scenario for the play called for the scene between Martin and Molly to be 'traPoetical' but the climax is brutal rather than tragic. Martin *'with imploring agony'* beseeches Molly not to shame him by telling Mary what he has confided in her. But Molly betrays his confidences prefiguring Pegeen who will also betray the Playboy ('God give you good rest', Pegeen tells him at the close of Act I, 'till I call you in the morning when the cocks will crow'). One critic remarks that in Synge's last three plays he 'rebukes the cruelty of beautiful women'.[18]

Act III features a debate between the tinker and the Saint, and, although Synge gives the time of the play as *'one or more centuries ago'*, there is a strong suggestion that the debate is really between paganism and Christianity in early Ireland. It is the same debate that Sir Samuel Ferguson (sympathetic to Ireland's druidic tradition) dramatised in his epic poem *Conal*, Yeats in *The Wanderings of Oisin* and *Supernatural Songs*, Joyce in the Druid/St. Patrick debates of *Finnegans Wake*. Martin's rejection of the Saint and Christianity is symbolised by his striking the tin can holding the holy water from the Saint's hand. But he loses Molly to the Saint and as he and Mary set out on the dangerous roads to the south the villagers pass through the ruined doorway of the church to witness the wedding of Molly to the 'almost elderly' Timmy the smith. The women of Ireland, Synge suggests again, sell themselves in marriage as Nora Burke sells herself to Dan Burke, Molly to the smith, Pegeen to Shawn Keogh.

In his programme notes for the 26 January 1907 premiere of *The Playboy of the Western World* Synge stressed that he had used 'very few words that I have not heard among the country people', further claiming that 'the same is true also, to some extent, of the actions and incidents I work with. The central incident of *The Playboy* was suggested by an actual occurrence in the west'. (*Plays*, II, p.363) It is instructive to compare the account of this incident as recorded by Synge in *The Aran Islands* with its recreation in *The Playboy* in order to gauge fully the audacity of his extravagant and morally nihilistic recreation of the original folk source.

In *The Aran Islands* account Synge, commenting on the psychology of the story of a parricide who was sheltered from the police by the islanders, makes three points. 'This impulse to protect the criminal is universal in the west' because of 'the association between justice and the hated English jurisdiction.' Secondly, these primitive people will only commit a crime when 'under the influence of a passion which is as irresponsible as a storm on the sea'. (*Prose*, p.95) The third point, Synge states admiringly, is that the islanders remained 'incorruptible' in spite of a reward which was offered. His changes to this account could hardly be more iconoclastic. In the Aran version the parricide is excused, in *The Playboy* it is glorified. With

Sophocles' *Oedipus Rex* as analogue, Synge celebrates what traditionally had been regarded as the most heinous of crimes — the killing of a parent. Where Oedipus had been punished by blinding and exile, the Playboy is rewarded by the approval of the villagers, the admiration of the local girls and the courtship of two fine women who want to marry him precisely *because* of his act of parricide. And here Synge daringly introduced a new motif totally lacking in the Aran account but present in his Sophoclean model — incest. Indeed Synge long played with the idea of having the Playboy marry the Widow Quin, a transparent surrogate for the Widow Casey who suckled him for six weeks.

Another radical difference shows how Synge changed the Aran account. There the islanders are innocent and idealised, as is proved by their loyalty in not informing on the parricide. But Synge's Mayo peasants are a degenerate, lawless and cruel breed who will betray the Playboy to the police to save themselves. At first glance Pegeen Mike may seem an exception to the people who surround her. She is Synge's finest female creation, a challenge to any young actress. But too many actresses, influenced by Christy's speeches praising her beauty, err in giving her a glamour and beauty she possesses only for the Playboy. If Pegeen is glamourised or if Christy is cast as a conventional romantic lead, the play will lack that brutality which Synge always felt was an essential element of the poetic. The actress Maire Nic Shiubhlaigh, writing in 1955, commented on this tendency to play the love scenes according to the conventions of romantic comedy. 'Produced nowadays, the play is done as a comedy — and is invariably successful. When it was given for the first time it was played seriously, almost sombrely, as though each character had been studied and its nastiness made apparent'.[19]

'Nastiness' may not be the fittest word to apply to Pegeen Mike's character — 'cruelty' seems more appropriate. She is a virago feared by all and the violence of her nature is expressed in images of brutality and torture. She is more cruel in her questioning of Christy about his crime than the men: 'You never hanged him, the way Jimmy Farrell hanged his dog from the licence and had it screeching and wriggling three hours at the butt of a string?' The scene at the opening of Act II where the village girls come bringing gifts to the Playboy has a sunny, idyllic quality to it which changes abruptly on the entry of Pegeen Mike, 'the fright of seven townlands' as she describes herself. Jealous of the village girls, Pegeen blackmails Christy with a description of the burial of a hanged criminal: 'When it's dead he is, they'd put him in a narrow grave, with cheap sacking wrapping him round, and pour down quicklime on his head, the way you'd see a woman pouring any frish-frash from a cup'. As Farrell hung his dog, she suggests, so will the law hang Christy: 'it'd make the green stones cry itself to think of you swaying and swiggling at the butt of a rope'. Pegeen, then, is acting entirely in character when she betrays Christy by handing him over to the law, the 'hated English jurisdiction' — 'or the lot of us will be likely put on trial for his deed to-day'. (*Plays*, II, p.169) — and when she binds him down and burns him with fire.

If we view Pegeen in this light, it is easier to see how *The Playboy* is of a piece with Synge's earlier plays. Christy is a solitary, a tramp, like Martin Doul who was stoned by the villagers and driven away, like Patch Darcy who went mad in the solitude of the Wicklow glens. It is precisely because Christy must not be incorporated into a brutal and degenerate society (as Molly Byrne was in *The Well of the Saints*) that Synge once again moves in Act III from domestic comedy to ironic comedy whose basic motif is the expulsion of the *pharmakos* or scapegoat from society. It is a mordant touch — a touch of genius — that the hero, Christy, is rescued by his 'dead' father from the heroine. But once again Synge, in thus switching genres, has imposed a severe burden on his audience because while the play represents Pegeen in this light, she is presented very differently, through Christy's eyes, in various speeches where the imagery suggests comparison with the Virgin Mary and with virginal Ireland herself. 'Amn't I after seeing the love-light of the star of knowledge shining from her brow', Christy declares, 'and hearing words would put you thinking on the holy Brigid speaking to the infant saints'. (*Plays*, II, pp.125–7) The phrase, 'star of knowledge', a direct borrowing from Hyde's *Love Songs of Connacht*, and the reference to St. Brigid, co-patron saint of Ireland, clearly suggest that Pegeen is a type of Irish womanhood.[20] But that she should turn out to be an informer (the most dreaded word in Ireland's political lexicon) was a shock to contemporary audiences, a shock both in terms of an aesthetic expectation denied and an historical and cultural expectation deflated. These different views of Pegeen are paralleled in Joyce's *Portrait* where Stephen debunks Davin's idealised vision of Ireland as Gaelic and Catholic: ' — Do you

know what Ireland is? asked Stephen with cold violence.
Ireland is the old sow that eats her farrow'.[21] In the same
exchange he indicates that he will try to escape from Ireland. In
like fashion Christy's escape from Pegeen represents the
triumph of a joyous pagan ethic over the debased Christianity
of the Mayoites. Seamus Deane puts the point well when he
describes the play's theme as 'the emergence of a Gaelic pagan
myth hero from a Christianised, anglicised and therefore
impoverished community'.[22]

It might seem, on first glance, that the epic story of Deirdre
lay outside the character of Synge's genius. He wrote to Molly
Allgood in December, 1906, of the new direction he proposed to
take. 'My next play must be quite different from the P.Boy I
want to do something quiet and stately and restrained ...'[23] But
Synge had long been attracted to the subject, having made a
translation of the Irish text, *The Fate of the Children of Uisneach*,
on Aran, 1900–1901, and when he reviewed Lady Gregory's
Cuchulain of Muirthemne he praised her version of Deirdre's
lament over the dead Naisi and his brothers as 'one of the finest
passages in the book'. (*Prose*, p.369) Then, too, he must have
been attracted by the central motif of the story, a prophecy that
the woman Deirdre would cause the death of the sons of Usna
and the destruction of Emain Macha. There were other
influences too we may speculate — the challenge offered by a
subject retold by such writers as Sir Samuel Ferguson, A.E., and
Yeats and by the realisation that in retelling the Deirdre legend
a writer was dealing with a myth central to Ireland's culture and
history. As one critic puts it,' ... the passive, mournful Deirdre
held some interior implication which made her a more
acceptable national figure than Grania. It was a poet's business
to explore the popular significance of Deirdre, as Yeats, A.E.,
and Synge did'.[24]

Although Synge had great difficulty in the composition of
Deirdre of the Sorrows, he never doubted the originality of his
approach. 'My treatment of the story of Deirdre', he said vis-à-
vis Yeats's and A.E.'s versions, 'wouldn't be like either of
theirs!'[25] It would be different because he was going to impose
on his source materials his own characteristic pre-occupations
and attitudes; his new, and final, play would be a recapitulation
of themes, motifs and dramatic methods that had coloured his
entire *oeuvre*. In most versions of the Deirdre legend, for
example, Naisi had played the dominant role, Deirdre a
subservient, passive one.[26] But in Synge's recension of the story

Deirdre is cast in the same masterful role as his other women —
Maurya, Nora Burke, Sarah Casey, Molly Byrne and Pegeen
Mike. She has the wilfulness of Sarah Casey and Molly Byrne
('When all's said it's her like will be the master till the ends of
time'), the melancholy of Nora Burke ('There's no safe place,
Naisi, on the ridge of the world ...'), the hard bitterness of
Maurya ('I'm well pleased there's no one this place to make a
story that Naisi was a laughing-stock the night he died'). The
brutality she shares with Pegeen Mike is apparent in her
seduction of Naisi where she plays off the intensity of present
passion against the dreadful fate that lies in store for them. 'I'm
a long while in the woods with my own self', she tempts him,
'and I'm in little dread of death, and it earned with richness
would made the sun red with envy'. (*Plays* II, p.211) The play
is structured by the same framing device Synge had used so
often — a wedding which closes Act I and the open grave of Act
III.

Act III was intended by Synge to be 'Rider-like' (*Plays*, II,
p.370), and its most astringent touch — the quarrel of Naisi and
Deirdre by the grave — parallels Maurya's quarrel with Bartley
when she refuses to bless him before he goes to the fair. Like
Maurya, Deirdre fears that she may be cheated of Naisi's death
and so be denied the mythic role in which she has cast herself
throughout the play. 'Go to your brothers', she commands
Naisi, '... the hardness of death has come between us' (*Plays*,
II, p.255), and when Naisi hesitates she denounces him for
cowardice and disowns their seven years in Alban as a 'dream'.
When Naisi, *frantic*, answers her, his language has the same
passion as that which characterised the violent exchange
between Martin Doul and his wife when they first saw each
other:

It's women that have loved are cruel only, and if I went on living from
this day I'd be putting a curse on the lot of them I'd meet walking in
the east or west, putting a curse on the sun that gave them beauty, and
on the madder and the stone-crop put red upon their cloaks.

(*Plays*, II, p.257)

What is characteristic also about Synge's treatment of the
legend is the way he once again imposes his own morbid view
of life on it. The dominant *leitmotif* of the play is a horror of life
which brings ageing, an inevitable loss of beauty, and a
consequent blighting of love. The motif of the first love scene
between Deirdre and Naisi is 'welcome to destruction' (*Plays*, II,

p.370) and, as in *Riders to the Sea*, life is continually described in images of decay, death in images of life. 'Draw back a little from Naisi who is young forever', Deirdre chants over the dead sons of Usna, and as Emain Macha burns in the background while she prepares her suicide, one has a sense of the charnel house and of a glorification by Synge of a death-wish which had always haunted his work.[27] One senses too that with *Deirdre of the Sorrows* Synge had come full circle, that in his final demythologising of Ireland Deirdre is as powerfully linked with death as Maurya, Nora Burke, Molly Byrne or Pegeen Mike. Consciously or unconsciously, Synge in delineating Ireland's features had drawn a portrait where she is revealed as Sheelagh na Gig summing up in herself sexuality and death, desire and horror.

NOTES

1 *J.M. Synge: Collected Works*, vol. IV, ed. Ann Saddlemyer, p.53. All quotations from Synge's published writings are taken from *J.M. Synge: Collected Works*, general editor Robin Skelton, vols. I–IV. Oxford: Oxford University Press, 1962–68. References will be included in the text.

2 Maurice Bourgeois, *John Millington Synge and the Irish Theatre*. New York: Blom, 1965, p.203.

3 See Seán Ó Súilleabháin, 'Synge's Use of Irish Folklore', in *J.M. Synge: Centenary Papers, 1971*, ed. Maurice Harmon. Dublin: The Dolmen Press, 1972, pp.18–34. Ó Súilleabháin's approach to Synge's use of Irish folklore is quite different to mine. For another view of Synge's treatment of women, see Ann Saddlemyer, 'Synge and the Nature of Woman', in *Woman in Irish Legend, Life and Literature*, ed. S.F. Gallagher. Gerrards Cross, Bucks: Colin Smythe, 1983, pp.58–73.

4 Seán Ó Tuama, 'Synge and the Idea of a National Literature', in *J.M. Synge: Centenary Papers, 1971*, p.9.

5 See Eugene Benson, *J.M. Synge*. London: Macmillan, 1982, pp.61–62.

6 Maire Nic Shiubhlaigh and Edward Kenny, *The Splendid Years*. Dublin: Duffy, 1955, p.55.

7 Seán Ó Tuama, *op.cit.*, p.7.

8 D.H. Greene and E.M. Stephens, *J.M. Synge, 1871–1909*. New York: Macmillan, 1959, p.148.

9 *The Collected Letters of John Millington Synge*, vol. I, 1871–1907, ed. Ann Saddlemyer. Oxford: Clarendon Press, 1983, p.106.

10 *Ibid.*, p.74

11 C.E. Montague, *Dramatic Values*, London: Methuen, 1911, p.54.

12 W.B. Yeats, *Essays and Introductions*. London: Macmillan, 1961, p.300.

13 Daniel Corkery, *Synge and Anglo-Irish Literature*. Cork: Mercier Paperbacks, 1966, p.128.

14 Ó Súilleabháin, *op.cit.*, p.19.

15 Quoted in Greene and Stephens, *op.cit.*, p.177.

16 *Collected Letters*, p.105.

17 James Joyce, *A Portrait of the Artist as a Young Man*, ed. Chester G. Anderson. New York: Viking Press, 1968, p.221.

18 Herbert Howarth, *The Irish Writers: Literature and Nationalism, 1880–1940*. New York: Hill and Wang, 1958, p.218.

19 Nic Shiubhlaigh, *op.cit.*, p.81.

20 Nicholas Grene, *Synge: A Critical study of the Plays*. London: Macmillan, 1975, pp.63–64.

21 Joyce, *op.cit.*, p.203.

22 Seamus Deane, 'Synge's Poetic Use of Language', in *J.M. Synge: Centenary Papers, 1971*, p.139.

23 *Collected Letters*, p.250.

24 Howarth, *op.cit.*, p.106.

25 Greene and Stephens, *op.cit.*, p.277.

26 For a detailed study of the Deirdre legend, see H.V. Fackler, *That Tragic Queen: The Deirdre Legend in Anglo-Irish Literature*. Salzburg: Universität Salzburg, 1978.

27 Howarth, p.236, speaks of a 'Götterdämmerung hue' to *Deirdre of the Sorrows*.

DRAMATISING THE LIFE OF SWIFT

RICHARD ALLEN CAVE

Writing a history play poses a considerable problem of balance: how to give an adequately detailed exposition of proven historical facts but to do so incisively and imaginatively enough that a thematic interpretation of those facts may evolve and develop, inviting the audience to reach beyond mere fact to engage with the process of history in ways that will illuminate their lives in present time. History plays must be felt to have a purpose. In some measure the problem is one faced with the composition of any play: the correct balancing of exposition and development, the presentation of circumstantial facts and the sensitive interpretation of them. But, unlike the wholly fictional subject, the exposition of historical events can be tested against external sources and if the dramatist wishes to gain a fair hearing for his interpretation of the lives of historical persons then he must be scrupulously accurate in his use of data. There is a further but related problem of decorum: the need to find an apt tone and language for the dialogues invented for historical figures, when often the outline of events seems powerful enough (one is inclined to write *dramatic* enough) in itself so that any attempt to realise it in theatrical terms seems doomed to failure. Decorum is again a problem facing any dramatist but the difficulty in composing a historical play is particularly acute. The risk of unintended bathos always looms close, similarly the jarring anachronism.

For the dramatist tackling the life of Swift as his subject, the difficulties are compounded by the enigmatic nature of the received facts; too much of the life is veiled in silence, perhaps deliberate secrecy. The known data are haphazard and the all-important connections between them a matter for conjecture. The dilemma is to find explanations that cover all the facts and not a random selection. This challenge is clearly part of the attraction of the subject and a surprising number of playwrights

17

have attempted it since Yeats's pioneering *The Words Upon The Window-pane* (first performed in November, 1930). Insofar as the enigmas relate to the most intimate details of Swift's life in his relations with Stella and Vanessa, while the known facts focus on his public self as Dean, politician and writer, attempts through the medium of drama to explain the pattern of his existence tend rapidly to define and evaluate the life in relation to the work. More precisely the plays tend to be exercises in judgement, where the life is weighed in the balance against the values and moral fervour explicit in Swift's work. Finding an explanation of the facts by this method, since the writer's chosen role is as castigator of human folly, vice and sickness, becomes a means of defining the value of Swift's achievement for the modern age. Swift's preferred literary mode was satire, the mode that more explicitly than most literary forms is an exercise in judgement. The extraordinary nature of some of the known facts of Swift's life and the alarming discrepancy between these and the professed attitudes of his writing has meant that much biographical study of Swift has tended sooner or later to place the Dean on trial. The Bible advises: Judge not that you be not judged[1] — a maxim that effectively explains the attraction of Swift's life as a subject for biographical or dramatic investigation and the dangers involved in such an undertaking. Dramatising the life of Swift is an exercise in judgement in every possible sense of the phrase: a high degree of scruple and decorum must obtain in the conception and the treatment of the subject, matched with a meticulous attention to the response of the audience. With any historical subject a decision must be made about how much exposition to include and how much knowledge one can assume an audience will bring to a play; in the case of Swift, fact, folk-myth, conjecture and opinion can exist in varying degrees in the minds of a potential audience (especially an Irish one). It is almost too easy for such an audience to *judge*. What the dramatist must do is to alert his audience to the dangers of holding to stock responses or reaching after quick conclusions; and instil in them too an awareness of the need for scruple and decorum, for fastidiousness and a respect for the complex niceties involved in judging the quality of another human life.

If the present essay in exploring these ideas further concentrates on but three of the many plays about Swift, it is because they exist as a conscious dialogue with each other: *Yahoo* was conceived in part as a reply to *The Words Upon The*

Window Pane and drew heavily for its theatrical technique on an early play of Denis Johnston's, *The Old Lady Says 'No!'*; Lord Longford's and Yeats's plays excited in Johnston a preoccupation with the details of Swift's biography (to which, significantly, he brought the mind of a trained barrister) that culminated over many years in *The Dreaming Dust*. Furthermore each play addresses itself to the tasks of guiding audience-opinion and defining the relation of a past age to the present by in varying ways exploiting then shattering the conventions of stage realism that normally in the nineteen-thirties and forties were employed in dramatising historical subjects. All three plays are unashamedly *theatrical* but purposefully so, the theatricality being metaphorical, symbolic of surreal, psychological and metaphysical apprehensions about the process of history that traditional modes of realism cannot readily convey. All three dramatists intimate their personal vision of the reality that is Swift through psychic shock, when their plays veer alarmingly away from the comfort of a predictable style towards a phantasmagoric world where enigma, inconsistency and paradox are the rule. The audience's predisposition to believe that character is a definable entity is held rigorously in question, the concept of a 'stable ego',[2] which alone would make viable the quest for precise explanations of Swift's conduct, is under fierce attack. Reality is shown to elude the mind obsessed with categories of behaviour; the flamboyant theatricality of the plays is designed rather to inspire more flexible and imaginative appreciations of Swift as man and author. If one is wary of applying the word 'compassion' to the plays, it is because all three dramatists make one aware that in writing about Swift they are dealing with experiences ultimately so tragic that they lie beyond the reach of anyone's pity. Compassion in such a context comes to seem a vulgar, demeaning response.

☆ ☆ ☆

When Yeats published *The Words Upon The Window Pane* he prefaced it with an introductory essay that is more a commentary on Swift's place in the history of ideas than on the play. These same opinions, quoted verbatim in the Intro-duction, are voiced in the play by a Cambridge student who is a caricature of a pedant in the making, comically obsessed with his thesis and his verdict about Swift. Enthusiastically, and with dogmatic emphasis, he propounds the view that Swift's life can be explained in terms of a fear of degeneration and madness not only personal but political: 'He foresaw democracy, he must have dreaded the future'.[3] Confronted by an experience of Swift during the seance, young Corbet's excitement knows no bounds: his hypotheses, he believes, have been confirmed. That Swift's spirit was weighed down with anguish, that his condition was the horror of knowing himself an eternal outcast, has made no impact on Corbet whatever: unabashed in the presence of such mental and spiritual pain, he rejoices in the accuracy of his own powers of reason. A sceptic to the last (Swift to him was after all 'the chief representative of the intellect of his epoch free at last from superstition'[4]), Corbet refuses to consider that anything miraculous has happened; instead he congratulates the medium as a brilliant actress and scholar; turning to the bewildered and exhausted woman as to an academic peer, he tries to debate with her in all seriousness: 'Was Swift mad? Or was it the intellect itself that was mad?'[5].

The preposterousness of the moment, pitched as it is between the comic and tragic, is characteristic of Yeats's strategy with this play. A grim epiphany is made manifest through the seance to a motley collection of individuals who miss the meaning of the event because they are deaf to all but the promptings of their own egos, seeing in it either the frustration of their petty hopes for enlightenment (Patterson anxiously seeks confirmation of the belief that 'they race horses and whippets in the other world'[6]) and spiritual guidance (Abraham Johnson seeks a blessing on his work 'as the work of Moody and Sankey was blessed'[7]) or the chance of a vicarious thrill like Miss MacKenna who longs to say with Job that the hair of her head stood up as a spirit passed before her face. They are all granted a vision of the after-life but it diverges so greatly from their expectations that they recoil from its impact and seek the shelter of their obsessions. Much of Yeats's drama is preoccupied with defining heroism as the power to transcend the frailties and follies of self-hood — Deirdre, Emer, Cuchulain, the Lame Man in *The Cat and the Moon* are all thus 'blessed'.[8] Not so the guests at Mrs. Henderson's seance: they are cranks dabbling in occult experiences beyond the reach of their imaginations or intellects. Yet all six roles — Dr. Trench, Miss MacKenna, Corbet, Patterson, Mrs. Mallet and Johnson — are wonderful character studies of a kind in which Abbey actors have always excelled. And this again would seem to be part of Yeats's strategy. For many years now the Abbey had ceased to be a stage where Yeats's visionary and heroic drama might be played; realism, and, as far as audience's preferences went, *comic* realism was the favoured house style. It was a nicely calculated effect to establish the situation of the seance in that comic mode to allay an audience's suspicions and allow their scepticism some play. Indeed Yeats's power to anticipate and control an audience's reactions throughout *The Words Upon The Window Pane* is masterly, especially at the point the seance begins. Mrs. Henderson, the medium, is no crank: she speaks with dignity in a voice that is calmly matter-of-fact explaining precisely what pattern the ritual will follow. That her 'control' is 'a dear little girl called Lulu who died when she was five or six years old'[9] who suddenly speaks *through* her in a high-pitched, ringing tone prompting the newcomer, Corbet, to mocking laughter ('Nobody must laugh. Lulu does her best but can't say big long words'[10]) deftly provokes, and so syphons off, any tendency to nervous giggling in the audience. The tone confidently sustained till now in the comic, satirical mode, suddenly begins to fluctuate wildly. Lulu summoning her first 'contact' (Mrs. Mallet's late husband) surprisingly jokes about his baldness and his odd appearance but then becomes hysterical at the approach of 'the bad man who spoilt everything last time'; everyone reacts with dismay, but Lulu is instantly calm again, distracted by a 'young lady' in strange clothes that she supposes with childish glee must be 'fancy dress'. The woman, says Lulu, is 'all bent down on floor' near to Dr. Trench, 'that old man with glasses'. Trench has preserved a bemused, avuncular aloofness from the other guests, though they have treated him with marked deference as a leading authority on spiritualism: his quiet response now — 'No, I do not recognise her'[11] — seemingly so simple yet so profound in its implications, eerily projects the play into a new dimension of awareness. Scarcely has the audience had time to respond to this before Lulu is shrieking helplessly at the return of 'that bad old man', her high-pitched terror being violently cut off by the intrusion through Mrs. Henderson's lips of a bass voice savage with pent-up fury.

Several of Yeats's Japanese-inspired dance-plays invite the audience to experience the drama by engaging with it in a creative relation, calling it all 'to the eye of the mind' so as to penetrate beyond the stylised surface and realise its metaphorical, symbolic dimensions. Trench clearly possesses that 'inner eye' that we call vision; and as a new play, (Yeats's

most daring experiment is stylisation) a play for the voices of
Swift and Vanessa, takes over the stage, the audience are tacitly
enjoined to develop that heightened sensitivity too. Yeats's
ideal drama was one where character is defined in a moment of
passionate intensity; such a drama intrudes here into the comic
realist mode, re-possessing the Abbey stage at the first
performance with an awesome power that immediately exposes
the spiritual triviality of the style it displaces. Try as the other
characters will to reassert a claim on our interest once the seance
is over, they are judged and found wanting for their insensitive
response to the play they have witnessed with us, wanting in
imaginative courage to face the truths to which the medium in
her trance gives them privileged access. The world of tragic
intensity having taken over the stage now has absolute
dominance: the guests hasten to depart; the medium, alone and
exhausted, tries to rest with a cup of tea but first her
consciousness and then her very form are possessed by the
spirit of Swift in its agony reaching out from beyond the grave,
even now as in his old age a being despised and rejected of men,
cursing the day of his birth yet avid for life not extinction. It is
a strange, troubling conclusion, like many of Yeats's endings
designed to go on resonating in the minds of the audience after
the fall of the curtain. In that sense we are as much *possessed*,
haunted by Swift's restless spirit as Mrs. Henderson. Whether
the moment affects us as more than melodrama depends on
how we interpret the play-within-the-play.

Two episodes occur: Swift arguing with Vanessa; Swift
meditating in Stella's silent presence; the one is fraught with
tormented and tormenting questions, the other relaxed, serene.
The tonal contrast is somewhat deceptive, for both episodes
illuminate the same quandary in Swift's mind. With Vanessa he
is seeking some explanation of her conduct in writing to ask
Stella if she is in truth Swift's wife, an act that shows passion
triumphing over decorum and self-control. The offence
astonishes, bewilders, outrages Swift: that the pupil whose
mind he stocked with classical virtues should stoop to the
behaviour of a 'common slut'! Vanessa excuses herself on the
grounds of her passion and appeals for understanding to the
passion in Swift. She longs to bear his child and seeks to cool
his rage by making him touch her body; but Swift cries out for
God's help to resist temptation so that 'he may leave to
posterity nothing but his intellect that came to him from
Heaven'[12]. His triumph, he claims, was to have 'rebuilt Rome'

in Vanessa's mind, so that, when they were together, 'it was as though I walked its streets'; but that was all a delusion; she was acting the model pupil simply to spend longer hours in his company; it was all a pose to feed her passion. She has outwitted him for all his brilliance of intellect[13]. Sensing his vulnerability and that she has him trapped, Vanessa's cajoling turns to a subtle form of blackmail: 'Jonathan — no man in Ireland is so passionate. That is why you need me, that is why you need children, nobody has greater need. You are growing old. An old man without children is very solitary. . . . but a few years if you turn away will make you an old miserable childless man'[14]. She has recognised in him the fear of loneliness and age that underlies his need for intimacy and she rebels against his self-control which will not allow him to satisfy that need, however pressing, except in a form of intimacy that is resolutely chaste and stoical. He speaks of a fear of latent madness and of passing that pollution on to a child but she argues that the essence of life is risk. That is to challenge his fundamental belief that the educated man can build Rome in the mind, can define for himself a pattern of living that transcends the accidental, the wayward, the impulsive. He refuses to live as she in the moment. Yet why does Swift not take refuge from his irrational fear and needs in a Rome re-built in his own mind? Why must he create in another the image of his ideal? With Vanessa the attempt failed; the creation was but an ill-fitting mask that, slipping awry, revealed a terrible reality.

If the hope Swift voices in this episode is a cruel delusion, so too is the serenity that quietens his spirit in Stella's company. Her birthday ode to Swift, whose words are etched upon the windowpane, celebrates his success in fashioning her in the image of his ideal:

> You taught how I might youth prolong
> By knowing what is right or wrong;
> How from my heart to bring supplies
> Of lustre to my fading eyes;
> How soon a beauteous mind repairs
> The loss of chang'd or falling hairs,
> How wit and virtue from within
> Can spread a smoothness o'er the skin.[15]

Unlike Vanessa, Stella has had the inner resources to transcend her passionate self, suppressing her subjective needs to meet and satisfy what she believes to be Swift's more urgent longing.

She is in a sense his masterwork, the creation of a woman such as Brutus and Cato would have loved, an embodiment of sacred not, like Vanessa, profane love, a woman loved according to the soul. That, unquestioning, unresisting, she gave her *self*, the consciousness that is her quintessential being, to Swift is an act of profound heroism. She has given all and asks for nothing — no children, lover, husband — offering a total intimacy beyond the limited pleasures of the flesh. Like Vanessa, Stella has intuitively divined Swift's innermost fear, as Swift with her can afford to admit: 'You understand that I am afraid of solitude, afraid of outliving my friends — and myself'[16]. Where Vanessa takes advantage of that knowledge, Stella responds creatively, which shows a greatness of courage and of heart. Recognising the extent of the sacrifice involved makes Swift doubt his own worthiness, especially given the fact of Vanessa's importance to him and his perverse attempt to exact from her what Stella willingly gave. The completeness of Stella's love throws into sharp relief the limitations of his own capacity for loving, rooted as it is in the negative emotion of fear. The continuing fact of her sacrifice eases his doubt that he has wronged her in accepting so rich a gift — not to accept would have been a greater wrong. But what if Stella die and her gift no longer sustain him? Again, as with Vanessa, his mind has no fortification against chance. Stella is his 'best' self and his most deep-seated dread is of outliving not only his friends, but *himself*. He may soften that dread with a vision of Stella presiding over his deathbed — 'Yes, you will close my eyes, Stella, but you will live long after me, dear Stella, for you are still a young woman, but you will close my eyes'[17] — but the anxious repetitions intimate the mind's awareness that it is hypnotising itself with delusions, giving itself up to the irrational. Stella died young and, deprived of her sustaining presence, fear and doubt took possession of Swift leaving him as we see him finally, an image of decay and dissolution, the Rome of the imagination sacked and in ruins. That ideal had always to be a *shared* ideal; and there lay its vulnerability.

Dr. Trench asserts that hostile influences at seances are usually occasioned by spirits caught in a passion of remorse. If that is Swift's condition then remorse is a misprizing of Stella's sacrifice. Love whether as Vanessa offers it or as Stella does, is a recognition of a human need; but Swift's Rome-inspired philosophy argues for a resoluteness that rises above human needs; the very gift of love is consequently a threat to his mind's rule. Swift's cursing like Job the day of his birth is an attempt to deny those human needs, all part of the hope that he will commit to posterity nothing but the fruits of his intellect. But as the play shows it is Swift, the man, that exerts a powerful fascination over future ages. His restless spirit reaches out from the past for understanding; yet a full understanding such as Stella showed demands imaginative sympathy, and sympathy implies awareness of an object in need of our charity. Yeats's Swift dreads solitude and loss, yet he excites nothing but detestation as a monster, a possessive ghost and bad, old man in the medium and her guests. But what of the theatre-audience? Confronted by Swift as he takes possession of Mrs. Henderson, an old man caught in the position of a foetus counting on his fingers relentlesly the many Ministers that were his friends who now are 'gone', how are we to respond? In the utterly subjective state of madness he is beyond the reach of pity; moreover compassion will invariably aggravate, not relieve, his condition. One is astonished in retrospect at the economy (in terms of dramatic structure and stage-time) with which Yeats has rendered so intricate a mind as Swift's, trapped in a labyrinth of guilt of its own devising that betrays itself to ever subtler forms of irrationality in its efforts to avoid acknowledging the necessary irrationality of so much human behaviour. Ultimately that mind finds guilt even in the fact of having been born and that is a denial not only of human need but of human worth. Swift 'outlives' himself to a most tragic extreme, a state to which, as Dr. Trench avows, only God can bring peace. Mrs. Henderson's final prayer in her own character expresses far more than she realises: 'It is sometimes a terrible thing to be out of the body, God help us all'[18].

☆   ☆   ☆

Lord Longford's *Yahoo* is in many ways a simpler, more traditional type of historical biography than Yeats's play; but it too has its strategies of surprise. As the title implies, Lord Longford calls more overtly than Yeats on Swift's writing to define his attitudes and behaviour. The play opens with Swift reading to Stella and Mrs. Dingley from *Gulliver's Travels*: 'But when I behold a lump of deformity and diseases, both in body and in mind, smitten with pride, it immediately breaks all the measures of my patience'[19]. The first act of the play enters the story at its climax with Vanessa's arrival at the Deanery with the fatal letter asking Stella to affirm or deny that she is Swift's wife; act two concentrates on Swift's ride to Celbridge and the return of the letter. This effectively brings the curtain down on a confrontation first with Stella, then with Vanessa, where Swift's patience twice breaks all measure.

Confronted in his home by a dishevelled Vanessa arguing 'You cannot forbid where my heart commands'[20], Swift cannot but agree to deliver the letter to Stella himself. He can maintain no dignity in her vengeful presence. She leaves; he reads the letter which is unsealed, summons Stella and offers her marriage on the express condition that their relations become no more intimate than they have ever been. They are married rapidly and secretly by Dr. Berkeley, whereupon Swift gives Stella the letter to which she writes a simple, accurate reply; she collapses briefly in sobs but by an exertion of will stands and departs, observing 'I will not earn the scorn of Dr. Swift as I have already earned his indifference'[21]. Swift, alone, prays: 'What have I done that I, of all men, should never know peace upon this earth?'[22] There is self-pity here, but why is it activated? Longford's technique is to offer a series of actions which through their very sequence gesture at explanations without precisely defining them. The marriage is undertaken in cold fury at Vanessa's act. It seems based on a careful, if rapid, calculation at first; but is the proper interpretation rather that Swift is asserting his authority over Stella, willing her into marriage merely as protection against Vanessa's wild emotionalism? His final anguish seems self-regarding; but is this because he has abused the sacrament of marriage in a way unworthy in one of his calling? or because he has abused Stella's trust, caused her infinite pain and compelled her to assume a Stoic indifference?

At Celbridge Swift finds a Vanessa who, vengeful before, is shameless now in defeat, and determined to make him admit 'you did right to make me love you'[23]. Their shared past pours forth as she demands an explanation of his treachery:

What claim has she to you, she, the cold prude with whom you might not speak alone, lest her icy virtue should be smirched? What claim has she that I have not? I have loved you, I have longed for you. You have sworn, too, that you loved me more than any living creature. You have left me without a shred of reputation, and then you say that I am less chaste than she, I, whose only desire was for marriage with the idol of my heart.[24]

When her rage becomes dangerous and vindictive — 'Do not kill me if you value your peace' — he takes refuge in his position as a clergyman: 'I am answerable to my Creator and not to any creature of His'. To her this is the ultimate insult — cant, which it doubtless would be in the average man but, as the play's opening intimated, Swift has tried always to live above the average man's nature, his Yahoo self, which it is beyond Vanessa's power to understand, swayed as she is by the tides of emotion. She can only interpret everything he says on a personal level ('Am I then as nothing in your sight?'), resorts to self-pity ('It is not my fault that I was born passionate') and finds solace shrewishly cursing Stella as 'the chaste Yahoo, the virtuous monster!'[25] Her hysteria having run free-rein through the gamut of negative emotions, she faints away leaving Swift horrified at her breakdown: 'Vanessa, have I done this to you?' It is a terrible awakening: implicit in that awareness of the need to accept responsibility for it all is a recognition that his philosophy can afford no lasting refuge from common humanity, that that humanity will judge him by its own standards as cruelly inhuman and not raise its standards to judge him on his own merits. The question to Vanessa is a dreadful admission of the gulf that has always existed between them.

The final act is preoccupied less with Vanessa's than with humanity's revenge on the Dean. To the throbbing of a drum like a wildly palpitating heart, time contracts and expands with the terrifying freedom of nightmare. Vanessa dies bequeathing *Cadenus and Vanessa* to posterity; Stella dying begs Swift to make public their marriage and is refused; jubilant crowds seen celebrating Swift as Nationalist hero over the Drapier letters disappear into a darkness peopled with cackling Yahoos; Vanessa's ghost howls in torment, while Death carries off Stella's corpse; hollow voices declaim the lists of Swift's dead friends; others, jeering, rehearse the names of his numerous biographers; in a spotlight a mother and uncle are seen enthusing over a Christmas edition of *The Little Folks's 'Gulliver'*; in another an academic lectures on Swift's 'dung complex'. When normality returns, Swift, insane and senile, is surrounded by a mob of eighteenth-century sightseers before whose indifference he pleads 'I am what I am.' Act III by shifting from realism to expressionism actualises the full horror of Swift's perception that concludes the previous act, in which momentarily he sees himself as others will judge him. It is a bitter spiritual journey he travels between that awakening and the moment he stands humiliated before the hostile mob. And what is the tone of that self-appraisal — 'I am what I am'? Defiance? Self-pity? Humility? Is the spirit that formerly had no patience with humanity proud still? or purged? Lord Longford believes more certainly than Yeats that Swift has gone 'where savage indignation can lacerate his heart no more' (thereby picking up interestingly the theme of Yeats's *The Countess Cathleen* that God judges by the motive not the deed). As darkness descends again a stentorian voice question, 'Dost thou repent thy sin?' and Swift, caught in a dim light, sits in judgement on himself, resolving all the enigmas, all those questions about tone and motive that the dramatic stucture of the play has invited us to ask:

> And I'll confess my folly and my hate,
> That yet proceeded from excess of love,
> And love and hate and folly I'll throw down
> Before Thy shining feet, all greatness gone,
> And ask for mercy on this little thing,
> The soul of Swift, this petty human soul,
> This soul that's weak and naked as all souls,
> That at the last is no more what I am,
> But a dim nothing in the Hand of God. [26]

☆   ☆   ☆

Denis Johnston is the only dramatist of the three with a precise theory about Swift's life (a theory that he has substantiated at length in a work of scholarship, *In Search of Swift*): that Swift was an illegitimate child of Sir William Temple's father and therefore Sir William's half-brother and consequently Stella's uncle, a fact he kept secret for fear of charges of incest being brought by his enemies against him and Stella, incest then being a capital crime. Johnston's *The Dreaming Dust* has a most flamboyantly complex dramatic structure, the brilliant theatricality having an incisive intellectual aim. A group of Dublin intelligentsia have come together to act a morality play about the Seven Deadly Sins to gain funds for St. Patrick's Cathedral and after the performance find themselves, prompted by the environment close to Swift's and Stella's graves, deep in a discussion about the Dean. The mood is tensely antagonistic; each is found to sympathise with one particular individual in Swift's story — Brennan, Stella, Vanessa, Mrs. Dingley, Berkeley, Tisdall or

Ford — but no one favours the Dean himself, though each actor feels free to offer an explanation of Swift's life from the standpoint of his own partiality. Which view is the accurate one? Each actor can substantiate his opinion by reference to a specific episode in Swift's life arguing that the moment defines the whole. They agree to improvise and play out their suppositions so each stage-manages the others in a presentation of the scene he personally feels is representative. A sinister pattern emerges: each actor shapes his episode so as to show Swift guilty of a particular sin; but each scene shows the historical personality most favoured by that actor to be subtly more guilty of the sin than Swift; ironically too the sin each accuses Swift of indulging is the one that actor played in the morality interlude — Brennan matches with Sloth; Anger with Vanessa; Envy with Berkeley; Pride with Stella; Gluttony with Tisdall; Avarice with Dingley; Lust with Ford. The theatrical idea of type-casting takes on symbolic resonance, illustrating how perception, and beyond that, judgement are subjectively conditioned reflexes, that acts of creative sympathy are rare movements in the human psyche. It is seen to be impossible not to stand judged oneself by one's mode of passing judgement and immensely difficult to achieve that state of detachment through which, perceiving this most profound of limitations in the self, one might admit (as Swift does at the play's end) 'I am that I am'.

Significantly it is Stella as Pride who breaks the deterministic pattern by literally disrupting the action, saying it is impossible to continue: she has no role to play worth speaking of. It is partly wounded professional vanity (as the leading actress she has had no 'big' scene) but it is more: in the various scenes Stella has been nothing but an attendant presence; confronted by a potentially 'big' moment — receiving Vanessa's famous letter — the actress is at a loss *how* to play; till now her parts have served a variety of dramatic functions for others but they add up to nothing out of which she could consistently 'build a character' in the Stanislavskian sense and find a logic and dramatic momentum which would help her intuitively to handle this particular crisis. Advised that she is being asked to behave in a fashion that has 'satisfied generations of biographers', she replies tartly: 'Swift's biographers — not hers'[27]. The actress's dilemma is the index of a greater moral and metaphysical dilemma which the play now seeks to resolve. Till now Swift's behaviour has appeared complex, quixotic, inconsistent, pantomimic, outrageous, cruel but always eluding the precise definitions imposed on it by the various actors. But the very dynamism, the unpredictability of his actions has excited attention. Pride chooses as her personal scene Stella's discussion with Swift whether she should marry Tisdall; arrogantly she insists it be played as a flashback interlude before she copes with the incident of Vanessa's letter. It is here that Johnston introduces his theory about Swift's paternity. Inevitably Stella asks why, if Tisdall is an unsuitable match, Swift does not wed her himself; she accuses him of pride: 'The vicar of Laracor could never condescend to marry a bastard'. When Swift prevaricates, sympathy wells up in her: 'I understand, and I would never reproach you, if only you would be honest'[28]. And Swift confesses the truth about their relationship and imposes secrecy on her for fear of the dangers that might ensue, given their long though chaste friendship. The question of Tisdall remains and, sensing Swift's detestation of the man, Stella decides to decline the offer and remain Swift's lifelong companion to his profound gratitude: 'Esther ... my star ... my dear, dear Stella. You are honouring me more than any man has ever been honoured, I am more deeply moved than I can say'[29]. With great clarity of mind she sees the difficulties before them but promises to honour the obligations of their chosen relationship. However — a subtle gesture of pride — she doubts Swift's strength of purpose: 'You are a man, Jonathan, and men sometimes need a love that I will not be able to give you'. The pride in her calls out the pride in him: 'I am *more* than man. I am Jonathan Swift, and I want nothing from any human being that I cannot get from you'[30]. A rash bargain — as years later the receipt of Vanessa's letter proves to Stella. Again pride governs her response: she agrees to be a martyr to Swift's needs, urges him to marry Vanessa but publish the fact of their blood-tie. She cannot be humiliated more after his marriage, but the publishing of his bastardy will expose him to humiliations he cannot face. The bargain binds them and he rejects Vanessa.[31] Pride works most deviously when its subject is personal honour.

Swift is seen by Johnston to be guilty of all the sins in part and yet that merely defines his essential humanity. As is seen most poignantly in the scenes with Pride, the working of sin is intricate: the unconscious sin that controls one character may impel that individual to create the circumstances in which another being may unwittingly succumb to the same sin; then what right has the one character to sit in judgement on the other for falling into temptation? All the characters are defined by more than the sum of their sins, just as they are more than the water and bones that the Sexton scoffingly says is the essence of man. To see merely the guilt in Swift is to miss the superhuman courage that their pact together exacted from both Stella and Swift, to fail to understand the self-disgust Swift felt at the emotional cost of it all to Stella and Vanessa, or to marvel that such a wide-ranging creative inspiration could have its roots in personal despair and antagonism. The Swift who utters 'I am that I am' is infinitely greater than the sum of travesty images of the Dean that the actors assemble. Johnston's control of his dramatic structure is that of a virtuoso as his series of fractured scenes shift with apparent effortlessness between different dimensions of reality in time present and time past, while he evolves a complex metaphysical conceit relating the processes of the theatre with the workings of the moral imagination. Like Yeats and Lord Longford, he ultimately exploits dramatic structure to define the limitations and dangers of the biographical impulse, conscious always that the biblical maxim — Judge not that ye be not judged — imposes a heavy burden of responsibility. The theatricality of all three plays is a means of ensuring that their audiences share that burden of moral awareness too. The theatricality of these dramatisations of the life of Swift is in each instance the index of the dramatist's integrity.

NOTES

1 St. Luke. vi. 37.

2 The term is D.H. Lawrence's and refers to dated, nineteenth-century conceptions of character in fiction, which his own novels sought to challenge.

3 W.B. Yeats: *The Words Upon The Window Pane*. Dublin: The Cuala Press, 1934. p.57. The play was first performed at the Abbey Theatre on 17 November 1930 in a production by Lennox Robinson; Yeats personally tutored May Craig in the role of Mrs. Henderson.

4 *Ibid*. p.57.

5 *Ibid*.

6 *Ibid*. p.36.

7 *Ibid*. p.40.

8 See a detailed discussion of this theme in the present writer's Chatterton Lecture, 'Yeats's Late Plays: "A High Grave Dignity and Strangeness" ', *Proceedings of the British Academy*. Volume LXVIII (1982) London: Oxford University Press, 1982. pp. 299–327.

9 *The Words Upon The Window Pane*. p.45.

10   *Ibid*. p.46.

11   *Ibid*. p.47.

12   *Ibid*. p.51.

13   Swift's misreading of Vanessa's character is as preposterous as Corbet's misjudgement of Mrs. Henderson and is one of many ironic parallels in the play.

14   *The Words Upon The Window Pane*. p.51.

15   *Ibid*. p.54.

16   *Ibid*.

17   *Ibid*. p.55.

18   *Ibid*. p.58.

19   Edward Pakenham, Lord Longford: *Yahoo*. Dublin: Hodges Figgis and Co., 1934. p.1. The play was first performed at the Gate Theatre in a production by Hilton Edwards, who also played Swift. Edwards's fine account of his production in 'Production', an essay he contributed to *The Gate Theatre, Dublin* (Edited by Bulmer Hobson, Dublin, 1934. pp.37–8) makes it clear how much Longford drew on Johnston's *The Old Lady Says 'No!'* which was an earlier success at the Gate and which Edwards describes at length in the same article, p.29.

20   *Yahoo*. p.18.

21   *Ibid*. p.26.

22   *Ibid*.

23   *Ibid*. p.36.

24   *Ibid*. p.35.

25   *Ibid*. pp.40–1.

26   *Ibid*. p.65.

27   Denis Johnston: 'The Dreaming Dust', *The Dramatic Works of Denis Johnston*. Volume 1. Gerrards Cross: Colin Smythe Ltd., 1977. p.296.

28   *Ibid*. p.298.

29   *Ibid*. p.300.

30   *Ibid*. p.300.

31   When Johnston reviewed *The Words Upon The Window-pane* for *The Spectator* (30 November, 1934) when the text of the play was published in *Wheels and Butterflies* he made a significant observation: 'As in Lord Longford's *Yahoo*, the author attempts to invent an imaginary conversation between the Dean and Vanessa on the occasion of his ferocious final visit to Celbridge — a conversation which of its very nature can never surpass the actual reported facts — the arrival, the letter flung down, and the silent departure'. With Stella, Johnston felt, Yeats was 'on firmer ground'. When Johnston came to devise his own Swift play, he cleverly allowed the power of the situation to speak for itself as he suggests here. In separate spotlights we see Vanessa anxiously awaiting Swift's appearance, convinced that he will come and determined to be 'ready with an answer for anything he may say', while Swift himself continually reiterates in time with hoof beats the phrase 'and I shall say ... I shall say'. The stage direction then reads: 'They meet in the centre of the frontstage. For a moment he stares at her in baffled torment'. After a long pause, Vanessa urges him, 'Speak to me. Haven't you got anything to say?' 'He throws down the letter and vanishes out of the light' Overwhelmed by the pain of the interview with Stella in which they have reaffirmed the importance of the pact to them both and with the pain of rejecting Vanessa whom he wishes to marry, Swift can say nothing.

ALL CHANGE: CONTEMPORARY FASHIONS IN THE IRISH THEATRE

EMELIE FITZGIBBON

The contemporary fashion collection from the House of Theatre, Ireland, (quite) Limited, indicates that confusion of styles and modes, that movement of top arbiters of taste from one house to another, in short, that ferment which indicates that some creative activity may be about to take place; so far however, no one is very sure what form it will take. But what is fashion? Perhaps it may be described as the external trappings in the search for a new and coherent style, an over-riding force which may ultimately give expression not only to the personal but also the national. Accordingly, the ferment, the multiplicity of fashions in the contemporary Irish theatre may be a good sign, a shake up of traditional pre-conceptions of selfhood and nationhood which may produce a new style of Irish theatre and drama at once indigenous and international: a style which has passed through the repressive constrictions of the mid-century and gives expression to an Ireland open to international influences as widely diverse as the impact of multinational industries and the colour symbolism of the pop-video. The presiding genius of the Irish Literary Theatre, which, like comfortable tweeds, has remained solid and secure in its self-image, rejecting what it perceived as 'trivial' changing styles from London, New York, Europe, is beginning to recede and with it goes, albeit very slowly, the dominance of a verbal, naturalist theatre. Dramatists and directors are increasingly becoming aware of the impact of the visual, the image, on their audiences, and there is a corresponding growth in the theatrical quality of Irish drama. The word is still dominant but at least the word is becoming embedded in the image.

Fashions, however, always go in cycles and there have been many attempts before this to extend the self-imposed parochial boundaries of the Irish theatre — Yeats looked to the international quality of Noh, Synge to atavistic roots in Greek and medieval literature, O'Casey to Expressionism, the early Gate Productions to the best of European stage and lighting design, Beckett to ... well, to Beckett — but the trend has always been back to naturalism and, of all the arts, theatre is most vulnerable to the dictates of fashions and audiences. The author or the painter may work in a garret if he has the minimum basic materials but the basic materials for the dramatist involve the expense of theatre, actors, designers and all the concomitant energies which are needed to transform script into theatrical image. Funding and education are, as ever, the necessary *données* which can, if the will is present, harness the renewed energies of the Irish Theatre and turn fashion into style; only through these can an audience be encouraged to attempt styles beyond the comfortable and the traditional and the manifest energies of the companies be sustained into a future. Funding dictates fashion, and few theatres, and no theatre companies, can continue existence without government grant aid.

... the ultimate arbiter

The dominating force in establishing theatrical style in Ireland at the moment is the Arts Council.[1] On the extremely limited amount of money made available to it from central government funding, a relatively new (1984) Arts Council is forced to parcel out its meagre offerings in order to keep professional theatre alive. The largest grant goes to the Abbey and its subsidiary, the Peacock, but the money is scarcely enough to keep a showcase national theatre alive let alone to encourage it in new developments. And the Abbey has problems within its own structure. It retains the legacy of its foundation as a state theatre in the anachronistic 'permanent and pensionable' status of its staff, a situation which is unreal in prevailing theatre economics. Under its last Artistic Director, Joe Dowling, the Abbey made some attempts to broaden its perspective and to move from its traditional naturalistic, verbal forms into styles and directions more attuned to Ireland of the 1980s. It gave a platform to some of the best modern Irish writing; it employed guest directors to extend the style of the company and gave audiences access to new modes, in, for example, Patrick Mason's inventive production of Tom McIntyre's *The Great Hunger* in 1983 or Michael Bogdanov's production of *Hamlet* in 1984; it encouraged young directors such as Ben Barnes or Raymond Yeates to work on new texts in the experimental Peacock Theatre; finally, it encouraged new emergent playwrights through its production of new full-length and one-act plays. A former script editor, Sean McCarthy, and, more recently, Christopher FitzSimon have brought into prominence the talents of Farrell, Donnelly, Reid, McGuinness and Aodhan Madden.

Unfortunately, at the time of writing, Joe Dowling has resigned as Artistic Director of the company, thus following a great tradition of imaginative artistic directors. The poor financial standing of the Abbey has forced the board into a conservative position: there has been a cut-back on the number of new plays to be staged and an embargo put on the employment of 'outside' directors and designers. In essence, unacceptably stringent conditions have mitigated against artistic considerations and, ultimately, it will be the image and standards of our national theatre which will suffer. Perhaps, however, it is also time to consider the nature and function of a national theatre, and, with the Abbey poised uneasily between white elephant and *eminence gris*, the theatrical institutions of Ireland should come under fresh and clear scrutiny from the Arts Council.

... '*Who's in, who's out*'

The fact that the Abbey soaks up a high percentage of the Arts Council's Drama budget means that the remainder is spread very thinly indeed, with preference given, quite rightly, to companies rather than to buildings. Consequently, second-guessing what particular fashion is favoured by the Arts Council has become almost an 'in-house' sport among theatre companies, where levels of funding are insecure and reviewed from year to year. 'In' in 1985 are the Druid Theatre Company from Galway, an outstandingly successful ensemble company built around the imaginative force of director Garry Hynes; Smock Alley, a newly formed group of actors working without a director on imaginative adaptations of classical scripts; Rough Magic, a very young company developed from Trinity Players and favouring new international work; and TEAM, the major theatre-in-education company in the republic. The Arts Council, in other words, encourages both alternative and conventional theatre, both metropolitan and regional, both established and newly formed. With no likelihood of an increase in its budget, however, indeed with an effective decrease, the Arts Council may be forced into a position where it will have to make unpalatable decisions and choose to invest its money in a small number of major companies rather than sharing meagre resources among the many deserving cases. If this happens, to the inevitable impoverishment of theatre in Ireland, then the government may finally be forced to emerge from behind the pious platitudes of the *soi-disant* Minister for the Arts and to confront the problem of Arts funding head on. The knock-on effect of inadequate funding is clearly observable. Central government allocated a small amount to the Arts; the Arts Council allocates a proportion of that to its Drama sub-committee; the sub-committee decides on the prevailing fashion houses; the fashion-houses decide on the fashionable dramatists. While the Arts Council at least tries to encourage a range of fashions it can keep the potential of new styles, companies, writers alive; if it is forced to consolidate it might well stultify the energies it had begun to generate.

... *Couturiers hauts et bas*

The great predominating fashion in Ireland for verbal theatre is still, unfortunately, the presiding design among Irish playwrights. Flashes of alternative, imagistic theatre are beginning to appear here and there, perhaps most notably in the works of Tom McIntyre, *The Great Hunger* (1983) and *The Bearded Lady* (1984), but still the fashion dictates that theatre communicates primarily through the word and, accordingly, the dramatist is the most important person in the theatrical hierarchy. Given that, one cannot but notice that, in the parade of fashionable dramatists, urban and, preferably, northern are definitely 'in', while southern and — heaven forbid — rural are decidely *passé* — unless directed by Garry Hynes at the Druid. Dramatists, then, are reflecting a new view of society in Ireland, a society which is shaped by socio-economic factors totally unlike those which formed its self-view in the past and many of the new plays are investigative of social and political issues. Frequently, the complex human relationships among a group of workers, the tensions and inter-personal difficulties they experience among themselves, are pitted against their mutual response to management figures, as in Frank McGuinness's *The Factory Girls* (1982) and Martin Lynch's *Dockers* (1982) and *Lay Up Your Ends* (1983), a vivid evocation of the lives of Belfast women working in the linen factories in the early part of the century. The forces which shape society, too, are also opened to examination: for example, the educational system over the past twenty years and the problems which its failure has created for both individual and society are ruthlessly exposed in Neil Donnelly's *Silver Dollar Boys* (1982), while the plight of teachers alienated by age, temperament and class from their pupils is aired in J. Graham Reid's *The Hidden Curriculum* (1982). Changing views of the place of women in what has been a heavily male-dominated society are reflected in plays which examine the status of women as well as the paradoxes within our own visions of ourselves, plays as widely different in style as Mary Halpin's *Semi-Private* (1983) and Mary Elizabeth Burke-Kennedy's *Women in Arms* (1984), in which she ironically sets today's women working in the meat department of a supermarket against the mythical armed women of the Tain saga. Plays on political issues tend to concentrate, inevitably, on the origins and results of the northern conflict, and texts are beginning to emerge which give expression to the political instability of the country and its dangerous tolerance of social and political violence. Equally inevitably such plays run the danger of stereotype and polemic: the 'message' overrides characterisation and plot; the background violence becomes a mere dramatic device to heighten the audience's sensibilities. Occasionally, however, plays emerge which give true dramatic expression to the terror, and these provide potent images of a society torn apart by itself. *The Interrogation of Ambrose Fogarty* (1981) by Martin Lynch, for example, attempts generally quite successfully, to contrast the 'ordinariness' of everybody involved in the interrogation with the horrendous dynamic generated by the situation itself; while the constant threat of terror provided a particularly resonant background to the appalling violence of J. Graham Reid's *The Closed Door* (1980) with its powerful central symbol: a door closed against knowledge, against emotion, against help. As always in Irish drama, the past is a territory where dramatists can better see the present, and playwrights continue to explore the origins of emotions and ideologies in plays such as Brian Friel's *Translations* (1980) and, more recently, Stewart Parker's *Northern Star* (1985) and Frank McGuinness's *Observe the Sons of Ulster Marching towards the Somme* (1985).

So much, then, for the subjects of our fashionable writers, but what of the writers themselves? One glance at the 1985 collections will indicate a definite hierarchy: the Paycocks; the Peacock Parade; the Birds of a Different Feather, and, finally, the Birds in the Bush. The Paycocks are the dramatists who are the immediate centre of attention; critics — and even other people — wait anxiously for their newest creations and there is much analysis of their designs, their quirks and their oddities. At the moment the Paycocks are three in number: Friel, Leonard and Murphy.

Brian Friel must rank as the major contemporary Irish dramatist and expresses in a style which is totally his own the conflicts of a society and of individuals undergoing an unprecedented and rapid period of change. And Friel is consistent in his visions. His Ireland is, like Gar in *Philadelphia, Here I Come!* (1964), split between private and public conceptions of itself; his people, too, are dislocated and ill at ease with themselves. As a dramatist, however, Friel is careful to avoid the trap of public statement except in so far as it is embodied in his characters; he delves into 'the dark and private places of individual souls'[2] in order to express their unease. His central characters are always individuals, individuals trapped by their background, their history and their language yet the dramatist is at pains to show us that none of these traps is fixed and definite but are structures which each individual makes for himself. The pattern was observable in the plays of the 1970s but has become more articulate and persuasive in his three latest plays *Translations, The Communication Cord* (1982) and his lyrical and evocative 'translation' of Chekov's *Three Sisters.* In these plays Friel shows language as well as society in a state of flux; meaning has little consistency in an ambiance where perceptions of reality are so coloured by individualism that they cannot be shared. *Three Sisters,* for example, depicts a society which holds within itself the inevitability of change and disintegration. In their small despairs, the characters are locked in separate worlds, never impinging, never giving, never receiving. His Russians are like his Irish balanced somewhere 'between the absurd and the momentous':[3] 'We Russians', says Vershinin, 'are a people whose aspirations are magnificent; it's just living we can't handle'.[4] And his living is bounded by change, societal and linguistic. In *Translations* the surrounding world of Gaelic Ireland is irrevocably changed by the linguistic regularisation of placenames and the move from a Gaelic and classical past into an anglicised future is accepted by the pragmatist and resented by the idealist, while the lovers are held apart by a barrier of communication, a barrier they cannot pass. In the first scene of the play a baptism, 'the ceremony of naming' is about to take place, and, ironically, what the play examines is the ritual of un-naming, the elimination of identity. It is a beautiful and a chilling play, an evocation of a recognisable landscape at the point of change and a startling and visual embodiment of the impossibility of true communication between people. Friel continues this investigation in his latest play, *The Communication Cord*, by inverting *Translations*, or rather by placing it in front of a distorting mirror where tragedy becomes farce, the ideal Ireland a 'restored' cottage, the voice of age and experience the cliches of an absurd politician. Communication is, naturally, impossible, and the central character Tim Gallagher — perilously close to a caricature of one of Friel's colleagues — can articulate paradoxically only by linguistic analysis: Tim can define a 'response cry' in words but cannot recognise it in reality. *The Communication Cord*, though uncharacteristically flawed in construction, is interesting in the questions it provokes. This society where people fail to understand one another, where politicians are locked in a false view of the glorious past, must, inevitably, like the cottage come tumbling down.

If Friel is concerned with the impossibility of communication between characters who are in themselves articulate, then Thomas Murphy aims, in Seamus Heaney's words, 'to raid the inarticulate',[5] to put on stage tortured beings who break the silence of the character only with great difficulty and yet who have individual dreams locked within themselves. In the depths of their distress, his characters have a vision, a yearning to sing, yet time and again they are forced to suppress the vision and to dam up the song. Murphy is an uneasy and a challenging dramatist. He frets against the constrainst of form and is never secure in his own voice, constantly changing and altering his plays as they go from performance to performance. In the last two years he revised that strange play *The Blue Macushla* for the Red Rex Company at the 1983 Dublin Theatre Festival; he reworked his 1968 play *Famine* for Druid Theatre Company; he has revised *The White House* for that company, under the title *Conversations on a Homecoming* (1985); he has also published a 'revised edition' of *Sanctuary Lamp* (1976, 1984). All these reworkings and revisions might seem to indicate a lack of coherent artistic vision but yet this is not so; Murphy's vision is coherent in its tortured expression of 'small' insignificant people, their torments thrown into sharp relief by whatever form of theatre he chooses to employ. Then, suddenly, in 1983, came *The Gigli Concert*, one of the most extraordinary plays to have been

written in Ireland for some time which immediately crystallised
all those longings, yearnings, inadequacies and despairs of his
earlier characters into the three potent characters of J.P.W. King,
an Irish Man and Mona. Murphy at his best discovers magic in
the ordinary. J.P.W. approaches the magical in his suicide
attempt, his attempt to uncover his soul: 'This night I'll conjure.
If man can bend a spoon with beady steadfast eye, I'll sing like
Gigli or I'll die'.[6] Perhaps there is a time for each person to sing
and Murphy like J.P.W. found his in *The Gigli Concert*: 'And
wait, wait, wait ... and wait ... until the silence is pregnant
with the tone urgent to be born'.[7]

In spite of the international status achieved by Hugh Leonard
his plays have currently somewhat slipped from fashion.
Leonard is a superb craftsman, as is evidenced from his earlier
plays *Da* (1973) and *A Life* (1979), but in his last two plays to
reach the national stage, *Kill* (1982), a satiric farce on Irish
political identity, and *Scorpions* (1983), three inter-related one-act
plays with 'a sting in the tail', craftsmanship did not conceal
somewhat threadbare ideas and impoverished characterisation.
Leonard, like Friel, writes predominantly in a naturalistic mode
and while he lacks warmth in his creations — and indeed has
created several memorable cold-blooded characters such as the
eponymous Da and Drumm in *A Life* — he is paradoxically a
gifted comic writer. Like his British counterpart, Alan
Ayckbourn, Leonard is always on the verge of a masterpiece,
constantly underrated, and, like Ayckbourn too, he chooses to
expose man's petty foibles and limitations largely through the
medium of comedy. He is also skilled at the adaptation of other
people's work both for television and the stage: his clever
version of Flann O'Brien's *The Dalkey Archive* called *The Saints go
Cycling in*, originally presented in 1965, was one of the most
successful revivals of 1984 in a production by the Gate Theatre
Company. Given his undoubted skill, his flair for looking 'quite
through the deeds of men', and his ear for dialogue, Leonard is
unlikely to be out of fashion for very long.

... the Peacock parade

Pride among the Peacocks, those dramatists whose work has
been encouraged by the Peacock Theatre, is Bernard Farrell.
Farrell's is a gentle and benevolent view of a changing Ireland,
his a tolerant voice which speaks of a new society familiar with
encounter sessions (*I Do not like thee, Dr. Fell*, 1979) holidays
abroad (*Canaries*, 1980), industrial disputes (*All in Favour said*

No!, 1981), pirate radio stations (*Then Moses Met Marconi*, 1983), and new middle class unemployment (*All the Way Back*, 1985). Characters from an older form of society haunt the peripheries of his plays but are largely ineffectual and merely reinforce the tolerant but inevitable stripping of human illusions which provides the essential comic material for his plays. His style is what John Barrett aptly calls 'thoughtful comedy'.[8] He does not aim to attack with polemic the erosion of values or the nouveau petty concerns of a comfortable middle class; rather, he allows his characters to achieve the satire for him, to expose themselves trapped by the triviality of their self-deceptions. Farrell has a firm grasp of dramatic structure and an ability to create characters who though bizarre and eccentric are still within the realms of the recognisable, and, above all, an ability to gauge his audience, to use as much satiric edge as will sharpen perception without alienating. Farrell may occasionally disappoint his critics, but never his audiences.

Next in the parade comes Frank McGuinness whose work is beginning to show signs of a break away from naturalism and the emergence of a strong and individual voice. His first, much acclaimed, play *Factory Girls* (1983) dealt with a sit-in in a factory by women workers. The characters were well drawn and the overall theme quite effective but, strangely, inadequacy in the creation of the male characters militated against a total credible dramatic conflict in terms either of equal opportunity, agitation or workers' rights. The experience, however, of working with TEAM theatre-in-education company in *Borderlands* (1984) may have made McGuinness aware of a more flexible style of theatre and audience response, and his latest plays *Observe the Sons of Ulster Marching towards the Somme* (1985) and *Baglady* (1985) exhibit a fluid, innovative and exciting approach to the medium. Neil Donnelly, also, has flirted with non-naturalistic forms as in his first version of *Silver Dollar Boys* in 1981. The 1982 version of the play, however, re-written for the Peacock, was 'controlled' back to a more naturalistic format. Donnelly, like J. Graham Reid, favours 'strong' situations predominantly involving males in which the underlying violence of Irish machismo is barely suppressed, ready to break out at crucial moments in his plays.

... the birds of a different feather

'Alternative' writers come in different guises. Tom McIntyre has worked at the creation of an Imagistic theatre style in which theatrical impact and communication is carried out largely through the medium of images created by the actors. The discovery in Patrick Mason of a director who could achieve what McIntyre wrote resulted in a stimulating, new style in two plays *The Great Hunger* (1983) and *The Bearded Lady* (1984). Another writer exploring national myths and ideologies through the medium of the image is Mary Elizabeth Burke-Kennedy whose haunting *Legends* (1981) and *Women in Arms* (1984) opened new possibilities for Irish narrative theatre. And collective scripts have become quite respectable. Generally socialist by persuasion, these plays have grown from the research of a company and give expression to the life of a community at a particular time in its history. *Lay Up Your Ends* (1983) and *Oul Delf and False Teeth* (1984) from Charabanc and the writer Martin Lynch, *The Kips, the Digs and the Village* (1982) from Dublin City Workshop and the writer/director Peter Sheridan all sought to communicate in a theatrically effective manner the feelings, the atmosphere, the social stratification of a community life now past. All these alternatives make the mixture of dramatic styles more rich and vivid and extend the possibilities of the medium.

... *the birds in the bush*

Several dramatists active in the 1970s have not yet produced their play of the '80s. Several, indeed, have fled to the greener pastures of television. Eugene McCabe's characteristic voice has been heard only in *Roma* (RTE 1980) and in television re-runs of his classic trilogy of the mid 1970s, *Victims*; John Boyd's *Speranza's Boy* (1982) received, at best, mixed notices; Ron Hutchinson's *Rat in the Skull* (1984) has been staged in London but not yet in Ireland; Desmond Forrestal's last play was *Kolbe* for the 1982 Dublin Theatre Festival and apart from his version of Chekov's *The Seagull* in 1979 Thomas Kilroy has produced no new dramatic work since *Talbot's Box* (1977). Stewart Parker, despite *Kingdom Come* at the Lyric Theatre in 1982, seemed to have moved to television but was obviously reserving his energies for the recently produced *Northern Star* (1985) which looks to be one of the best works to date.

Traditional or avant-garde, Irish playwrights have produced a great deal of interesting new work in the past few years. But what is new work if it does not find an audience? And is there a life after Dublin for high quality theatre old and new?

... *An assured local provenance*

Irish theatre outside the major centres has long had a vital life and style of its own. It may not seek to emulate the newest fads and fashions but it is open to change and diversity. Amateur drama groups exist in plenty and various annual drama festivals encourage high standards of expectation in production and presentation. In addition to the amateur movement, and, indeed, probably because of it, provincial Ireland has had for many years a tradition of touring companies bringing the 'wonders' of professional theatre to a public educated by its own theatrical activities. The extraordinary phenomenon of the 'fit-ups', those bands of travelling players which existed up to the 1950s, may have vanished but a new and no-less interesting form of touring theatre has taken their place. The formation of the Irish Theatre Company in the 1970s was a bold — if somewhat paternalistic — move to provide state-sponsored theatre for the provinces. Based in Dublin, the ITC's brief was to tour provincial areas with productions whose quality would be similar to that achieved by the national theatres. In the years of its operation, the company established that the highest standards of production and design could be attained by a touring company, and it is this which has been the company's most valuable and abiding legacy to the Irish theatre. The demise of the ITC in 1982 was, however, probably a blessing in disguise and freed Arts Council funding to encourage new, smaller and most cost-effective structures in the place of a monolith. With the monies released from the ITC the Arts Council set up a National Touring Agency (June 1982) which finances touring 'product' from a variety of companies. The result has been that a wider range of styles and plays is available to audiences outside Dublin and small alternative theatre companies as well as major companies have a chance to tour their plays. The growing realisation by the Arts Council of the value of indigenous theatre has been matched by the growth of new, small, tightly-knit professional companies which tour to new, compact and effective venues. Well-equipped theatres such as the Belltable in Limerick (established in 1981), the Hawk's Well in Sligo (established in 1982), the Everyman and the Ivernia (established in 1982) in Cork, the Theatre Royal, Waterford, Siamsa Tire in Tralee, the Druid in Galway, as well as countless local halls, provide a comprehensive circuit for touring both new and classical works to a growing public. The range of drama and theatre available outside Dublin may be assessed by a look at a selection of plays on the touring circuit — some centrally funded, others not — during the period autumn 1983 to spring 1985: *The Gigli Concert*, a new play by Thomas Murphy produced by the Abbey Theatre Company; *A Midsummer Night's Dream* and *Love for Love*, inventive adaptations of classical texts by Smock Alley Theatre Company; *Famine* by Thomas Murphy produced by Druid Theatre Company; *Indian Summer*, a new play by Jennifer Johnston produced by Cork Theatre Company; *Upstarts* by Neil Donnelly produced by the Actors and Playwrights Company; *Boat People*, a new play by Dilly Keane, and *Facade*, a new play by Trish McMenamin both by Gemini Productions; *Peer Gynt*, a new adaptation of Ibsen's text by Declan Burke-Kennedy and *Women in Arms*, a new play by Mary Elizabeth Burke-Kennedy both produced by Cork Theatre Company; *The Riot Act* by Tom Paulin after Sophocles and *High Time* by Derek Mahon after Molière both produced by Field Day Theatre Company; *The Blue Macushla*, a rewritten version of his earlier play by Thomas Murphy produced by Red Rex Theatre Company; *The Glass Menagerie* by Tennessee Williams, produced by the Abbey Theatre Company; *Oul Delf and False Teeth* by Martin Lynch produced by Charabanc Theatre Company; *Sexual Perversity in Chicago* by David Mamet, produced by Rough Magic Theatre Company. Certainly a range and variety of texts, styles and tastes which attest to a vital audience and an encouragement to playwrights and companies that an audience for their works exists countrywide and is not confined to the eastern seaboard. The metropolis, it must be admitted, however, does play a major part in cultivating the growing internationalism of the Irish theatre.

... *A flavour of the international scene*

One of the greatest forces in encouraging the change and expansion of theatrical tastes has been the Dublin Theatre Festival. It has provided an opportunity for those working in or interested in the Irish theatre to view the best of international styles and to present a showcase of their own work. Viewing itself in the highly critical mirror of international standards has made the Irish theatre more aware of its own criteria and annually renews determination to emulate the best of what it has seen without slavishly copying it. At the last festival in 1983 Kasimierz Braun, the controversial Polish director, directed an extraordinary piece of environmental theatre, *The Old Woman Broods* at the Project Arts Centre while, down the road at Trinity College, Druid Theatre Company staged an imaginative revival of M.J. Molloy's *The Wood of the Whispering;* Thomas Murphy's *The Gigli Concert* received its premiere at the Abbey while the Colletivo di Parma performed their wonderful *Hamleto* at the Gate Theatre; dance, mime, collective performances, virtuoso directors, new styles, new works, the inevitable high excitement of controversial reviews provides what Lynda Henderson has referred to as 'the annual adrenalin' of the Theatre Festival.[9] In short, the Dublin Theatre Festival alerts an insular theatrical tradition to the fact that even as the message changes with a changing society so too must the medium. The haunting resonance of images achieved in *Macunaima* (Brazilian Theatre Company, 1982) or *Anna Livia* (Wroclaw Contemporary Theatre, 1982) may have helped Irish audiences to accept such potent Irish images as the mother icon in Tom McIntyre's *The Great Hunger* or to remain open to the atavistic power of the long individual mime sequence which is the climactic point of *The Gigli Concert.*

... signs of the times

The possibilities of growth and development are all there; the changing fashions, the production talents, the inventive minds are all vital and energetic in their potential. Other vital signs that theatre in Ireland may well be entering a new and creative phase are: the encouragement by the Arts Council itself of new works by hitherto unknown writers in the form of their recently established playwright/director workshops; the initiation in 1984 of a degree programme in Drama and Theatre Studies — the first in the Republic — under Professor John McCormick in Trinity College Dublin and the establishment of a Drama Centre in the same university; the foundation, also in 1984, of the Association of Critics of the Irish Theatre, an affiliated branch of the international association which unites academic and the journalistic theatre and drama critics in a mutual exchange of views and ideas; the publication since 1982 of an all-Ireland theatre magazine, *Theatre Ireland*, edited and produced in Northern Ireland but drawing funding from both Northern and Southern Arts Councils. Articles in *Theatre Ireland* cover not only issues relevant to theatre in Ireland but also raise wider issues and stimulate enquiry into international styles and standards.

Maybe a lack of government commitment to a coherent policy of arts funding will stifle the potential, maybe the creative ferment is merely a comforting illusion concealing mere fretful activity, maybe the audience for new work will fail to materialise and stay by their television sets. Only time will tell, but at least there appears to be in the theatre in Ireland in 1985, to misquote Robert Hogan, if not exactly a deluge of genius, more than a trickle of talent.[10]

NOTES

1 This essay deals with fashions in the Republic of Ireland only. The Northern Ireland Arts Council is a completely separate body with a different funding policy and, consequently, different criteria apply to fashion in the north.
2 Quoted from Friel's 'sporadic diary' in an article on Brian Friel by Fintan O'Toole in *Brian Friel: The Healing Art, Magill* magazine, January 1985, p.34.
3 Brian Friel, *Faith Healer* published in Brian Friel, *Selected Plays.* Faber & Faber, London, 1984, p.336.
4 Brian Friel, *Three Sisters.* Gallery Press, Dublin, 1981, p.43.
5 Seamus Heaney, *Preoccupations.* Faber and Faber, London, 1980, p.47.
6 Thomas Murphy, *The Gigli Concert.* Gallery Press, Dublin, 1984, p.74.
7 *Ibid.*
8 John Barret, 'The Thoughtful Comedy of Bernard Farrell'. *Theatre Ireland,* No.3, 1983.
9 Lynda Henderson, 'Annual Adrenelin: The Dublin Theatre Festival'. *Theatre Ireland,* No.4 1983.
10 Robert Hogan, 'Since O'Casey', essay on Irish Theatre in *Since O'Casey and Other Essays,* Irish Literary Studies 15. Colin Smythe, 1983, p.154. 'Despite economics and timidity and sheer bad taste, some interesting plays are somehow being produced and published. It is not exactly a deluge of genius, but it is much more than a trickle of talent'.

DISTANCING DRAMA: SEAN O'CASEY TO BRIAN FRIEL

NICHOLAS GRENE

Because with us the sensational has become almost commonplace, it has been too easy to analyse the Irish question not just in political terms but in terms of the politics of violence. We in Ireland are all in a sense children of the revolution — more precisely, of the revolutionary decade 1912 to 1922 — and for the past sixty years scholars and states-men alike seem to have been mesmerized by the Easter Rising of 1916. [1]

F.S.L. Lyons writes here of a situation which he, and many other recent Irish historians, have worked hard to change. There has been a deliberate and concerted effort to turn Irish historical studies away from an obsessive focus on the politics of the national question to an analysis of the underlying social, economic and cultural experience. [2] What the historians have been seeking is a view of Irish history which adequately renders its complexity and does not merely reduce it to a narrative of its most sensational political events. The sensational might seem to be the very stuff of drama, and yet twentieth-century Irish playwrights, also, have tried to de-sensationalise, one might almost say to de-dramatise, the images of political violence. Sean O'Casey, Denis Johnston, Brendan Behan and Brian Friel, each in their distinctive ways, have challenged the bold simplicities of violent and dramatic action with complicating and distancing ironies.

The object of this essay is to look at four plays — *The Plough and the Stars* (1926), *The Moon in the Yellow River* (1931), *The Hostage* (1958) and *The Freedom of the City* (1973) — and to analyse within them the relationship between theatrical technique and political statement. It will explore the varying ironic strategies with which O'Casey, Johnston, Behan and Friel distance their audiences from that mesmerising image of Easter 1916 and its legacy for the Irish 'children of the revolution'. The four plays,

written over a span of nearly fifty years, seem to have certain
striking similarities. They are all more or less centrally
concerned with political violence, yet that violence is hardly
ever allowed to hold the centre-stage. It is constantly upstaged,
underplayed or undercut by an anarchic dramatic context which
deliberately disrupts the spectacular and the sensational. At
times, as with *The Plough and the Stars*, this disruption mimics
the comic and the trivial disorder of ordinary life as against the
high drama of the violent action. Yet none of the plays, not even
O'Casey's, offers this mixed mode as merely realistic. The
setting in each case, whether it be Dublin tenement or disused
fort, brothel or Derry Guildhall, symbolises far more than it
represents. The plays suggest images of the nation not just of a
specific group or community. Historically the events represented take us from Easter 1916 to Bloody Sunday 1972 and can be
identified with the moods of the specific periods in which the
plays were written. And yet there are congruences in style and
attitude which are remarkable in dramatists from such diverse
generations and cultural backgrounds and which suggest a
distinctive theatrical tradition.

The Plough and the Stars

'You have disgraced yourselves again', thundered Yeats from
the stage of the Abbey at the audience which had expressed
vociferous displeasure at an early performance of *The Plough and
the Stars*. But what did he expect would be the response to that
play performed at that period in Ireland's national theatre?[3] In
1926, just a decade after the Easter Rising, and only four years
after the establishment of the Irish Free State, it was surely not
surprising that the Irish public should react against such an
aggressively anti-nationalist play. The surprise is rather that it
was received enthusiastically on the opening night and that it
was not until the fourth showing that the real trouble broke
out.[4] It is easy now to smile at the absurdity of the objections
raised to the play — the outrage at the appearance of the
Tricolour in a pub, the pious denial that anyone plying Rosie
Redmond's trade existed in the sacred city of Dublin. But we
should not underestimate the provocation represented by
O'Casey's iconoclastic attack on the ideals associated with the
Rising. He told the audience who venerated the memory of the
men who died for Ireland that those men were cowards afraid
to confess that they were afraid. He made a brilliantly malicious

selection of the more sanguinary passages of the speeches and writings of Padraig Pearse and created from them a grotesque and terrifying parody of Pearse's Messianic rhetoric. The second act of *The Plough and the Stars* is a great set-piece of anti-nationalist satire, comparable to the Citizen episode in Joyce's *Ulysses*. The Tricolour in the pub is the least of it. There is the link between patriotic afflatus and the thirst for alcohol — 'A meetin' like this always makes me feel as if I could dhrink Lock Erinn dry'; there is the equation of the militant idealism of the Speaker with the bar-room belligerence of the drinkers; there is the strutting-match between Fluther and the Covey suggesting that the fervour of the rebels — 'Ireland is greater than a wife' — is only a sublimated form of the sexuality which takes Fluther home with Rosie. All of these combine to subvert fundamentally the principles which led to the Easter 1916 Rising.

The orthodox explanation of O'Casey's anti-nationalism is that it was based on his commitment to the labour movement. O'Casey resigned from the Irish Citizen Army in 1914 in protest against Countess Markiewicz continuing to be involved in the nationalist Irish Volunteers as well as the Citizen Army.[5] The decision of the Citizen Army to join force with the Volunteers represented a sell-out of the labour interests. This point of view is, of course, expressed in the play. The banner of the Plough and the Stars is disgraced 'Because it's a Labour flag, an' was never meant for politics. . . . It's a flag that should only be used when we're buildin' th' barricades to fight for a Workers' Republic'.[6] But the Speaker here is the Covey who, with his crudely doctrinaire socialism drawn from 'Jenersky's thesis' and his obvious cowardice, renders ridiculous sentiments which we might otherwise be tempted to identify as O'Casey's own. If there are signs of a left-wing critique of the nationalist movement in *The Plough* in glancing asides such as the English corporal's profession — 'I'm a Sowcialist moiself, but I 'as to do my dooty' — these never amount to a systematic and consistent political point of view.

It has been suggested by Desmond Greaves that 'the deep hidden trauma of O'Casey's political life was that he was not out in 1916'. This he argues, is 'the emotional fulcrum of *The Plough*. It is 1916 seen through the eyes of those who did not take part'.[7] Whether we accept this view that O'Casey denigrates the Rising in order to justify his own failure to join it, we should certainly go carefully about oversimplifying his political and emotional attitudes within the play. It is, for instance, a critical commonplace to see O'Casey's pacifism represented by the heroic suffering women in his plays as against the empty and destructive braggadocio of the men. But Nora in *The Plough*, often included in a line-up of such heroic and suffering women, is treated nearly as critically as her husband, the weak and vain Commandant Clitheroe. Her possessive attempts to hold on to him, to exclude entirely the outer world and re-create endlessly the schmaltz of the honeymoon, are portrayed as at best pitiable, at worst foolish and deluded. Nora's saccharine romanticism coupled with Rosie Redmond's down-at-heel sexiness should effectively stop us from interpreting the play as an injunction to make love not war.

There is a significant ambiguity in O'Casey's handling of Nora Clitheroe in the opening act of the play. We are shown the tenement flat which she has done her best to 'improve' and given the sardonic comments of the other tenement-dwellers on her improvements. The print of 'The Sleeping Venus' raises shocked eyebrows — 'Oh, th' one that got that taken, she must have been a prime lassie'; the newly-delivered parcel is opened and the expensive hat is disapprovingly examined — 'Such notions of upperosity she's gettin' '; the lock which Fluther is fitting arouses the wrath of Bessie Burgess — 'Puttin' a new lock on her door ... afraid her poor neighbours ud break through an' steal'. As so often with the figures in his Dublin plays who aspire beyond the tenements, O'Casey seems to invite a double response in the audience. There is more than a little pathos in Nora's efforts to make a home out of the tenement rooms which she shares with two other men besides her husband. Her pictures on the walls, her lock on the door cannot be for us the objects of derision that they are for her fellow lodgers in the tenement. And yet to some extent we do share their belittling laughter in the theatre.

O'Casey here shows the mixed feelings common to many working-class writers. To become a writer at all is to develop needs which can hardly be met in the writer's original milieu, needs for books, music and painting, for leisure and privacy. In Donal Davoren, for instance, O'Casey's mocking self-portrait in *The Shadow of a Gunman*, we see the plight of a poet constantly interrupted by the casual incursions of tenement visitation. It is not only the woman writer who needs a room of her own. But the impulse towards privacy, towards the development of a consciously chosen individual way of life as against the communal norm, can also be viewed as a bourgeois aspiration to be regarded with suspicion. O'Casey the writer, therefore, necessarily has some sympathy for Nora's desire to put up barriers against the levelling social anarchy of the tenements; and yet at the same time his loyalty to the people makes him join in their mocking hostility to her 'upperosity'.

Seamus Deane, in an acerbic essay on 'Irish politics and O'Casey's theatre', argues that O'Casey fails to develop a critique of Irish history or politics'.[8] That may well be true. But the peculiar strength of *The Plough* lies not in the articulation of a consistent social and political attitude but in its complexity of dramatic texture. Act II most obviously works through multiple theatrical ironies with its interplay between the foreground images of the pub and the looming appearances of the Speaker at the back. But other less clearly structured scenes in the play have a comparably complicated dramatic effect. In Act III, in the midst of the glorious comedy of the looting, we have the deeply disturbing reunion of the Clitheroes. O'Casey here takes on a stock theatrical situation, the conflict between love and duty, and turns it into something very different. To start with, Nora's hysterical language, though touching, is almost as embarrassing to the audience as it is to Clitheroe:

Jack, Jack, Jack; God be thanked ... be thanked ... He has been kind and merciful to His poor handmaiden ... My Jack, my own Jack, that I thought was lost is found, that I thought was dead is alive again! ... Oh, God be praised for ever, evermore! ... My poor Jack. ... Kiss me, kiss me, Jack, kiss your own Nora![9]

Although we may sympathise with Nora's feelings here, we shrink from her public demonstration of them; our instincts are like Clitheroe's — 'for God's sake, Nora, don't make a scene'. This area of discomfort is deliberately counterpointed with others. There is the equally raw quality of the language of the wounded Langon, whose situation makes it so urgent for Clitheroe to leave:

Oh, if I'd kep' down only a little longer, I mightn't ha' been hit! Everyone else escapin', an' me gettin' me belly ripped asundher! ... I couldn't scream, couldn't even scream. ... D'ye think I'm really badly wounded, Bill? Me clothes seem to be all soakin' wet. ... It's blood ... My God, it must be me own blood![10]

This does more than provide a grim contrast to the metaphorical and sacramental blood of the Speaker in Act II — 'the red wine of the battlefields'. It gives us an all too convincing sense of the ordinarily unheroic reaction to violent physical pain. And presiding over the whole scene from an upper window is Bessie Burgess, with her vengeful and tasteless chorus of jeers:

Th' Minsthrel Boys aren't feelin' very comfortable now. The big guns has knocked all th' harps out of their hands. General Clitheroe'd rather be unlacin' his wife's bodice than standin' at a barricade ... An' th' professor of chicken-butcherin' there, finds he's up against somethin' a little tougher even than his own chickens, an' that's sayin' a lot![11]

This is a merciless scene, in which ugliness and indecorum deny to the audience any sort of aesthetic catharsis. We are forced to face the truth of what we watch without either the luxury of emotional identification or the security of dramatic distance.

The complex and pervasive ironies of *The Plough* often crystallise around the singing of songs. The Covey in the first act, for instance, delights in 'twartin' and tormentin' ' Peter Flynn by his sarcastic singing of Moore's Melodies — 'When proudly, me own island harp, I unbound thee' or 'Oh, where's th' slave so lowly'. Moore's faded rhetoric aptly represents Uncle Peter's do-nothing nationalism of uniforms and parades. It is less clear just how ironically we are to take the sentimental love-song which Clitheroe sings to Nora a little later in the act. Even though the lyrics are O'Casey's own, it is tempting to see in this insipid and banal piece of crooning a comment on the fragility of the relationship which Nora fights so hard to preserve. Certainly its very banality adds pathos when Nora, in delirium, sings a reprise of it in the last act. Act I ends to the strains of 'It's a Long Way to Tipperary' coming from the Dublin Fusiliers on their way to the front. The song, so closely identified with the British troops in the Great War, with its nostalgia for Tipperary and its farewells to Piccadilly and Leicester Square, reminds us of the integral part played by Irish soldiers in a war fought in defence of the British Empire. By contrast, Act II ends with the deliberate bathos of Rosie Redmond's bawdy ballad cutting into the off-stage mobilisation of the Volunteers and the Citizen Army.

Nowhere in the play does O'Casey show a surer dramatic touch than in his handling of Bessie Burgess's hymns in Act IV. Bessie is characterised at the beginning of the play as a black Protestant whose drunken hymn-signing is a provocative offence to her Catholic neighbours. Ironically it is with Newman's hymn 'Lead, kindly light' that she lulls Nora in her illness — Nora who used to complain of her rowdy singing. Bessie dies saving Nora, but with the hymn she sings as she dies, she makes a specifically Protestant profession of faith.

> I do believe, I will believe
> That Jesus died for me;
> That on th' cross He shed His blood
> From sin to set me free. [12]

O'Casey, however, does not let the play end with such an emotional climax but introduces a final ironic twist with the offstage singing of 'Keep the Home Fires Burning' by the British soldiers, joined in by Sergeant Tinley and Corporal Stoddart as they sit down to their cups of tea. The two men are enjoying the home fire of the woman whom they have just shot. And yet this is not partisan irony. The emotion which the song expresses is real and we are aware that, in Ireland as in France, these men are strangers away from home, entitled to what consolation they can get from the sentiment of Ivor Novello.

These are organic ironies which O'Casey develops from the songs in *The Plough*. As Maik Hamburger concludes in his study of songs in other early O'Casey plays, 'they are not deliberately alienated in a Brechtian fashion, but they do provide a distancing effect in their own way in correlation with the other components of the play'. [13] Through them O'Casey holds in dramatic tension the human conflicts endemic in the Irish situation, conflicts between private and public life, between the several religious and political factions, between the Great War beyond Ireland and the little war within. The play is not mere 'slice-of-life' naturalism, but neither is it the pacifist or anti-nationalist polemic which it is sometimes considered. It opposes no alternative value-system to the heroic code which it attacks. The tenement characters are real anti-heroes; in them ordinary virtues — compassion, toughness, good humour — are matched by ordinary shortcomings — ignorance, vindictiveness, stupidity. *The Plough* has its weaknesses, particularly in the self-conscious working of O'Casey's ornately comic language. But its greatness lies in the way in which it resists the simplifications of emotional and political attitudes, in the panoramic irony with which its dramatic world is created.

The Moon in the Yellow River

In *The Moon in the Yellow River* the limited independence of the

Treaty has been won and the Irish Free State established. With the disused fort which is the play's setting and the power-house nearby, Johnston chose images appropriate for the new state. The fort, 'a relic of the Napoleon scare', had been long unoccupied before Dobelle took it over, so we are discouraged from seeing it as a direct symbol of the British military presence withdrawn in 1922. As always with Johnston there are literary echoes — Captain Shotover's converted ship in *Heartbreak House,* Joyce's Martello tower in *Ulysses.* There is also a suggestion of the anomaly of the Anglo-Irish still remaining in Ireland, the so-called 'Garrison' in a country no longer occupied. The power-house, however, has a much more obvious significance. Suggested by the Shannon scheme of the 1920s which provided the country with cheap hydro-electricity, the works run by the German engineer Tausch represents the force of international modernisation which followed independence. For the die-hard Republican Darrell Blake, Tausch and his works stand for a type of colonisation to be opposed just as strongly as the political domination of the British. This may not be historically particularly accurate — Republican dissent from the Treaty settlement in the 1920s focussed almost exclusively on the political issues of Partition and the oath to the Crown — but there was undoubtedly an isolationist, anti-industrial element within the Republican tradition, and Johnston chose to highlight the clash between this and the modernising cosmopolitanism of Tausch.

Johnston's memories of 1916, as the schoolboy son of a judge held hostage with his family for three days, are recorded in the Preface to his play about the Rising, *The Scythe and the Sunset.*

My recollections of the week are personal and undramatic. Of the rebels, I principally remember their charm, their civility, their doubts, and their fantastic misinformation about everything that was going on.[14]

The charm and the inefficiency are transferred to the Republicans of *The Moon* who at times appear to be straight out of comic opera. With the explosives which have been left out in the rain and the shells which fail to detonate, the theatrical key-note is anti-melodrama. And yet Johnston is playing cat-and-mouse games with audience expectations, setting up suspense only to deflate it yet reactivating the threat of violence once we have been lulled into comic complacency. There is real and biting irony in the stage image as Tausch declaims on the benefits his works can bring to Ireland:

what might can equal electrical power at one farthing a unit? *(On the blinds appears the shadow of a man in an overcoat holding something in his hand that closely resembles a revolver.)* I see in my mind's eye this land of the future — transformed and redeemed by power — from the sordid trivialities of peasant life to something newer and better. [15]

A serious and sombre point is made: the masked gunman is a force to oppose the might of 'electrical power at one farthing a unit' and he stands in the way of Tausch's modern Utopia. But of course as soon as the masked gunman is unmasked as the dunderheaded Willie Reilly and is violently scolded by his mother, the formidable Agnes, for his failure to wipe his boots, the audience are let off the hook again and can relax into relieved laughter. Yet we are never safe — guns will be used, bangs will go off before the play is over.

Tausch is used throughout the play as Johnston's and the audience's butt, the straight man as against the variety of zanies, clowns and wits who populate the action. There is a special enjoyment for an Irish audience in the alienating discomfiture he undergoes as the well-bred German visitor faced with the craziness of the Dobelle household. Such oddity we are prepared to take to ourselves in delighted mockery of the earnest and idealistic foreigner. But there is a more uncomfortable edge to Dobelle's serious mock-warning to Tausch about Ireland's bogey men:

here we have bogey men, fierce and terrible bogey men, who breathe fire from their nostrils and vanish in the smoke.
Tausch. You have what?
Dobelle. And we have vampires in shimmering black that feed on blood and bear bombs instead of brats. And enormous fat crows that will never rest until they have pecked out your eyes and left you blind and dumb with terror.
Tausch. Come, come, Mr. Dobelle.
Dobelle. And in the mists that creep down from the mountains you will meet monsters that glare back at you with your own face. [16]

Here and throughout the dramatic action of the play itself, Johnston is trying to define the strain in Irish life which seems too absurd, too grotesque, simply too funny to be real and yet is no less terribly real for all that. The crucial demonstration of this is of course the murder of Blake at the end of the second act.

As Blake concludes his bravura performance at the piano, Tausch bursts out in exasperation, 'This is no country! It is a damned debating society! Everybody will talk — talk — talk — ... But nothing ever happens'. And at that instant 'Lanigan without any demonstration shoots Blake dead'.[17]

Darrell Blake is not altogether successfully realised as a character in the play, but the spirit of the characterisation is significant. Johnston portrays him as brilliant, attractive, but ultimately impossible — so impossible that he has to be destroyed. We are allowed to feel the charm of his actorly daring in just the spirit of Yeats's 'Meditations in Time of Civil War':

> An affable Irregular,
> A heavily-built Falstaffian man,
> Comes cracking jokes of civil war
> As though to die by gunshot were
> The finest play under the sun.[18]

And yet ultimately we are aligned with the brutal forces which can not allow Blake's form of anarchic individualism to survive. Lanigan's horribly frank apologia comes home to us as it does to the outraged Tausch:

I'm a gunman. I always was and I always will be. And if you ask me why, I declare to God I don't know. There's no glamour on my side, nowadays. But God help you all if I wasn't. It may be brains and inspiration that makes the country at the start, but it's my help you're always telephoning for before the end.[19]

The link is made between the modernised society of the Free State and the violent force necessary to sustain it. Dobelle emphasises the point to Tausch:

Tausch ... You wish me to believe that Lanigan's shot was part of my world — that he and I are truly on the same side.
Dobelle. More than that. Lanigan is just yourself. He is your finger on the trigger.[20]

Lanigan is one of the bogey men who 'glare back at you with your own face' and that holds good for us in the audience as well as Tausch.

Johnston's technique in *The Moon* is by breaking down the expected continuities of dramatic action to break down also the audience's shaping sense of themselves and their society. The Shavianism of the play has often been noticed, in particular its evident debt to *Heartbreak House*.[21] But where Shaw's aim is to divert action into discussion, Johnston denies Shavian force and direction even to the discussion. Thus in the second act when Blake organises the debate over whether or not to blow up the works, in the midst of the various absurd opinions expressed in the mini-poll, we sense that Dobelle's contribution will be the key. Sure enough his is the casting vote against the works, but when he winds himself up to give the expected Shavian-type set speech expounding his reasons, no-one will listen to him and the scene settles back into ridiculous cross-purposes. *Heartbreak House* ends dramatically with the Zeppelin raid which, as an image of apocalypse, stimulates and challenges both the characters on stage and the audience in the theatre. In *The Moon* instead we get the purely arbitrary accident by which the works is blown up after all. Nothing dramatic could be contrived to have less significance.

We may detect in *The Moon* on Johnston's part a degree of political discomfort which is close to despair. He tells in the preface to the play of how Captain Jack White, founder of the Irish Citizen Army, reproached him for his justification of the brutal repression of the Republicans by the Free State.

> I invited him to tell me what the proper answer was . . .
> 'There is no answer', said Jack White, 'and you know it. That is why you are a traitor and a renegade'.[22]

Even though Johnston maintains an attitude of quizzical amusement in telling the story, he does not altogether succeed in setting aside the charge. What he does in the play, through the figure of Dobelle, is to try to suggest the possibility of personal renewal even at the moment of political despair. The circumstances of the death of Dobelle's wife which led him to renounce any relationship with his daughter may seem a bit too plotted for an otherwise plotless play. But the moment at which he 'sees' Blanaid for the first time is a moving one. It contributes to Dobelle's new understanding of the need for an openness to feeling which includes the vulnerability to pain. He is forced to renounce the defensiveness of an embittered disillusionment in words which paraphrase O'Casey: 'take away this cursed gift of laughter and give us tears instead'. The ending of the play could be accused of sentimentalism, maybe even of a degree of evasiveness on Johnston's part, a refusal to face the implications of the political and social dilemmas he has exposed. But what he is seeking is a dramatic image which can delicately and subtly

relate the personal to the political. The housekeeper Agnes and
her preoccupation with the long-drawn-out off-stage labour of
Mrs. Mulpeter, have provided a sort of grotesque running gag
through the play. That protracted labour is given allegorical
colouring — 'the birth of a nation is no immaculate conception'.
It is thus a complex form of emotional coda which is represented
by the final stage tableau as Dobelle and Blanaid fall asleep and
Agnes enters:

It is morning outside and the sunlight floods into the room from behind
her. She crosses to the window and opens the shutters with a sigh of
intense satisfaction and smiles out at the flowers and the ivy that grow
around the frame. Nodding her head, and with an approving click of
her tongue, she softly hums a lullaby and surveys a new day. That is
the end of this play.[23]

This is very fragile but perhaps just sufficiently understated to
work theatrically. It is no up-beat ending but as much of human
hope as Johnston feels he can salvage from his bleakly funny
look at the aftermath of revolution.

The Hostage

The Hostage by Brendan Behan — or from an original script by
Brendan Behan? This is the critical question which has been
constantly canvassed because of the involvement of Joan
Littlewood and her Theatre Workshop company in its
production. Comparisons with Behan's first version, the Irish
play *An Giall*, have shown how extensively it was altered to
become *The Hostage* and more than one critic has argued that the
changes were not for the better. Ulick O'Connor, Behan's
biographer, claims that '*The Hostage* as it was performed in the
West End and Paris version is a blown-up hotch-potch
compared with the original version which is a small masterpiece
and the best thing Behan wrote for the theatre'.[24] While
allowance is made for Joan Littlewood's extraordinary theatrical
talents, it is felt that what she did was to camp up the play for
a London audience while Behan was too drunk to care. It is
certainly true that the additions and changes made were all such
as to suit the Theatre Workshop house-style. The extra
characters — Rio Rita, Princess Grace, Miss Gilchrist and Mr.
Mulleady with chorus of whores and clients — enlarged the cast
and made possible the ensemble playing which was a Joan
Littlewood hallmark. The added songs, the risqué jokes, the

topical allusions and the sub-Brechtian anti-illusionism all helped to make it a distinctively Stratford East product. These features in the printed text do date it quite badly, so that it seems in some ways embarrassingly of its period. Yet there is much in the play which is significantly Behan's — many of the original lines are translated more or less literally — and the final published version is of real interest in the context of the Irish dramatic tradition.

In Act II as Meg finishes singing an aggressively Republican song to the assembled company, she throws in an extra-dramatic in-joke:

The author should have sung that one.
Pat. That's if the thing has an author.
Soldier. Brendan Behan, he's too anti-British.
Officer. Too anti-Irish, you mean. Bejasus, wait till we get him back home. We'll give him what-for for making fun of the Movement.
Soldier (to audience). He doesn't mind coming over here and taking your money.
Pat. He'd sell his country for a pint.[25]

Behan — if it is Behan — here sends himself up and pre-empts a whole range of critical reactions to himself and his play. There is the charge that he did not really write it — 'that's if the thing has an author' — there is his former reputation as a convicted I.R.A. terrorist and his current reputation as a rowdy ballad-singing stage-Irish drunk playing to an English audience. Whether the lines were Behan's own or a company contribution, they skillfully deal with what must at some level have been real anxieties. By the 1950s Behan had moved away from the Republican beliefs which had earned him years in English and Irish prisons. The thrust of *The Hostage* is anti-Republican in so far as it identifies the movement with a crazy fringe of fanatics and nuts. Behan must have been aware of how good anti-I.R.A. propaganda such a play was coming as it did from a former I.R.A. man. It is hard to believe that he felt no discomfort at entertaining the English so successfully with the ridiculous antics of his former comrades or that he did not anticipate Republican reactions like that of the Officer — 'we'll give him what-for for making fun of the Movement'.

Behan partly tries to rationalise his repudiation of Republicanism by making a distinction between the 'old' I.R.A. and the 'new' I.R.A. Such a distinction has been a regular feature of public opinion in Ireland since independence for those who wish to distance themselves from continuing violence while preserving pious respect for the principles of 1916. In Behan's case it is a rather different sort of opposition. The Officer is presented as a caricature of the new I.R.A. — fanatical, puritanical and right-wing — and as such he is relentlessly mocked by Pat, the old I.R.A. man.

Officer. In the old days there were nothing but Communists in the I.R.A.
Pat. There were some. What of that?
Officer. Today the movement is purged of the old dross. It has found its spiritual strength.
Pat. Where did it find that?
Officer. ''The man who is most loyal to the faith is the one who is most loyal to the cause''.
Pat. Haven't you got your initials mixed up? Are you in the I.R.A. or the F.B.I.?[26]

Pat, hard-bitten and realistic but humane and loyal to his former comrade Monsewer, seems to be set up for our approval by contrast. It is true that Behan, through Meg, deflates Pat's fantasies of the heroic action in which he lost his leg:

Pat. It was a savage and barbarous battle. All we had was rifles and revolvers. They had Lewis guns, Thompsons, and landmines — bloody great landmines — the town was nothing but red fire and black smoke and the dead were piled high on the roads ...
Meg. You told me there was only one man killed.
Pat. What?
Meg. And he was the County Surveyor out measuring the road and not interfering with politics one way or another.[27]

This is to reduce the time of the War of Independence to the same status as the present: in both it is the innocent victims that suffer. And yet Behan is closely involved with Pat as he jeers at the Officer. 'You know, there are two kinds of gunmen. The earnest, religious-minded ones like you, and the laughing boys'. Behan here identifies with the old I.R.A. — Michael Collins, the ablest guerrilla leader to emerge from the Troubles was known as the 'Laughing Boy' — and stigmatises the modern movement as humourless and inhuman. Pat plays his part in the action which results in the death of Leslie, and his disabling commitment to the past is diagnosed accusingly by Teresa at the end: 'It wasn't the Belfast Jail or the Six Counties that was troubling you, but your lost youth and your crippled leg'. Yet Behan was trying here, not altogether successfully, to disengage himself from attitudes which at some level he continued to share with Pat.

The addition of queers and whores, Russians and blacks to the cast of *The Hostage* has generally been considered part of Joan Littlewood's broadening of the focus of Behan's original play for the benefit of non-Irish audiences. The gamey mélange which results shifts the play away from an exclusive concern with the 'Irish question'. The Dublin brothel becomes not merely a hide-out for I.R.A. sympathisers but a haven for all sorts and conditions of the socially unacceptable. The rather arch daring with which this is treated —

> We're here because we're queer
> Because we're queer because we're here —

the sanatised jokiness, are now among the dated features of the play's style. And yet there is more here than mere 1950s camp. Behan, himself quite possibly bisexual, with all of his experience of the underworld of prison life, makes the 'gaieties' of the play speak for him. There is an outstanding theatrical moment in Act III as Miss Gilchrist and the Soldier sing their duet:

As the song goes on, the whores and queers sort themselves out into a dance for all the outcasts of this world. It is a slow sad dance in which Ropeen dances with Colette and Princess Grace dances first with Mulleady and then with Rio Rita. There is jealousy and comfort in the dance.[28]

In this Behan moves beyond nationalism, beyond even the apolitical humanism which opposes nationalism. There is a spiritual strain in all of his work, and here we may find a specifically Christian identification with the morally and socially dispossessed.

The Hostage was written against the background of the I.R.A. Border raids of the 1950s. The play contrives to suggest the futility and absurdity of the continuing Anglo-Irish conflict in a world of larger and even more frightening conflicts. As Pat says, 'It's the H bomb. It is such a big bomb it's got me scared of the little bombs'. The image of Republican Ireland is of the seedy brothel, owned by the mad Monsewer, the English convert to Irish nationalism (a far from unrepresentative type) who is frozen in an imaginary past of heroic struggle. The play attempts even-handedly to subvert all orthodoxies, all social and political pieties in the interests of a fully humane iconoclasm. And yet with historical hindsight it may seem that what is most seriously dated about *The Hostage* is the way it underrates the continuing strength and importance of the Republican tradition. There is an assumption underlying the play that the remaining Republicans, whether 'old' or 'new' I.R.A., are deranged relics of a past that is gone. In the 1950s that may have seemed a reasonable assumption to make. In the 1980s it looks distinctly complacent. With continuing violence which has gone on for sixteen years, and a whole new generation of the I.R.A. who are neither 'earnest and religious-minded' nor 'laughing boys' but extremely efficient urban terrorists our view of *The Hostage* must necessarily be altered.

The Freedom of the City

Brian Friel's *The Freedom of the City* is unlike the other plays considered in this essay in that it was written out of an immediate reaction to the historical event which inspired it. On Bloody Sunday, 30 January 1972, thirteen civilians on a banned Civil Rights march in Derry were shot dead by British troops. A tribunal of enquiry presided over by Lord Widgery reported later in the year, exonerating the soldiers involved. Friel's play was very obviously written out of the emotions generated by Bloody Sunday and the Widgery report, and it was ready for production in the Abbey by February 1973. It is not, therefore, distanced from its subject in time, as, for instance, *The Plough* is, nor does Friel have the authorial detachment of Johnston in *The Moon* or Behan in *The Hostage*. Whereas O'Casey and Behan had both moved away from allegiance to a political cause and *The Plough* and *The Hostage* express their disenchantment, *The Freedom of the City* was the first work of Friel's to concern itself directly with political conflict, as though the events of 1972 had forced a previously apolitical writer to adopt a committed political stance. In structural terms, also, *The Freedom* is out of line with the other three plays. In them death comes arbitrarily, unexpectedly, at or towards the end of the play, out of an incongruously comic dramatic atmosphere. With *The Freedom*, true to its emotional origins, death is the given, the dead bodies lying on stage are what we start from, and only from there do we move back to explore the experience which led up to the outcome of death. And yet for all these obvious dissimilarities, *The Freedom* can be seen as significantly parallel to the works of O'Casey, Johnston and Behan.

Friel's play was written out of anger, double anger at the suffering of an oppressed minority and at the hypocrisy of their oppressors. The plot and setting of the play are in themselves polemically symbolic, with the accidental occupation of Derry's Guildhall by three of Derry's Catholic citizens. Derry is a largely Catholic city but by skillful manipulation of electoral boundaries and voting rights, its local government had for years been kept in the hands of Protestant Unionists and, as the mock news report in the play has it, the Guildhall was 'regarded by the minority as a symbol of Unionist domination'. When Skinner, Lily and Michael award themselves the freedom of the city in a mock ceremony in the 'Mayor's parlour' of the Guildhall, they take a freedom of which they have been signally deprived. In an incident which Lily relates from the Civil Rights march, Friel bitterly underlines the irony:

I was at the back of the crowd, beside wee Johnny Duffy — you know — the window cleaner — Johnny the Tumbler — and I'm telling him what the speakers is saying 'cos he hears hardly anything now since he fell off the ladder last time. And I'm just after telling him 'The streets is ours and nobody's going to move us' when I turn round and Jesus, Mary and Joseph there's this big Saracen right behind me. Of course, I took to my heels. And when I look back there's Johnny the Tumbler standing there with his fists in the air and him shouting, 'The streets is ours and nobody's going to move us!' [29]

The little deaf window-cleaner mouthing the slogans of democratic liberty, dwarfed by the oncoming tank, is Friel's savagely satiric image of the political situation. As Brigadier Johnson-Hansbury, the commander-in-chief of the security forces, lists the massive array of military strength which he has at his disposal against the three Civil Rights marchers in the Guildhall, we are reminded of Fluther's indignant protest in *The Plough* to Sergeant Tinley's complaint that the Irish rebels won't 'foight fair':

Fight fair! A few hundhred scrawls o' chaps with a couple o' guns an' Rosary beads, again' a hundhred thousand thrained men with horse, fut, an' artillery . . . an' he wants us to fight fair! D'ye want us to come out in our skins an' throw stones? [30]

As much as the deaths in Derry on Bloody Sunday what shocked even moderate Irish opinion in 1972 was what appeared to be the whitewash of the Widgery tribunal report. It deeply offended many Irish people who still retained some belief in the principles of British justice. Friel voices this sense of outrage in his deliberate parody of the Widgery proceedings in the play. His Judge is at pains to disclaim bias, to delimit the objective of the tribunal:

It is essentially a fact-finding exercise; and our concern is with that period of time when these three people came together, seized possession of a civic building, and openly defied the security forces. The facts we garner over the coming days may indicate that the deceased were callous terrorists who had planned to seize the Guildhall weeks before the events of February 10th; or the facts may indicate that the misguided scheme occurred to them on that very day while they listened to revolutionary speeches. But whatever conclusion may seem to emerge, it must be understood that it is none of our function to make moral judgements.[31]

As we are to find out in the course of the play, this supposedly factual, judiciously dispassionate statement is prejudiced in every word. The three people did not 'come together' except by accident, they did not 'seize possession' of the Guildhall but were driven into it blinded by tear-gas and water-cannon, they were anything but 'callous terrorists' and had no scheme, misguided or otherwise. The very terms in which the Justice frames his opening preamble, grossly prejudges the issue.

Yet *The Freedom* is not as aggressively committed politically as it might seem to be, and as it was thought to be at the time of its first production.[32] Friel is concerned in the play with the relation between the actual experience of the three central characters and a whole range of misrepresentations of that experience, not only the prejudiced tribunal view. There is the instant apotheosis into nationalist legend which is represented by the drunken Balladeer —

A hundred Irish heroes one February day
Took over Derry's Guildhall, beside old Derry's quay.

There is the slippery journalist's rhetoric of the RTE newsman as he describes the funeral of the three, attended for public relations reasons by all the Southern Irish political dignitaries. There are the contrasting sermons in which the deaths are turned into moralised exempla for and against revolutionary violence. In each case we see the lives and deaths of the characters we know as Lily, Michael and Skinner transformed into something else. Besides the various distortions of the local perspectives, Friel weaves into the ironic fabric of the play a sociological lecture on urban poverty for which the characters serve as involuntarily apt illustration. The reality of their language exposes the inauthenticity of the sociologist's, even if we recognise the general accuracy of what he says.[33]

Through much of this work, Friel is concerned with the tension between the fixity of any dramatic action and the essential fluidity of real human experience. His technique in *The Freedom,* as in many of his other plays, is retrospective. It is not merely the tribunal which attempts the reconstruction of what really happened, it is the play itself. And in the collage of the various sorts of misrepresentation with the immediacy of the lived events, he makes us aware of how much less clear-cut the truth is than the plausible travesty. Within the several fake external investigations of the significance of the characters, we are allowed to explore for ourselves their real dramatic meaning. Friel has deliberately chosen three characters to represent different attitudes towards their common social and political situation, rather as O'Casey gives a spectrum of opinion within his tenement cast. Michael believes sincerely in the objectives of the Civil Rights movement of the 1960s — 'a decent job, a decent place to live, a decent town to bring up our children in', 'fair play . . . so that no matter what our religion is, no matter what our politics is, we have the same chances and the same opportunities as the next fella'.[34] They are honourable objectives and Michael believes that if they are honourably pursued by peaceful means, they can be achieved. The play exposes this belief as cruel delusion as Michael's trust in the basic reasonableness of the social authorities is devastatingly betrayed. Skinner, of whom Michael is deeply suspicious, is far more cynical and shows intermittently beneath his mask of satiric wit a much more aggressively anti-authoritarian stance. Lily is without any very definite political or social views, and mothers both Michael and Skinner indifferently out of a habit of motherliness which derives as much from her temperament as her eleven children.

Friel set his play back in time to February 1970. It was this winter of 1969–70 which saw the first violent disruption of the Civil Rights marches and the emergence of the Provisional I.R.A. In the dialectic set-up between Michael and Skinner we see reflected this historical moment. If Michael represents habits of mind characteristic of the Civil Rights movement and in his death suggests their inadequacy, Skinner shows us a potential Provo in the making. His last thoughts as he faces death from

the British soldiers are 'how seriously they took us and how
unpardonably casual we were about them; and that to match
their seriousness would demand a total dedication, a solemnity
as formal as theirs'. [35] Such 'total dedication' was to come from
the Provisionals who in the 1970s were in a position to re-
activate Republicanism as a militant struggle to the death
against the British. Skinner is given a vision of international
revolution which has latterly become an important element
within the I.R.A. movement. He defines for Lily the reasons
why she marches:

Because you live with eleven kids and a sick husband in two rooms that
aren't fit for animals. Because you exist on a state subsistence that's
about enough to keep you alive but too small to fire your guts. Because
you know your children are caught in the same morass. Because for the
first time in your life you grumbled and someone else grumbled and
someone else, and you heard each other, and became aware that there
were hundreds, thousands, millions of us all over the world, and in a
vague groping way you were outraged. That's what it's all about, Lily.
It has nothing to do with doctors and accountants and teachers and
dignity and boy scout honour. It's about us — the poor — the majority
— stirring in our sleep. [36]

It is a strong speech and together with Skinner's general
attractiveness and his superior intelligence and insight might
suggest that the play's main thrust was to support this militant
attitude. But Friel takes pains to off-set this impression by
following Skinner's speech with Lily's confession as to the
actual reason why she marches — for her mongol child Declan:

it's for him I go on all the civil rights marches. Isn't that stupid? You
and him *(Michael)* and everybody else marching and protesting about
sensible things like politics and stuff and me in the middle of you all,
marching for Declan. Isn't that the stupidest thing you ever heard? [37]

Friel gives to Lily a motive completely without political
significance. Downs' syndrome, as a genetic defect, could not
even be attributed to the poor conditions in which Lily has to
live. What is suggested here is that there is a level of human
pain and need which no political panacea can satisfy, suffering
that no change of government could allay.

The structure of *The Freedom* is designed to show the necessary
disproportion between lived actuality and interpretation,
whether it is political, sociological or rhetorical. The audience is
privileged in being given access to that Mayor's parlour and

seeing the reality which excluded outsiders fictionalise for their own purposes. Yet at times we may feel that Friel pushes that privilege too far. In a stylised sequence near the beginning of the second act, each of the three dead characters voice their final thoughts, sum up their individual tragedies. The stage direction is that they should speak 'calmly, without emotion, in neutral accents'. In dramatic context this seems like a false note. Friel as dramatist has taken over the role of interpreter, denying to the characters their dramatic sovereignty, and substituting his own more articulate, more self-conscious voice for theirs. In a play which has set the authenticity of the central characters against the abstracting distortions of interpretation, this appears a mistake. Indeed if the play has a principal weakness it is perhaps in the sense of control and purposefulness with which it is all put together. The superficially disparate images and angles on the main action are never in fact random and we are constantly aware of their artful disposition. In Friel the sheer virtuosity of technique threatens the central immediacy of experience which it the purpose of the play to dramatise.

Conclusion

Parnell came down the road, he said to a cheering man:
'Ireland shall get her freedom and you still break stone' — Yeats, 'Parnell'[38]

the Free State didn't change anything more than the badges on the warders' caps. — Behan, *The Quare Fellow.* [39]

The Plough and the Stars, The Moon in the Yellow River, The Hostage and *The Freedom of the City* are all in a sense counter-revolutionary plays in their profound scepticism about the effect and effectiveness of political liberation. Whatever happens, power remains vested in a system which leaves the people powerless. O'Casey's British soldier may be a socialist but he has to do his duty. As George, the 'Christian Communist' of *The Moon* observes 'every time that the people try to be free and happy and peaceful it seems ... that somebody comes along and stops them with big guns'. George's comic effort to make a big gun to defend the people ends significantly with its confiscation by the Free State authorities. Leslie, the hostage, is scornful at the idea that the British government will be concerned about his fate:

I suppose you think they're all sitting around in the West End clubs with handkerchiefs over their eyes, dropping tears into their double whiskies. Yeah, I can just see the Secretary of State for War now waking up his missus in the night: "Oh Isabel-Cynthia love, I can hardly get a wink of sleep wondering what's happening to that poor bleeder Williams".[40]

Skinner speaks movingly of the poor 'stirring in their sleep', but the only effect of the deaths in *The Freedom* is to make political capital for those already in power, whether it is the British who brand them as terrorists or the Southern Irish notables who attend their funerals as martyrs.

And yet the recurrent protest against the powerlessness of the people does not represent a fully socialist attitude in any one of the plays. All four of them resist political commitment, suggest indeed that such commitment is incompatible with understanding. O'Casey may be anti-nationalist in *The Plough*, Friel anti-British in *The Freedom* but neither of them any more than Johnston or Behan can give themselves to an alternative political ideology. There are some signs of uneasiness on the part of the authors with this lack of commitment in the polarities of the Irish situation. We may detect in O'Casey and Behan a reaction against former loyalties, in Johnston the discomfort of detached neutrality, in Friel the pressure to stand up for his own community. It is easy to sentimentalise these plays as protests against violence. We can all be assumed to be against violence as we are against sin. Part of what makes these four plays important and impressive is the sense of creative struggle which was necessary to write them. What Thomas Kilroy has said of O'Casey's plays is true also of those of Behan, Johnston and Friel: 'they arose from contemporary dynamic forces within Irish society, from a need to engage in the process of history'.[41]

Counterpointing the bold images of dramatic action with song, dance, above all with the play of language, the four dramatists achieve a whole range of ironic effects. The militant rhetoric of the Speaker in the second act of *The Plough* is undercut by the demotic speech of those in the pub; the shadow of the gunman in *The Moon* threatens the naive idealism of Tausch's hymn to electricity; the soldier with his quiet entry into the mad dance which ends the first act of *The Hostage* changes the significance of the scene; the sociologist Dodds, burbling on about how 'present-orientated living ... may sharpen one's attitude for spontaneity' leads straight into the apparition of Skinner in full Mayoral regalia. The interplay of language and theatrical image offers to the audience some of the comic consolations of irony. The very vividness of colloquial speech and its absurdity acts as a reassurance of life. The plays, however, with their various dislocations and discontinuities, leave us peculiarly conscious of the menace of violence and death, and of the arbitrariness with which they destroy meaning. O'Casey makes us feel the literal obscenity of the real suffering caused by the Rising, as against the sacramental metaphors of blood-sacrifice. The suddenness of Blake's murder in *The Moon* figures the blank inscrutability of death itself. Leslie Williams at the end of *The Hostage* is allowed to rise to his feet and sing 'Oh death where is thy sting' with the rest of the cast, but the effect is only to reinforce the contrast with the world outside the theatre where corpses do not get up and sing.[42] One of the horrors of *The Freedom* is to hear the pathologist detail the multiple wounds in the dead bodies of the very live characters with whom we are dramatically engaged. The purpose of these four plays is not primarily pacifist; they do not oppose simple principles of peace and brotherhood to the politics of violence. But in distancing us from the drama of politics, in presenting it with the obliqueness of ironic perspectives, in focussing on the victims and the survivors, they create powerful tragicomedy out of the tragicomic history of Ireland.

NOTES

1 F.S.L. Lyons, *Culture and Anarchy in Ireland 1890–1939*. Oxford: Clarendon Press, 1979, p.1.
2 Terence Brown speaks of 'a quiet revolution' in the writing of history in Ireland. See *Ireland: a Social and Cultural History 1922–79*. London: Collins, 1981, p.291.
3 James Simmons suggests that Yeats 'certainly relished' the disturbance and 'may even have stage-managed it' — *Sean O'Casey*. London: Macmillan, 1983, p.17.
4 Hugh Hunt has assembled much of the evidence of what took place in the theatre that night in *The Abbey: Ireland's National Theatre 1904–1979*. Dublin: Gill & Macmillan, 1979, pp.124–30.
5 For a critical account of O'Casey's version of his resignation see C. Desmond Greaves, *Sean O'Casey: Politics and Art*. London: Lawrence & Wishart, 1979, pp.75–6.
6 Sean O'Casey, *Three Plays*. London: Macmillan, 1957, p.151.
7 Greaves, *Sean O'Casey: Politics and Art*, p.120.
8 Thomas Kilroy (ed.), *Sean O'Casey: A Collection of Critical Essays*. Englewood Cliffs. New Jersey: Prentice-Hall, 1975, p.149.
9 *Three Plays*, p.194.
10 *Ibid.*, p.195.
11 *Ibid.*, p.194.
12 *Ibid.*, p.216.

13 Maik Hamburger, 'Anti-illusionism and the use of song in the early plays of Sean O'Casey', *O'Casey Annual No. 2*, ed. Robert G. Lowery. London: Macmillan, 1983, p.26.

14 *The Dramatic Works of Denis Johnston*, I. Gerrards Cross: Colin Smythe Ltd, 1977, p.87.

15 *The Dramatic Works of Denis Johnston*, II. Gerrards Cross: Colin Smythe Ltd, 1979, p.109.

16 *Ibid.*

17 *Ibid.*, p.142.

18 W.B. Yeats, *Collected Poems*. London: Macmillan, 1950, p.229.

19 *Dramatic Works*, II, pp.150–1.

20 *Ibid.*, p.153.

21 See Thomas Kilroy's valuable essay, *'The Moon in the Yellow River*: Denis Johnston's Shavianism' in *Denis Johnston: a Retrospective*. ed. Joseph Ronsley. Gerrards Cross: Colin Smythe Ltd, 1981, pp.49–58.

22 *Dramatic Works*, II, p.82.

23 *Ibid.*, p.158.

24 Ulick O'Connor, *Brendan Behan*. London: Panther, 1979, p.200. Richard Wall takes a similar view in his comparison of *An Giall* and *The Hostage* in *The Art of Brendan Behan*, ed. E.H. Mikhail. London: Vision Press, 1979, pp. 138–146. Colbert Kearney is more cautious: 'It is not suggested that the existing text of *The Hostage* is not the work of Behan, but that the principles of the play are those of Miss Littlewood rather than the author of *An Giall*', in *The Writings of Brendan Behan*. Dublin: Gill & Macmillan, 1977, p. 133.

25 Brendan Behan, *The Complete Plays*. London: Methuen, 1978, p.204.

26 *Ibid.*, p.160.

27 *Ibid.*, p.210.

28 *Ibid.*, p.226.

29 Brian Friel, *Selected Plays*. London: Faber & Faber, 1984, p. 114.

30 O'Casey, *Three Plays*, p.213.

31 Friel, *Selected Plays*, pp.109–10.

32 Seamus Deane, in his Introduction to the *Selected Plays*, p.19, says that 'Friel was accused . . . of defending the IRA by his attacks upon the British Army and the whole system of authority which that army was there to defend'.

33 Such ironic subleties can be missed. I saw a production of the play in Liverpool where some drunken Trotskyites kept barracking the sociologist's lecture with shouts of 'Bourgeois revisionist'.

34 *Selected Plays*, p.160.

35 *Ibid.*, p.150.

36 *Ibid.*, p.154.

37 *Ibid.*, p.155.

38 *Collected Poems*, p.359.

39 Behan, *The Complete Plays*, p.59.

40 *Ibid.*, p.217.

41 Kilroy, *Sean O'Casey: A Collection of Critical Essays*, p.2.

42 Philip Edwards speaks eloquently of the effect of this theatrical moment in *Threshold of a Nation*. Cambridge: Cambridge University Press, 1979, pp.236–7. Throughout this essay I am indebted to Edwards's extremely illuminating analysis.

JUNO AND THE PLAYWRIGHTS: THE INFLUENCE OF SEAN O'CASEY ON TWENTIETH-CENTURY DRAMA

HEINZ KOSOK

I come from the same area as Sean O'Casey about whom I don't intend to say anything for the simple reason that it would be like praising the Lakes of Killarney — a piece of impertinence. As far as I'm concerned, all I can say is that O'Casey's like champagne, one's wedding night, or the Aurora Borealis or whatever you call them — all them lights.[1]

This is how an Irish fellow dramatist, Brendan Behan, reacted to the plays of Sean O'Casey, whom he considered 'the greatest playwright living in my opinion',[2] and whom he defended vigorously against O'Casey's Irish critics:

In the United States, O'Casey is studied and praised in schools and universities all over the country. In the U.S.S.R. he is a highly respected artist. O'Casey is one of the few remaining unifying influences in a divided world. Why the hell should he care about a few crawthumpers in Ireland?[3]

Behan's praise, even if worded somewhat exuberantly, is fairly typical of the reaction of many twentieth-century dramatists to the plays of Sean O'Casey. John Arden (to cite a few highly diverse playwrights) confessed: '... I have been continuously inspired and excited by his plays — from all periods of his work ...' and he defended O'Casey as an experimental playwright and as a European rather than an Irishman.[4] Equally, Arnold Wesker stated: 'I can only say he was among my loves and influences'.[5] Arthur Adamov insisted on his attachment to the plays of O'Casey whose 'tenderness' he singled out for special praise as O'Casey's most exceptional merit;[6] and he even placed O'Casey on the same level as Brecht.[7] Bertolt Brecht more than once referred approvingly to the plays of O'Casey.[8]

And Brian Friel stated quite simply: 'We all came out from under his overcoat.'[9]

Eugene O'Neill and Denis Johnston also spoke very highly of O'Casey's early plays, even if they were not prepared to accept his later departure from the realities of the Dublin slums. O'Neill grumbled after he had read *The Star Turns Red*: ' . . . O'Casey is an artist and the soap box is no place for his great talent. The hell of it seems to be, when an artist starts saving the world, he starts losing himself'.[10] And Johnston fired a whole barrage of articles against O'Casey's later plays while conferring upon his earlier ones the greatest honour a writer has to give, that of parodying them. Not only did he insist 'The consummate craftsman who could create the second Act of *The Plough and the Stars* clearly knows as much as need be known about the English language . . .',[11] he also called his own play about the Easter Rising *The Scythe and the Sunset,* and in *The Old Lady Says 'No!'* he even brought a worker playwright named O'Cooney on stage who is a replica of O'Casey at the time of his early fame.

Distinctly negative pronouncements are less easy to discover. The shrillest of them is that made by Brinsley MacNamara who, when he was a director of the Abbey Theatre, denounced his fellow directors and the Dublin audience in 1935 for their 'wholly uncritical, and I might say, almost insane admiration for the vulgar and worthless plays of Mr. O'Casey'.[12]

If O'Casey found widespread acclaim among his fellow dramatists, the question remains whether their pronouncements are indicative of an influence that O'Casey may have exerted on their plays. Did he in any way shape the work of his contemporaries (as artists, if not in age) such as Brecht or O'Neill, or did a younger generation — Behan, Arden, Wesker and others — follow him as a model? And if such an influence is discovered, how does one measure it? It is of course highly dangerous to set down every superficial parallel as a possible influence; serious research into literary influences has often been discredited by source-hunting of this kind.

Literary critics have usually been just as vague on the subject of a possible O'Caseyan influence as O'Casey's fellow dramatists. If John Arden, for instance, is characterised as 'a writer whose theatrical genius is strangely similar to that of O'Casey',[13] it hardly helps to pinpoint concrete influences. Usually, critics have not taken the question any further than the following statement which is quite useless as criticism:

... O'Casey extended his experiment by mixing realistic and non-realistic techniques in his plays — a mingled form which he was to use in all his later plays, and which has subsequently been used by most modern dramatists, to mention some representative examples, Obey's *Noah* (1931), Wilder's *Our Town* (1938), Giraudoux's *Madwoman of Chaillot* (1945), Williams's *The Glass Menagerie* (1944), Miller's *Death of a Salesman* (1949).[14]

What, if anything, one is inclined to ask, do these playwrights have in common with O'Casey; are they supposed to have consciously or subconsciously imitated him; and was there nobody given to 'mixing realistic and non-realistic techniques' (whatever these may be) *before* O'Casey? Even when his influence is seen as limited to one particular group of playwrights, it is still described in far from precise terms, as in the following statement:

... his working-class origin, and apprenticeship as a labourer rather than an intellectual, made him a culture hero of the new English dramatists of 1956. Worthy on his record of the highest official honours, here was a world-famous man of the theatre who, even in old age, made no concessions to established authority. . . . You can read his influence most obviously, of course, in *The Quare Fellow* and *The Hostage* by Brendan Behan. But O'Casey's influence goes much further than that. It extends to Arden, Wesker, Delaney, Rudkin, Alun Owen and a dozen others, wherever in fact urban dialect is shaped, selected and built up to the purposes of serious drama, wherever the rejects of society, the soldiers in *Serjeant Musgrave's Dance* or the rustics in *Afore Night Come*, are put in the centre of the stage and given a voice. They copied his faults, too, whenever they cultivated a folksy togetherness or let feeble stereotypes put the case for the ruling classes.[15]

The question of literary influence is certainly a difficult one. It is difficult not only where the technical problem of detecting and documenting such influence is concerned. It also encompasses the question of evaluation. Does a writer's importance depend on the amount of influence he has exerted on others? Would it be possible to argue, in other words, that a writer's literary qualities could be measured in terms of his influence? Or could one say, conversely, that the truly great artist is so special that he cannot be copied or imitated or even taken as a model by others? In the field of twentieth-century drama, Strindberg, Ibsen, Chekhov, Wilder and Brecht can be seen as examples of the first case, while Hauptmann, O'Neill, Shaw and Anouilh illustrate the second. The influence of Brecht, to take an example, upon a host of other writers was perhaps even greater than the literary quality of his works would have warranted; it is not too much to say that the whole course of twentieth-century drama would have been different if it had not been for the model of Brecht — a model that often was not even realised as such. On the other hand, O'Neill remained a lonely giant without followers, whose greatness seems to stand out even more because he did not initiate any tradition whatsoever.

Where O'Casey is concerned, both arguments could be used with equal conviction. O'Casey wrote highly diverse plays, which renders it practically impossible to make general statements about his work. If one sub-divides his career as a playwright into five phases,[16] it is only the first one, with his great 'Dublin' plays like *Juno and the Paycock* and *The Plough and the Stars*, that can be shown to have been influential for other dramatists. In his later plays, especially in masterpieces like *The Silver Tassie, Red Roses for Me* and *Cock-a-doodle Dandy*, O'Casey was moving in a direction where apparently nobody wanted to, or was able to, follow him. As far as his plays written after 1926 are concerned, the question of his influence on other writers could be answered in one brief sentence: it was largely non-existent.

A variety of reasons can be cited to account for this statement. First, O'Casey's exceptional life history made it difficult for him to come into close contact with other writers. He was forty-three when his first play reached the stage; consequently he was always at least half a generation older than his 'contemporary' fellow dramatists. This is partly why he never had access to a larger circle of writers. In addition, his social status and his fragmentary, largely autodidactic education prevented him from being accepted as a 'man of letters'. When he settled down in Devon in 1938, he isolated himself in a geographic as well as a social sense from the literary scenes of London and Dublin. It was only during his sojourn of slightly more than ten years in or near London that he had a chance to make closer contact with other writers, but even then he seems not to have availed himself more than occasionally of this opportunity. Therefore younger playwrights had little chance of being closely acquainted with him; an influence on the immediate personal level was practically impossible.

Second, after 1926, when O'Casey had moved to England, he also lacked direct contact with a particular theatre that could have staged model productions of his plays, as did the Abbey

Theatre with his early works. An influence like the one exerted by Brecht through the Theater am Schiffbauerdamm was impossible for him after 1926.

Third, again with the exception of his early plays, O'Casey's writings did not gain any great influence through the theatre, simply because they were not acted frequently enough. Most of his plays after *The Plough and the Stars* received only one or two productions during his life-time in the English-speaking world, and several of these took place in provincial or even amateur theatres, far removed from the beaten track of critics and the general public alike. Consequently, younger playwrights whom he might have induced to learn from him did not have a chance of seeing more than an accidental selection of his writings on stage.

Fourth, O'Casey did not develop any coherent dramatic theory. His various statements on the drama, the theatre, and on literary theory in general are highly relevant to an understanding of his own works; they are always interesting, often amusing and sometimes remarkably astute, but they do not add up to any organic system of critical insights.

And fifth, because he lacked any basic dramatic theory, his plays are markedly divergent, even more so perhaps than those of such fellow dramatists as Hauptmann or O'Neill. Few of them are based in any way on insights derived from the preceding work; in the second and third phases of his career especially, each play constitutes a new departure and tries to solve new problems. This variety makes O'Casey a truly experimental playwright, but it has certainly reduced his influence on others, and it makes it practically impossible to recognize any influence derived from the whole body of his work. Instead, one has to look for the influence of individual plays.

An example of such isolated influence by an individual play can perhaps be seen in T.S. Eliot's *The Family Reunion*, the choric technique of which may well have been modelled on O'Casey's *Within the Gates*. Eliot had seen the London production of *Within the Gates* in 1934, and had shown himself impressed by O'Casey's use of chants in his play; he later thought that he might have been unconsciously influenced by O'Casey.[17]

Such individual influences of O'Casey's later plays dwindle into insignificance however in comparison with the unmistakable impact of the early plays, especially *The Shadow of a Gunman, Juno and the Paycock,* and *The Plough and the Stars.* Not surprisingly, such influence makes itself felt most of all in Anglo-Irish drama. Here, his influence seems to have worked in two ways, not only in the form of direct imitation, which is, of course, predominant, but also as an impulse to be as different as possible from O'Casey, the desire not at any cost to be taken as a follower. O'Casey's importance as a model *and* also an anti-model for the whole of Anglo-Irish drama since the twenties can be appreciated when one observes that the only history of drama to cover this field, Robert Hogan's *After the Irish Renaissance,* cites O'Casey on almost every page as a standard of evaluation for all other playwrights.

For a while it had looked as if the O'Caseyan influence would produce a flood of melodramatic plays about the Irish War of Independence and the Civil War. This is underlined by an amusing review of a long-forgotten play, Gerald Brosnan's *Before Midnight,* of 1928, written at a time when O'Casey had already turned away from this material:

I do not suppose that the spiritual father of the Abbey gunmen, C.I.D. men and prostitutes who has recently forsaken his offspring will claim the literary paternity of Mr. Gerald Brosnan, or that Mr. Brosnan will acknowledge any relationship with him. I do not suppose, either, that the Abbey audience will accept *Before Midnight* even as a drop of O'Casey war-substitute. But I do plead for a Kellog pact of dramatic disarmament and the blowing-up of dumps. In art there is no such thing as a successful school. O'Casey, as a man of genius, closed the door he opened. It makes a strong man blench to think of an O'Casey school, to think of the myriad of Mr. Brosnan's unproduced colleagues who are raiding Dublin tenement houses, stuffing their plays in vain with revolvers and prostitutes and C.I.D. men.[18]

Fortunately the reviewer's misgivings did not come true. A few works only of this particular tradition have been preserved. The most remarkable among them is undoubtedly Brendan Behan's *The Hostage* which has been called 'a gaily subversive play in the O'Casey tradition'[19] and had the greatest success of all Irish works in that mould.

Behan's indebtedness to O'Casey can fully be gauged only when one considers the original Gaelic version, *An Giall,* in addition to Joan Littlewood's English adaptation. Here the action has not yet been broken up into 'alienating' music-hall acts, and the parallels to O'Casey are much more obvious. It is not, however, sufficient to speak simply of an influence on the part of O'Casey, for Behan in many respects went beyond his model, developing and sometimes exaggerating O'Caseyan motifs. As in *The Shadow of a Gunman, Juno and the Paycock* and parts of *The Plough and the Stars*, the scenery of *The Hostage* is a room in a tenement house; like O'Casey, Behan was thinking of a definite house in Dublin. Several of his characters are immediately reminiscent of O'Casey's figures; the humorous, sceptical, quarrelsome and nevertheless helpful Pat cannot be imagined without the model of Fluther Good, and Teresa, in her strange mixture of fairy-tale naiveté, shyness, healthy self-confidence, practical altruism, courage and affection is closely related to Minnie Powell. It is also tempting to see Monsewer, who in his ridiculous kilt haunts the play as a symbol of the dead past and is treated by everybody with mock respect, as a relation of the Man in the Kilts in *Kathleen Listen In*; yet it is unlikely that Behan knew O'Casey's early play, for it was not published until 1961. It is more certain, however, that he refers to Rosie Redmond from *The Plough and the Stars*, the first and most famous prostitute on the Irish stage, when, in characteristic exaggeration of his model, he depicts a whole brothel whose inmates, prostitutes, pimps, homosexuals, are treated with the same humour, understanding and compassion as was Rosie.

The stage events in *The Hostage* are projected onto a politico-military background action that repeatedly erupts on the stage, immediately affecting the stage characters. Behan, however, is much more critical of the historical process than his predecessor. The I.R.A. activities of the nineteen-fifties, as an anachronistic continuation of the struggle for independence, are not only, as in O'Casey, criticised by some of the stage-figures, but are disparaged by the action itself: the senseless and accidental death of young Leslie condemns those who are responsible for his kidnapping. In addition, the guerilla fighters are, in contrast to O'Casey, shown here in a decidedly negative light. On the other hand, the real struggle for independence which is constantly present in the conversation of the stage figures, is treated with a similar objectivity to that found in O'Casey. In both cases, however, it is not the politico-military action but its effects on individual, well-defined characters that is at the centre of the play. In his juxtaposition of serious and comic elements, Behan goes beyond O'Casey, although at the time of *Juno and the Paycock* this must have appeared hardly possible. There is no doubt that Behan could achieve this extreme blending of styles only after the path had been prepared for him by O'Casey.

The Hostage, as a late reaction to O'Casey's plays of the Revolution and the Civil War, takes up an exceptional position. In the meantime, O'Casey's early plays had been much more influential in another field of Irish drama. O'Casey was the first to introduce the world of the Dublin slums to world literature, and the specific tradition he created is that of the family play set in the slums. Once the tradition had been established, dozens of plays were set in the tenements around Mountjoy Square. Only a few of them have appeared in print; Seamus de Burca's *The Howards* (1960), Robert Collis's *Marrowbone Lane* (1939) and Brendan Behan's short-play *Moving Out* (1952) may be cited as examples. All three deal with family histories from the Dublin slums and belong to the O'Casey tradition in a wider sense, although they do not show any specific indebtedness to O'Casey.

Several plays, however, written under the influence of O'Casey's works derive more directly from *Juno and the Paycock.* Louis D'Alton's *The Mousetrap* (1938), for instance, depicts a family strongly reminiscent of *Juno and the Paycock,* with a sneering and domineering but unsuccessful father, a long-suffering mother, a son who through one rash action mars his whole future and is finally arrested for murder, and a daughter who is left pregnant by the intruder from the outside world. Like O'Casey's play, *The Mousetrap* is realistic in intention, with roughly sketched characters and nicely observed dialogue, but the plot is far too contrived, the disasters succeeding each other with improbable rapidity because, unlike O'Casey, the author tries to confine his action within the classically acceptable 24 hours limit. At the time of its publication the author's obvious sympathy for the 'fallen' girl, and his understanding for the seducer, together with his contempt for the upholders of conventional morality, apparently made the play unacceptable for the Irish stage, while its model has become a staple of the Irish theatrical repertoire.

Walter Macken's *Mungo's Mansion* (1946) transfers O'Casey's characters from the Dublin tenements to the slums of Galway. The unemployed Mungo is another 'Captain' Boyle, seen slightly less critically, whose excitability is motivated at least in part by a previous accident. His love-hate relationship to the ragged Mowleogs is immediately reminiscent of Boyle and Joxer, a similarity underlined by the unexpected win in the sweep-stake. As in O'Casey, this play, under the rather repulsive surface of quarrels and egoism, hides a great deal of attachment, helpfulness and uncomplicated humanity. The chief differences are the absence of a character comparable to Juno and the absence of a politico-military background action.[20]

A Juno-like character is present, however, in a play that transfers the atmosphere of O'Casey's drama to yet another town, a poor area of Waterford: this is James Cheasty's *Francey* (1961). Again, as in *Mungo's Mansion*, the conflict between the care-worn, protective mother and her spendthrift husband is intensified by the presence of a parasitic character, a direct successor of Joxer, revealingly named Jock, who exploits the title character, a direct successor of 'Captain' Boyle, and turns against him when the source has fallen dry. There is also a hare-brained neighbour addicted to the lowest type of gossip, whose words could have come directly from O'Casey's Mrs. Madigan, without, however, taking on her thematic function in the play. Francey himself is another braggart who lives in a world of fantasy and cares nothing for his wife, senselessly spending the compensation money he has received after a road-accident, until his married life, as well as his children, are ruined. Unlike O'Casey's play the motif of unexpected, destructive wealth has become central, triggering off a melodramatic action that leads to an unmitigated catastrophe. The protective forces embodied in Juno are here not strong enough to counteract the destructive forces of 'Captain' Boyle. Obviously the author has taken over the individual ingredients of O'Casey's play without grasping their contextual, supra-individual meaning. It is, perhaps, the absence of a more general background action, more than anything else, that leads Cheasty into the double abyss of sentimentality and sensationalism.

Both the Juno-character and the general background action are present in a work that more than any other resembles the O'Casey play: Joseph Tomelty's *The End House* (1944). In this case it is sufficient to characterise Tomelty's work, without any explicit comparison, in order to draw attention to the obvious parallels with *Juno and the Paycock*. *The End House* is set in a poor, Catholic quarter of Belfast, the historical background being the Troubles of 1938. The central characters are the unemployed braggart and show-off MacAstocker, his wife Sar Alice, who throughout her life has been struggling for the survival of her family and does not expect any more from life than to provide enough to eat for her relations, her daughter Monica, who hopes to achieve a higher station in life and wants to leave the influence of the slums behind her, and her son Seamus, who

has just been released from a prison sentence for his member-
ship in the illegal I.R.A. The initial situation of the play concerns
the death of a neighbour who has been shot by I.R.A. men
because he had betrayed one of them to the police. The audience
learns about his death when a newspaper article is read at the
beginning of the play. This event is succeeded by a series of
catastrophes: Sar Alice loses her insurance money, MacAstocker
is injured in an accident, Monica falls in love with an English
soldier who deserts with the money borrowed from her and
leaves her helpless, possibly pregnant, Seamus is probably
involved in the killing of the neighbour and is himself shot
during a raid. Sar Alice and Monica remain as the victims, who
are not even able to repay the money they borrowed from their
neighbours and thus lose their good name.

In view of these parallels, which are supported by many
minor details, it is necessary to emphasise the differences
between the two plays in order to protect Tomelty from the
accusation of straightforward plagiarism. The characters in *The
End House* are seen less critically. MacAstocker is less
depreciated by his actions than Boyle, and there is no character
comparable to Joxer. In his place, Tomelty has introduced two
'positive' helpful neighbours, and the cornet player Stewartie is
his most interesting innovation. Because of the absence of a
Joxer-like character, *The End House* lacks a great deal of the
humour of *Juno and the Paycock*; its emotional tone, therefore, is
more homogeneous. It is stamped by the author's compassion
for the victims of the political situation. Although there is no
attempt to make the theme explicit, as O'Casey had in Juno's
prayer, the author's purpose in the play is more obvious and
more unified. Where all the stage characters are seen with
sympathy, and are presented as innocent victims, the
responsibility for such a situation must fall entirely on the
existing political system, which is additionally criticised here in
the brutality and despotism of the police.

A direct continuation of *The End House* may be seen in John
Boyd's *The Flats* (1971), set in the Belfast of 1969. The 'end
house' has here been replaced by the 'end flat', situated in a
strategic position in a block of flats. It is commandeered both by
the British Army and by the Civil Defence Committee, at a time
when a Protestant mob threatens to attack the flats inhabited
predominantly by Catholics. This situation gives rise to
extended discussions of various political viewpoints: militant
republicanism, moderate nationalism, pacifism, socialism, the

self-styled neutrality of the British Army, and a wholly understandable individualism concerned only with personal survival. Whereas the political background events have thus been updated, the mechanism for projecting them onto the stage is still that provided by O'Casey in *Juno and the Paycock*. The list of *dramatis personae* again reads like a description of O'Casey's play. There is the same constellation of the unemployed father who neglects his family, the care-worn mother untiring in her efforts to keep the family together, the outsider son who engages in subversive activities, and the disillusioned daughter who hopes for an escape from the slums through her fiancé who comes over from England. It is true that Boyd has omitted the time-worn motifs of seduction and unexpected riches, but the whole atmosphere of slum life under the pressure of a military conflict is closely reminiscent of *Juno and the Paycock*, and so is Boyd's use of test situations to distinguish between various attitudes to life, even to the point where a British soldier is to be given a cup of tea, and the characters react in various ways to this challenge, just as Johnny's demand for a glass of water in O'Casey's play had helped to distinguish between Juno and Mary. Even if Joe Donellan is not such a despicable good-for-nothing as 'Captain' Boyle, numerous details (including Kathleen's concluding prayer) point to the immense influence of O'Casey's work. It is a measure of O'Casey's success that his play is so much more convincing, unified, life-like, moving and universal than its successors and will be remembered when all the others are forgotten.

The literary reactions to *Juno and the Paycock*, however, were not limited to Anglo-Irish drama. In fact, the influence of this play could hardly have been more widespread geographically as well as chronologically. It was O'Casey's only work to have initiated a new and still living literary tradition, that of the family play set in the slums. This type of play undoubtedly owed something to the tradition of bourgeois tragedy, but it is precisely those traits that O'Casey added to the tradition, especially the transfer of the events into the squalid world of big-city slums, that were widely imitated. If *Juno and the Paycock* was not the first play with such a setting, it was the first that was internationally successful. Moreover, O'Casey provided a specific combination of characters, plot elements and motifs which reappeared in a number of plays, rendering a concrete influence in each case more than probable. Four examples may be briefly described to illustrate this point.

One of the best-known English plays between the two world wars, justly appreciated by audiences throughout Britain, was *Love on the Dole* (1934) by Ronald Gow and Walter Greenwood, a play set in the world of the unemployed, a working-class quarter of Salford, Lancashire. Its constellation of *dramatis personae*, however, is that of *Juno and the Paycock*: the unemployed father, the indefatigable mother who alone keeps the family together, the daughter striving for 'higher' values. As in *Juno and the Paycock* the action is determined by the dual motifs of seduction and of unexpected wealth that disappears as soon as it has been won, and it is interspersed with comic elements. As in O'Casey's play, the necessity of strikes and demonstrations is discussed. Although none of these elements alone would suffice to constitute an influence, their combination points quite clearly to O'Casey.

Clifford Odets's *Awake and Sing!* (1935) belongs to the same period as *Love on the Dole*. Of this play it has been said: '*Awake and Sing!*, though not so great a play, is *Juno and the Paycock* transposed from the Dublin slums to the Jewish Bronx of New York. It has the same pattern of coarseness and sensibility, the quality that can send poetry, like a shaft of sunlight, through the squalor of a tenement'.[21] The specific Dublin milieu, unique in language and characters, has here been replaced by another, equally specific milieu. It is true that in O'Casey's Dublin the Berger family's standard of living would hardly qualify them as the inhabitants of a slum, but the higher material demands of the American way of life classify them as members of the lowest social class whose existence is constantly threatened by unemployment. It is significant that the descriptions of the *dramatis personae* with which Odets prefaces his play, could be transferred, with very slight modifications, to the characters in *Juno and the Paycock*. The relationship of Bessie to Juno, for instance, can hardly be overlooked:

BESSIE BERGER, as she herself states, is not only the mother in this home but also the father. She is constantly arranging and taking care of her family. She loves life, likes to laugh, has great resourcefulness, and enjoys living from day to day. A high degree of energy accounts for her quick exasperation at ineptitude. She is a shrewd judge of realistic qualities in people in the sense of being able to gauge quickly their effectiveness. In her eyes all of the people in the house are equal. She is naive and quick in emotional response. She is afraid of utter poverty. She is proper according to her own standards, which are fairly close to those of most middle-class families. She knows that when one lives in the jungle one must look out for the wild life.[22]

She tyrannises her family because she is deeply concerned about their happiness. She asserts herself against her husband who has been defeated by life and lives in fruitless memories of the past, as well as against her son who rebels against a purely materialistic attitude, and she cares for her self-confident daughter who would like to dissociate herself from the family, when she expects an illegitimate child and finds that no other refuge is left to her. Like the motif of seduction, the motif of unexpected wealth (Jacob's insurance money when he kills himself), point to the model of O'Casey's play. Even more reminiscent of O'Casey is the fact that this family in the process of disintegration, shaken by various catastrophes, entirely cut off from the world outside and thrown upon itself, is nevertheless not presented as an image of hopelessness and despair. Small gestures of affection are still capable of fending off the apparently all-powerful fate of poverty, and the final victory of Juno's humanity is here paralleled in Ralph's defeat of resignation and material dependence, even though Odets's solution seems to be less organic than O'Casey's.

Arnold Wesker's early play *Chicken Soup with Barley* (1958) is set in a similar and equally well-defined social context as *Awake and Sing!*, the world of East European Jewish emigrants in London. Although it appeared more than twenty years later, it has its starting point in the same historical situation, the thirties, a period overshadowed by economic crises and mass unemployment that seemed to predict an imminent end to the capitalist bourgeois way of life. In *Chicken Soup with Barley* the familiar constellation of *dramatis personae* from *Juno and the Paycock* is again clearly recognizable (in the other two plays of the *Chicken Soup Trilogy* it is still present, though less obvious).[23] The resolute and optimistic mother who fights for the material welfare of her family, the resigned, passive, egocentric father, the son who is engaged in political activities and his elder sister, initially equally active but later disillusioned, all owe their existence as much to the model of the Boyle family as to Wesker's personal experience. The relationship is sometimes underlined in conspicuous details. Ada, for instance, turns one of 'Captain' Boyle's favourite terms against her father, who is so closely related to Boyle: 'Daddy — you are the world's biggest procrastinator'. And Sarah's indefatigable care for her family's welfare is symbolised in the same action as Juno's motherliness: her never-tiring readiness to make tea as a spontaneous cure-all for problems, sorrows and disease:

SARAH: Sit down, both of you; I'll get the kettle on [*Goes off to kitchen.*]
MOUNTY: [*to Bessie*] Always put the kettle on — that was the first thing Sarah always did. Am I right, Harry? I'm right, aren't I? [*shouting to Sarah*] Remember, Sarah? It was always a cup of tea first.[24]

Juno reacts in an identical way:

MRS. BOYLE: There, now; go back an' lie down again, an'Ill bring you in a nice cup o' tay.
JOHNNY: Tay, tay, tay! You're always thinkin' o' tay. If a man was dyin' you'd thry to make him swally a cup o' tay![25]

Even more important is the fact that *Chicken Soup with Barley*, like *Juno and the Paycock*, is projected onto a historical background action which intensifies the stage events and raises them to a universal plane. The changing role of socialism in the England of the thirties, forties and fifties that dominates the discussions of the stage characters and is occasionally projected on stage when they take part in demonstrations and, like Johnny, are wounded, is depicted with the same sceptical objectivity as the civil war in *Juno and the Paycock*, the author refraining from restricting his characters' individuality by imposing any opinion of his own. *Chicken Soup with Barley* is the most remarkable example of the far-reaching influence that O'Casey exerted, without, however, in any way constraining his successors' originality of creation.

Another, not quite so conspicuous example is Errol John's *Moon on a Rainbow Shawl* (1958), of which Doris Lessing has said with some exaggeration: '. . . it is nearer to O'Casey than anything else in our language'.[26] O'Casey's Dublin tenement milieu has here undergone a more unusual transformation, and yet the ugly slums of Port of Spain, Trinidad, show surprising parallels to the world of 'Captain' Boyle, underlining the universality of O'Casey's play. The precise representation of a world of poverty characterised by its dialect, habits and types of persons is equally reminiscent of O'Casey, as is the unsentimental poetisation of this world. As in *Juno and the Paycock*, brutal egoism exists side by side with a most admirable altruism, and one finds the resigned adaptation to apparently unavoidable necessities as well as the attempt at revolt. The situation of Mary has been shared between two characters, Rosa who will be alone to care for her child, and Esther, who has not (yet?) given up the struggle against the repressive forces of her surroundings. The clearest O'Casey influence is, however, again to be found in the parents: Sophia has been made ruthless and angry by the responsibilities that have been forced upon her, but she takes her role as the protectress of the family as seriously as Juno, while Charlie in his resignation escapes from his duties into drunkenness and the reminiscences of his past as a cricket star.

The influence of Sean O'Casey on twentieth-century drama has, therefore, not been as extensive as that of some other play-wrights, like Ibsen, Chekhov or Brecht. As a basically optimistic playwright he stood little chance of widespread imitation at a time when pessimism had become the vogue even in popular entertainment. As an experimental playwright he could not build up a tradition of O'Casey plays, because he tended to question the technique of each of his own plays in the following works. And as a playwright who combined highly diverse styles — the tragic and the farcical, the realistic and the fantastic, the poetic and the allegorical — he did not project a unified image that could be followed by less gifted writers.

He did, however, exert a strong influence in a few clearly circumscribed fields. He introduced the slums of Dublin to the stage and made them acceptable as a literary milieu. He encouraged Irish authors to write about the tenement dwellers, and to do so with the typical O'Caseyan mixture of humour, understanding and compassion. And most of all, he created in *Juno and the Paycock* a play that could be followed, in its over-all structure as well as in many details of characterisation, plot motifs, and theme, in many parts of the world, a play, moreover, that presents one of the most important links between traditional bourgeois tragedy and modern proletarian drama. In addition to his own plays, this basic pattern of *Juno and the Paycock* was O'Casey's most valuable gift to the world of literature.

NOTES

1 *Brendan Behan's Island: An Irish Sketch-book.* London: Transworld Publishers, 1965, pp.12–14.

2 *Confessions of an Irish Rebel.* London: Hutchinson, 1965, p.30.

3 Letter to the *Irish Times* (29 August 1961), quoted by John O'Riordan, 'O'Casey's Dublin Critics', *Library Review,* 21, ii (1967), 63.

4 Letter to the *Observer* (27 September 1964), quoted *ibid.*

5 Quoted in Bernard Leroy, 'Two Committed Playwrights: Wesker and O'Casey', in: Patrick Rafroidi, Raymonde Popot and William Parker (eds), *Aspects of the Irish Theatre.* Lille: Editions Universitaires, 1972, p.116.

6 'J'ai souvent dit et répeté mon attachement à l'oeuvre de Sean O'Casey, où l'ambiguité des situations et des personnages n'entrainent presque jamais confusions et équivoques, et où la sévérité, non plus, ne devient pas hargneuse. La tendresse d'O'Casey pour ses personnages me frappe à chaque nouvelle représentation, et c'est peut-être là que se trouve son plus exceptionnel mérite.' Arthur Adamov, 'La femme avenir de l'homme' dans l'oeuvre de Sean O'Casey', *Lettres Francaises*, no. 1028 (1964).

7 *Sinn und Form*, 13 (1961), 938–939.

8 See Beate Lahrmann-Hartung, *Sean O'Casey und das epische Theater Bertolt Brechts*, Neue Studien zur Anglistik und Amerikanistik, 28. Frankfurt: Lang, 1983, p.10.

9 *Sean O'Casey Review*, 4 (1978), 87.

10 Quoted in Arthur and Barbara Gelb, *O'Neill*. New York: Harper & Row, 2nd ed. 1973, p.830.

11 'Joxer in Totnes: A Study in Sean O'Casey', *Irish Writing*, no. 13 (Dec. 1950), 52.

12 Quoted by Robert Hogan, *After the Irish Renaissance: A Critical History of the Irish Drama since 'The Plough and the Stars'*. London: Macmillan, 1968, p.32.

13 Kevin Casey, 'The Excitements and the Disappointments', in: Sean McCann (ed.) *The World of Sean O'Casey*. London: Four Square Books, 1966, p.218.

14 David Krause, *Sean O'Casey: The Man and His Work*. London: MacGibbon & Kee, 1960, p.99.

15 Laurence Kitchin, *Drama in the Sixties: Form and Interpretation*. London: Faber, 1966, pp.105–106.

16 For details of his career, see the present author's *O'Casey the Dramatist*. Gerrards Cross: Colin Smythe, 1985.

17 Ronald Ayling, 'The Poetic Drama of T.S. Eliot', *English Studies in Africa*, 2 (1959), 247–250.

18 C.P.C., 'Before Midnight', *Irish Statesman* (July 21, 1928), 392.

19 Kitchin, *Drama in the Sixties*, p.98.

20 On the personal relationship between Macken and O'Casey, see Heinz Kosok, 'O'Casey and An Taibhdhearc', *O'Casey Annual*, 3 (1984), 115–123.

21 Audrey Williamson, *Theatre of Two Decades*. London: Rockliff, 1951, p.165.

22 Clifford Odets, *Golden Boy, Awake and Sing!, The Big Knife*. Harmondsworth: Penguin Books, 1963, p.117.

23 For comparisons between the two plays, see for instance, Margery M. Morgan, 'Arnold Wesker: The Celebrated Instinct', in: Hedwig Bock and Albert Wertheim (eds.), *Essays on Contemporary British Drama* (München: Hueber, 1981), p.34; and Robert Fricker, *Das moderne englische Drama* (Göttingen: Vandenhoeck und Ruprecht, 2nd ed. 1964), pp.148–149, 153.

24 *The Wesker Trilogy*. Harmondsworth: Penguin Books, rev. ed. 1979, pp.40, 58.

25 Sean O'Casey, *Collected Plays*, vol. I. London: Macmillan, 1957, p.7.

26 Quoted on the cover of Errol John, *Moon on a Rainbow Shawl*. London: Faber, 2nd ed. 1963.

BRENDAN BEHAN'S THEATRE

DESMOND MAXWELL

I

'We're off, in this order: the Governor, the Chief, two screws Regan and Crimmin, the quare fellow between them, two more screws and three runners from across the Channel, getting well in front, now the Canon. He's making a big effort for the last two furlongs. He's got the white pudding bag on his head, just a short distance to go. He's in. [*A clock begins to chime the hour. Each quarter sounds louder.*] His feet to the chalk line. He'll be pinioned, his feet together. The bag will be pulled down over his face. The screws come off the trap and steady him. Himself goes to the lever and ...

The hour strikes. The WARDERS *cross themselves and put on their caps. From the* PRISONERS *comes a ferocious howling.*

— *The Quare Fellow*

This burlesque of a radio sports commentary, sardonically transferred to a condemned man's approaching the scaffold, had its first audience on 19 November 1954 at the Pike Theatre Club, Dublin. The next year the Pike presented Beckett's *Waiting for Godot*, a premiere shared with the production by the Arts Theatre Club, London. The work of Behan and Beckett was, of course, to become widely accessible. Still, there was at least a symbolic value in their Dublin presentation.

Both plays were directed by Alan Simpson, who with Carolyn Swift founded the Pike in 1953. Their intention was 'to stir up the theatrical lethargy of post-war Ireland'.[1] In that cause, if only for these two pioneering productions, the Pike has an importance out of proportion to its minute size. It represented an imaginative energy notably absent elsewhere in Dublin theatre. The established companies would have nothing to do with Behan, nor with Beckett. The former was disreputable, the latter riskily *avant-garde*.

Yet without making extravagant claims for Behan, it is fair to say that *The Quare Fellow* addressed its audiences with a good

87

deal more urgency than the rather circumspect bill of fare then commonly on offer: Shaw (*St. Joan, The Doctor's Dilemma*), a Eugene O'Neill (*Anna Christie*), an Elmer Rice (*Not for Children*); from the home dramatists Lady Longford's *The Hill of Quirke*, Joseph Tomelty's *Is The Priest at Home?*, M. J. Molloy's *The Will and the Way*, and *Twenty Years A-Wooing* by John McCann, a prolific and popular writer of soap operas: revivals, safe new works, potboilers. Though Behan's career as a playwright was brief — he wrote only two considerable plays — it greatly enlivened this predictable scene; and was a harbinger of the revival of Irish theatre in the early sixties, when Behan was to make an unexpected posthumous appearance.

By way of comment on his own plays, Behan has had his word on Beckett. 'When Samuel Beckett', he said, 'was in Trinity College listening to lectures, I was in the Queen's Theatre, my uncle's music hall. That is why my plays are music hall and his are university lectures'.[2] It is a near-sighted view of Beckett, whose characters have a good deal of Laurel and Hardy in them. Applied to Behan's own plays it also calls for some reserve.

The Hostage is its obvious verification. It demonstrates Behan's affinity with — perhaps subservience to — Joan Littlewood's improvisational theatre, of which he said, 'the thing to aim... for [is] to amuse people and any time they get bored, divert them with a song or a dance'.[3] Behan in the Littlewood orbit supplied *The Hostage* with an abundance of those vaudeville ingredients. Her 1958 production at Stratford East used the original script as a diagram for elaboration — spontaneous dance, the introduction of songs, of topical references — even of dialogue, an opportunity still embedded in the published text: 'The lines of this scene are largely improvised to suit the occasion'.

It was in a way a marriage of minds. The method suited Behan. Seated in a pub opposite the Theatre Royal during rehearsals, he was perfectly happy to supply a song, a scene, a snatch of dialogue on demand. The danger of the method is its potential for indiscipline, Behan's affliction. The authority of the playwright's words and design abates; parts acquire a momentum of their own. *The Hostage*, then, is not so much Behan as a joint Behan/Littlewood creation, and to the consequences of that relationship we shall return.

II

Behan's first play, *The Quare Fellow*, is a very different matter.

It began as a one-act play in Gaelic, *Casadh Sugáin Eile (The Twisting of Another Rope)*. The Abbey rejected it, and also its three-act version, as did Hilton Edwards for the Gate Theatre. When Alan Simpson finally took it up, he found Behan, like Joan Littlewood after him, an easygoing collaborator — 'not', he says directorially, 'one of those playwrights who see everything differently to the director, or try to mess him around'. The manuscript was a mess, the play's structure sprawling and uneconomical, but Simpson had no doubt of its quality. His editorial intervention was much more modest than Joan Littlewood's, however. As he puts it:

We re-arranged rather than re-wrote some of the play. I still have a copy of the original script, which is very rambling. A character would change subjects as though in a genuine conversation. We made Brendan sort it out so that one subject was dealt with at a time. We probably made cuts; in fact, I am sure we did, and we tied up loose ends such as curtain lines.[4]

The play ran for a month and brought Behan forty or fifty pounds. None of the larger Dublin theatres would house it. *The Quare Fellow* went to Joan Littlewood at Stratford East.

The critics of the 1958 New York production responded without enthusiasm. *The New York Times* complained of Behan's 'uncertain command of the theatre medium' and of the play's looseness of design; the *Herald Tribune* of its triteness.[5] These are curious opinions. The play is tightly knit and almost classically unified. Behan was perfectly capable, in 1954, of the kind of remaking suggested to him by Simpson.

Before curtain rise, the prisoner's sardonic lament, 'that old triangle', gives human voice to the stage set's images of confinement: the severe lines of metal cell doors and the administrative circle, the women's section visible but beyond reach, the notice in Victorian lettering which says, 'SILENCE'. All except the voice is institutional, correctional. The play, like the voice, challenges the restraints. Their physical duress — unsentimentally observed — represents the crude moral arbitrations of the prison. Sequences of action also dramatise the basic tension between the system and its creatures, routine and individuality, warders and prisoners:

WARDER REGAN. Right, B. Wing, bang out your doors. B.I. get in off your steps and bang out your doors, into your cells and bang out your doors. Get locked up. BANG THEM DOORS! GET INSIDE AND BANG OUT THEM DOORS![6]

The scenes of morning stand-to, the line-up for inspection, the filing out to dig the grave should be played to suggest the prisoners' minimal obedience to the forms. These dreary rituals, paid mocking observance, stand against the antic caperings of the two Young Prisoners, who 'samba out with their brushes for partners humming the Wedding Samba': the play's only 'routine'. Like the choreographed coal-stealing in Wesker's *Chips With Everything* (1962), the drill in McGrath's *Events While Guarding the Bofors Gun* (1966), *The Quare Fellow*'s chores and curbs evade the intention of their supervisors. 'By the left, laugh', as Dunlavin says. Elsewhere in the play, effects akin to those of music hall are immediately part of the action. As the quare fellow's last, superior meal is brought to him, the prisoners crowd round the yard with a kind of farewell, patter chorus:

PRISONER A:	Pork chops.
PRISONER B:	Pig's feet.
PRISONER A:	Salmon.
NEIGHBOUR:	Fish and chips.
MICKSER:	Jelly and custard.
NEIGHBOUR:	Roast lamb.
PRISONER A:	Plum pudding.
PRISONER B:	Turkey.
NEIGHBOUR:	Goose.
PRISONERS A, B, and NEIGHBOUR:	Rashers and eggs.
ALL:	Rashers and eggs, rashers and eggs, and eggs and rashers and eggs and rashers it is.

(p.84)

The Quare Fellow entirely avoids the pantomime extravagances of *The Hostage*. One song, 'that old triangle,' sounds the play's strict chronology, from 'To begin the morning/The warder bawling' through 'On a fine spring evening/The lag lay dreaming' to 'The day was dying and the wind was sighing'. Apart from that there are a few snatches only. Thus discreetly used, the harsh, haunting song generalises on the passage of time, which is the main 'action' of the play. The prison inmates return obsessively to it — particularly the coming hour of execution, but generally as the focus of their lives: 'Healy is coming up today', 'the small hours of this morning', 'long months here', 'out again this day week', 'three days of No. 1', 'the death watch coming on at twelve o'clock'. Hardly a page lacks such a confining definition by hours, days, years. Time and space impose their restrictions, brought together in the final song:

> In the female prison
> There are seventy women
> I wish it was with them that I did dwell,
> Then that old triangle
> Could jingle jangle
> Along the banks of the Royal Canal. (p.124)

The crude song, in the diminuendo after the hanging, revives the sexual antithesis to death, with an artistic decorum which *The Hostage* vulgarises.

Behan was well aware from his own experience that these confinements neither eradicated individuality nor formed any liberal ethic in the prisoners. While he was in Mountjoy Jail after 1942 he worked on a play called *The Landlady*, which involved suicide and prostitution. It never had a chance to shock the bourgeois, as it certainly would have. It did shock a number of Behan's fellow-convicts, who forcibly prevented its staging in Mountjoy. The prisoners in *The Quare Fellow* are no more tolerant. Dunlavin is horrified that the cell next to him is to be occupied by a sexual offender, not the reprieved murderer: 'Killing your wife is a natural class of a thing could happen to the best of us. But this other dirty animal on me left . . .'. For the prisoners, the Quare Fellow is not a Cause. He is a victim, a sacrifice, the ceremonies of his death detailed in their minds. Through the prisoners the audience has entrance to the condemned cell and to knowledge of its occupant, who is divested of the idiosyncrasies of self.

Much of the conversation about the Quare Fellow refers to him only indirectly, through prison lore of the gruesome mechanics of hanging and the hours before it. He is all the Quare Fellows who have met this death. Warders and prisoners agree on, to put the matter mildly, its messiness. What do we learn of it? The duty warders make futile attempts to conceal the passage of time. The washer is put beneath the condemned man's ear, the hood is donned. The prisoner's build may be wrongly estimated: decapitation or strangulation — 'his head was all twisted and his face black, but the two eyes were the worst; like a rabbit's; it was fear that had done it'.

The execution becomes an exercise in terror for almost all concerned in it; that or a bureaucratic necessity. The prisoners' view of it is unsentimental, almost clinical, with a colour of macabre fascination. Most feel some compassion, Prisoner C deeply. But the compassion is for a man recognised, on the whole, as the agent of his own execution — 'Begod, he's not being topped for nothing — to cut his own brother up and butcher him like a pig'.

These responses are far from the absolutes of reformist discourse. Their power is the greater for an anguish — and an appetite — which does not come from a received Virtue Crucified. The personification is not to suggest any symbolic association between the Quare Fellow and Christ. Christ, however, did have to share his crucifixion with two outcasts more of the Quare Fellow's persuasion. Without urging an extension of that kind, Behan's play does interpolate exercises of observance which hint at the extension.

The prisoners' chorus makes a ceremony of the Quare Fellow's meal. The hangman, drunk, and his sober attendant deliver a litany which tastelessly but formally solemnises the soul and body of the Quare Fellow:

JENKINSON [*sings*]: My brother, sit and think.
                While yet some time is left to thee
                Kneel to thy God who from thee does not shrink
                And lay thy sins on Him who died for thee.

HANGMAN: Take a fourteen-stone man as a basis and giving him a
          drop of eight foot...

                                                          (p.117)

Finally, the prisoners enter the rite. Their wordless howling at the moment of execution, and Mickser's parody of a race-course commentator, determine their presence at a mystery, not a demonstration against capital punishment. The play, for all its essentially naturalistic manner, invites these larger understandings.

Colbert Kearney has remarked that *The Quare Fellow*

is a play within a play, and structurally much more sophisticated than it is often thought. There are two audiences: those in the theatre watch those on the stage who witness the externals of the closet-drama .... The theatre audience cannot resist judging the behaviour of those on stage and invariably they laugh at the black humour of the prisoners and dissociate themselves from the strict principles of the prison regime. At some point during or after the play the theatre-audience must realise that they have been tricked into a position which is critical of the very institution which they support outside the theatre.[7]

The point about the play's structure is well taken, and as

Kearney argues, *The Quare Fellow* 'lacks the simplicity of propaganda'. He rightly disputes the criticism that the play is, a 'rather shallow bit of propaganda directed largely towards the evils of capital punishment'. Its effect should be felt, Kearney argues, 'wherever there is an imperfect society which, in its desire to organise itself for the good of the majority, makes imperfect laws which alienate the exceptions, the unusual, the 'quare' fellows.'[8]

The play reaches into the condition of the outcast and the social defences erected against him. With considerable perception it represents the psychological defences which people set up against violent death, and at an even deeper level its fascination. The emotions which welcome barbaric revenge in whatever form — execution, feud, assassination, war — enter the play's ambit, observed with a remarkable neutrality of tone. Even Warder Regan, who comes closest to explicit condemnation of the whole process, never fully interrogates its motives. One of his speeches, towards the end, refers to the pandering to a lust for death and spectacle, now hypocritically muted with the hanging removed from public to private view, from mass audience to secular and ecclesiastical representatives. Almost shouting, Regan says, 'I think the whole show should be put on in Croke Park; after all, it's at the public expense and they let it go on. They should have something more for their money than a bit of paper stuck up on the gate'(p.114). But he continues in his office: '[The hangman] has no more to do with it than you or I or the people that pay us, and that's every man or woman that pays taxes or votes in elections. If they don't like it, they needn't have it'. Regan is part of the 'they'. His dual position of critic and participant shades him away from a merely propagandist voice.

The Quare Fellow epitomises Behan's achievement in theatre. It is localised by language, through which it escapes to its wider applications. The music-hall styles are there — cross-talk, song, slapstick — but refined to subtler purpose. The play has a message, but the message is not the play. The play is entertainment, but entertainment is not its substance. *The Quare Fellow*, classically restricted to one day's action, takes us into the presence of individuals who merge into a voice beyond their individualities.

Unlike *The Hostage*, *The Quare Fellow* adroitly deploys not intrusions but analogues of music-hall forms: of cross-talk, 'routines', dance, patter. In *The Hostage*, Behan's concern to avoid boredom interferes with muted effects. He, or Joan Littlewood, will not leave alone the moving conversation between Teresa and Meg about the young boy who is to be hanged in Belfast. 'Come on, Kate', Meg must say, 'give us a bit of music', and a wild dance takes over. Some of the interference is less self-indulgent. The song, 'I will give a golden ball' emerges congenially enough from Teresa's and Leslie's halting declarations of love. The song leads them to bed together, a bed for two individuals, not vaudeville turns. 'I know I wasn't much good to you', Leslie says later (p.229).

The Hostage has its points of control: the setting, an old house, once a Republican sanctuary, now a brothel, which has seen the Ascendancy days of Monsewer's,

> Tea and toast and muffin rings,
> Old ladies with stern faces,
> And the Captains and the Kings (p.193).

The location entertains the themes of internal Irish disputes, English/Irish antagonisms, and countering these the communion between Teresa and Leslie. The play's jumble of styles, however, confuses their presentation. Comedy and pathos never reach into each other. Behan manipulates his characters and situations to sudden reversals of effect as unfeelingly as Public Good, National Security, The Cause — his targets — manipulate their real-life counterparts.

The Hostage began as *An Giall* (The Hostage) a play in Irish commissioned by Gael-Linn and performed in 1958. Behan then wrote a translation for Joan Littlewood, which by the time it appeared in London had acquired another half-dozen characters and become 'a drastically modified version'.[9] *An Giall's* immediate origin was an incident during the British invasion of the Suez Canal Zone in 1956. A British officer captured by the Egyptians was later found dead, suffocated in a cupboard — Leslie's fate in *An Giall*.

The event fastened on Behan's imagination how large, public occasions reduce individuals to objects; and the imperative to resist this diminishment. His play, he said, 'is basically about the ordinariness of people — which is an extraordinary thing at such times ... All that I am trying to show in my play is that one man's death can be more significant than the issues involved':[10] sober thoughts, which *An Giall* embodies in its Irish setting. Richard Wall's examination of the two plays demonstrates conclusively that *The Hostage* vulgarises *An Giall's* delicacies, achieving 'the destruction of [its] integrity, a drastic alteration of its tone, and a reduction of the impact of its most striking feature: the tender romance between Teresa ... and Leslie ... in a brutal world'.[11]

Behan declared his approval of Joan Littlewood's rendering. He dismissed the original production as 'of the school of Abbey Theatre naturalism of which I'm not a pupil'.[12] Whether this is genuine conviction or the self-deception of success it is impossible to say. Certainly, *The Hostage* is flawed; and *An Giall* is in the line of *The Quare Fellow*'s naturalism, which as in the Abbey tradition at its best pushes the convention beyond simply imitative designs.

III

In 1967, three years after Behan's death, the Abbey Theatre presented *Borstal Boy*, an adaptation of Behan's novel by Frank McMahon, directed by Tomás MacAnna. The transference from the one to the other form is a case history of the requirements imposed by the shift of medium. Changes in narrative tone, attitude, point of view in the novel must find equivalents on the stage among characters and settings literally present to the audience. The theatre demands a telescoping, a reduction, and in a sense a simplifying of the novel's expansiveness and its highly mobile chronology.

The dramatisation of *Borstal Boy* is remarkably coherent with both the quite complex scheme of the novel, and the style of Behan's theatre. It is lavish with song (as is the novel) and employs a good deal of intricately choreographed movement: much, one might think, like *The Hostage*. In *Borstal Boy*, however, these elements are not just beguiling interludes. They are translations from the language of the novel, they are under the authority of a clearly developed interpretation, and they are subject to MacAnna's belief in a final, inviolable script which embodies his view of the novel's statement.

Behan's novel — the most convenient term for it — is somewhat fictionalised autobiography, a kind of *Portrait of the Artist as a Young I.R.A. Man. Borstal Boy* is not only, in a documentary way, a classic of 'prison literature'. As Colbert Kearney remarks, Behan wrote 'an imaginative autobiography ... just as Joyce did in the *Portrait*'.[13] It is Behan's most controlled and most self-sustained work, a novel of adolescence, of experience finding a literary style for its meaning. Gradually, it unfolds a mutation in the author's view of himself, and of views outside him.

Despite its location in English jails (where Behan has a rough time) and for its greater part, the more humane Hollesley Bay Borstal, *Borstal Boy* never loses sight — or sound — of Ireland, Dublin particularly. The Irish past enters the present of the jails in reminiscence of a scene or an episode:

The house we lived in was a great lord's town house before it was a tenement, and there was a big black Kilkenny marble fireplace before my bed. If the souls in Purgatory really came back, it was out of there they would come. A Hail Mary was all right, but there was more comfort in the sound of the trams. There were lights and people on them. Old fellows, a bit jarred and singing, and fellows leaving their mots home to Drumcondra after the pictures.[14]

There was a similar piece of sculpture over Kilmainham Prison. I had often passed it with my father, taking me for a walk on Sunday mornings. It was where he had first seen me, from his cell window, during the Civil War. I was born after he was captured, and when I was six weeks old my mother brought me up to the jail and held me up, on the road outside, for him to see from the cell window. (p.38)

... in Kerry, where the arbutus grows and the fuchsia glows on the dusty hedges in the soft light of the summer evening. *'Deorini De'* — 'The Tears of God' — they called the fuchsia in Kerry, where it ran wild as a weed. (p.61)

The recollections are of an experience and an inheritance which the alien scene is modifying. The reflexes of the rehearsed 'Irish rebel', without ever disappearing, adjust to new facts. Fresh experience re-directs the ingrained set of attitudes. *Borstal Boy* is about this interaction and its outcome. While political dogma softens, language in interesting ways acquires dominance.

The Irish earthing of the book is mainly in its language, in Behan's heightened Dublin idiom. Much of it is more or less transcription of authentic argot: ' "They said that", said I, "and they'd say Mass if they knew the Latin" '; ' "The blessings of God on you", said I, "and may the giving hand never falter".'; ' "You've a neck like a jockey's ballocks". ' The same Dublin cant informs the language of narrative, meditation, judgement. It takes place — a recurrent phrase — 'in my own mind'. Cant, however, in its extended periods ('in my own mind') ascends to High Cant, deriving recognisably still from a vernacular model, but transformed beyond its normal usages. As Behan is doing his 'Number One and solitary', his dinnertime frustration issues in a memorable, unspoken invocation to an Ireland that might do better by him:

Oh, come up at once, the publican would say, what kind of men are you at all? Have you no decency of spirit about you, that wouldn't make way for one of the Felons of our Land? Come on, son, till herself gives you this plate of bacon and cabbage, and the blessings of Jasus on you, and on everyone like you. It's my own dinner I'm giving you, for you were not expected and you amongst that parcel of white-livered, thin-lipped, paper-waving, key-rattling hangmen. And, come on; after your dinner there's a pint to wash it down, aye, and a glass of malt if you fancy it. Give us up a song there. Yous have enough of songs out of yous about the boys that faced the Saxon foe, but, bejasus, when there's one of them here among you, the real Ally Dally, the real goat's genollickers, yous are silent as the tomb. Sing up, yous whores gets. (pp.93-4)

Unmistakably Dublin patter, the speech outsoars imitation to a Platonic Ideal. It assembles slang ('whores gets'), cliché ('Felons of our Land'), invention ('white-livered, thin-lipped, paper-waving, key-rattling hangmen'), formality ('the publican would say') into an individualised, breakneck rhetoric. It is a rhetoric which looks beyond its native origins, assimilating new possibilities. Behan has a curiosity about language and remarks his dealings with forms of it new to him.

Behan is very conscious of his ear for accent and idiom. He claims to speak English like a native ('Smashing, china') after two days and a bit in the country; his house master at Hollesley Bay compliments him on his command of rhyming slang. We see the process of acquisition at work. Behan notes: how Charlie says 'dawncing' and 'pipah'; the phrase, smoking 'as Charlie said, "like lords' bastards" ', an expression forty pages later appropriated into Behan's talk; the warders; 'Ill Kerr-ect, sir'; the Chief's 'chuckle, as it's called'; 'the Borstal Warders as 'better gentlemen, in the way that word is used'. A cohabitation of dialects comes about. Almost as a figure of the book's design, the English imitate Behan's accent, and he theirs. The absorption of each by the other, of all that language signifies of a way of life, reflects a mutation in the received sentiments of Behan's Republicanism: 'I was saving up to be a coward and if I'd fight for anyone it'd be for myself'.

Living within the essential vernaculars are passages in more formal style, dealing in mood and description, as in the evocation of the Kerry fuchsia. Their formality and heightened diction never bleach the colloquial pigment:

The autumn got weaker and beaten, and the leaves all fell, and a bloody awful east wind that was up before us and we on our way to work in the morning, sweeping down off the top of the North Sea, which in the distance looked like a bitter band of deadly blue steel out along the length of the horizon, around the freezing marshes, the dirty grey shore, the gunmetal sea, and over us the sky, lead-coloured for a few hours, till the dark fell and the wind rose, and we went down the road from work at five o'clock in the perishing night. (p.359)

The sense of cold and deprivation moves from 'bloody awful', in a sinewy sentence, to a sensuous elaboration of what constitutes 'bloody awful', making of it a fully articulated experience. *Borstal Boy* is a work of art whose language subtly enacts a development of feeling and imagination. Though it has not the complexity of manners of Joyce's *Portrait* it marks out a linguistic territory synonymous with the experiences that occupy it.

The reporting voice, manipulating its discourse, is an acquisition of the older Behan, a medium of retrospective judgment. The retrospective utterance gives experience a shape concealed in its past actuality. Underlying the whole book is the older Behan who has found the words that crystallise perceptions into meaning. The novel has a continuous double focus. That of the mature, sardonic, reflective Behan puts in perspective the events which for the sixteen-year old Behan are undergone, not fully apprehended and judged, a youth now regarded with amusement, irony, envy.

IV

The adaptation of *Borstal Boy* had its genesis in Iceland where in 1962 MacAnna was directing *The Hostage*. Its translator suggested that there might be dramatic value in *Borstal Boy*. On his return to Dublin MacAnna asked Frank McMahon to prepare a script. According to MacAnna, this turned out to be a straight-forward working through the novel, employing flashbacks as the novel — frequently — has them. There was in consequence a multiplicity of short scenes, and the playing time would have been much too long. The final shape came out of a close collaboration between MacAnna and McMahon over the four-week rehearsal period.

There are three available texts. The Irish and American published versions are largely identical, the latter rather shorter and with a few Americanised idioms. The Abbey working

typescript is the longest and technically the most interesting. Its
stage directions are the amplest, and accompanied by extensive
handwritten notes, the director's detailed instructions for the
players' movements. Its fascination, not to the purpose here, is
that from it we can anatomise the progress, by elisions and
compoundings, to the final text, which most clearly shows the
nature of the translation from the novel.

The most compelling effect in the adaptation is its transference
of the older/younger duality in the novel. Both the younger self,
as Brendan, and the older, as Behan, are represented on stage.
Once seen, the device appears inevitable. In fact it came to
MacAnna only gradually, from a feeling that some necessary
depth in the novel, a distancing of the young Behan, was absent
from the early drafts. The older Behan, as a voice over, the first
solution, lacked substance.

Then serendipity played a part. The actor Niall Toibín
happened to call in MacAnna's office and MacAnna,
remembering him as a good friend of Behan, saw him in the
play as the older man: as it turned out, an uncannily accurate
stage resurrection of its subject. So the disembodied became the
embodied, and the play found its point of control. Brendan as
a separate character is freed to act throughout the play as a
young boy, subject to extreme responses. The older Behan
carries most of the tensions of the novel's narrator, recollecting
with both irony and regret. The interactions between the two
versions of self establish varied moods from which the audience
views the action.

The flashbacks of the novel are absorbed into the interchanges
between the two Behans. As the action moves forward for
Brendan, these exchanges with his older self suggest a kind of
timeless present. The present time that we see on stage is the
young Behan's past, framed by his future, the elder Behan he
will become, looking back. In the end, the effects are far from
simple, and transfer perfectly the double focus of the novel.

As to construction, Brecht supplied MacAnna with, as he calls
it, the strip-cartoon approach: a series of pictures in simple, or
apparently simple, chronological order. But the scenes run so
fluidly into each other that there is no sense of the 'real' time
that has passed. The passage of time is subordinate to the
passages of feeling, reflected in delicate gradations of lighting,
where MacAnna's mentor was Adolphe Appia: 'the setting for
a play is light and little else'. All these elements — the dual
Behan, the Brechtian structure, the lighting — are the medium

whose function is to accommodate on the stage the words of the novel.

The play's reliance on the words of the novel demonstrates its fidelity to its source. Of about 1100 lines of dialogue in Act I, just over two hundred are original to the play. The spare additional dialogue serves to conflate episodes separated in the novel. So two church scenes, one at Hollesley, one at Feltham jail — a location omitted from the play — become one, and the novel's dispersed comments on the various Borstal boys are unified into the single scene introducing them as they disembark at Hollesley.

The play bridges, associates, economises. An inventive care marks its editorial manoeuvrings within the novel. For example, on p.107 of the play, Behan's comment on the boys' innocent appearance closes a scene taken from pp.231–3 of the novel. 'Reposed and innocent', he says, 'they look now, every mother's son of them'. The sentiment is drawn partly from p.200. 'Reposed and innocent,' however, comes from p.349. So too the Assizes scene in Act I ranges over pp.28, 41, 93, 124, 132, and 143–4 of the novel. All the exhanges in the court itself come in pp.143–4, mostly in reported speech. The particular event is made, in a perfectly organic union, to entertain a synthesis of Brendan/Behan's attitudes to the law and to Ireland.

A simpler amalgamation illustrates the thoroughness of the editing. Brendan twice sings 'The sea, oh, the sea' in the novel, pp.212 and 333. The play uses it once, during the gardening work-party. This scene takes its dialogue from pp.212 and 333 to introduce and round off the song, and combines political deflation with it, a sardonic comment on romanticised Irish attitudes to the land — 'our family's land was all in window boxes', lifted from p.234. Enveloping that content is a brief surge of emotional release through the coastal vista, open fields and bright sunlight suggested by the stage lighting. Moving through these scenes, both immediate and remembered, like the two Gars of Brian Friel's *Philadephia, Here I Come!*, Brendan and Behan are not merely in plain contrast. At various moments in the play they share a feeling, a memory, a judgment. As Brendan is going off to solitary they infect each other with enthusiastic defiance, and join in a union of abuse:

BEHAN: Make way there, you with the face, and let in the man
            that's doing jail for Ireland, and suffering hunger and
            abuse amongst that parcel of white-livered —

BRENDAN: — thin-lipped —
BEHAN: — paper-waving —
BRENDAN: — key-rattling hangmen.

As the play advances they reach towards identity, so that at the end, separating, they echo each other:

IMMIGRATION MAN: It must be wonderful to be free.
BRENDAN: It must.
(He goes. BEHAN is left alone, gazing after BRENDAN.)
BEHAN: It must indeed ... *(Sings.)*
Is go dteighidh tu, a mhuirnin slan

V

Critics now are looking at Behan with a colder eye than when his reputation for both work and riot was at its height, when he seemed, as according to Fintan O'Toole he no longer seems, assured of a 'place in the automatic hierarchy of ... Wilde, Shaw and O'Casey'. Behan left behind him, O'Toole concludes, 'a brilliant book of autobiography, two interesting but minor plays, a handful of fine short stories'.[15] Beyond that, O'Toole associates Behan with 'a glow of life in the dullness of Dublin ... an energy that was important to his times'.

However, the importance of *Borstal Boy*, novel and play, resides not so much in the flamboyant being whose creation it is as in the interplay which the work sustains between the man and the deliberating mask. The indiscipline of the life surrenders to an ordering vision. Part of its allure is that while it contains it does not muffle the disruptive impulse. Brendan Behan, the 'I' of the novel, Brendan/Behan the double 'I' of the play, is preserved in the one as a form of words, in the other as that form conveyed to the theatre.

Strictly speaking, of course, *Borstal Boy* is not part of Behan's dramatic work, and Alan Simpson rightly excludes it from the *Complete Plays*. But the Abbey's *Borstal Boy* renews the characteristics of Behan's own plays. Its dialogue is Behan's. It has as many songs as *The Hostage* but deploys them with the structural control of *The Quare Fellow*. It renders Behan's concern with individuals, not abstractions and causes — or with abstractions and causes implied in the individuals whose brief lives are paramount. *Borstal Boy*, like Behan's theatre, is densely populated, fluent in vernacular, fluid with movement, shifting in mood. It re-enters Behan's world of the outcast, with all its sardonic compassion.

As Behan in the mid-fifties enlivened a lethargic Irish theatre, in the mid-sixties he appropriately took posthumous part in an Irish dramatic revival. Tom Murphy's *A Whistle in the Dark* played in London in 1961; Brian Friel's *Philadelphia, Here I Come!* at the Dublin Theatre Festival of 1964, his *Lovers* at the Gate Theatre in 1967; Tom Kilroy's *The Death and Resurrection of Mr. Roche* at the 1968 Festival. The production of *Borstal Boy* signified, too, a revitalisation of the Abbey itself, a self-confidence in the potential of the manifold resources of its new theatre, which it occupied in 1966; and it honoured the harbinger of this renaissance, the dramatist who extended yet again the Abbey's tradition of imaginative excursions within an essentially realist style.

NOTES

1. Alan Simpson, *Beckett and Behan and a Theatre in Dublin*, London: Routledge & Kegan Paul 1962. p.1.
2. Seamus de Burca, *Brendan Behan: A Memoir*, Newark: Proscenium Press, 1971. p.12.
3. *Brendan Behan's Island*, London: Transworld Publishers, 1965.
4. Alan Simpson, 'Behan: The Last Laugh' in Des Hickey and Gus Smith (eds.) *A Paler Shade of Green*, London: Leslie Frewin, 1972. p.214.
5. They were by contrast ecstatic over *The Hostage*.
6. *The Complete Flap*, ed Alan Simpson London: Eyre Methuen 1978. p.87. subsequent references are to this edition.
7. *The Writing of Brendan Behan*, Dublin: Gill & McMillan, 1977. p.79.
8. *Ibid*, p.169.
9. Richard Wall, '*An Giall* and *The Hostage* Compared,' *Modern Drama*, Vol. XVIII, No.2, June 1975, p.165.
10. Rae Jeffs, *Brendan Behan—Man and Showman*, London: Hutchinson, 1966. p.35.
11. Wall, p.171.
12. *Brendan Behan's Island*, p.17.
13. Kearney, p.94.
14. *Borstal Boy*, London: Transworld Publishers, 1961, p.27. Subsequent references are to this edition.
15. 'The Laughing Boy,' *Sunday Tribune*, 18 March 1984.

NEW WINE, OLD BOTTLES: SHAW AND THE DUBLIN THEATRE TRADITION

VIVIAN MERCIER

You Never Can Tell (1897), fourth of the 'pleasant' plays, was ultimately called a 'shameless' pot-boiler by Shaw.[1] Nevertheless, it deserves attention as his first moderately successful attempt at comedy of manners, a genre that he later explored — and expanded to fit his genius — in *Man and Superman, Misalliance, Pygmalion* and *Heartbreak House.*[2] One can't escape the feeling that in *You Never Can Tell* Shaw was trying to fill the gap left by a once immensely successful Irish playwright, Oscar Wilde, who in 1897 was completing his two-year sentence in Reading Gaol. What's more, parts of this play seem to be written in conscious imitation of *The Importance of Being Earnest,* a work which Shaw, both as moralist and dramatic critic, had professed to despise.[3]

In Shaw's earliest dramatic works, the three 'unpleasant' plays, there is always at least one threatening woman character. The bad-tempered Blanche Sartorius of *Widowers' Houses* (1892) and Julia Craven in *The Philanderer* (written 1893) were both probably based on Shaw's first mistress, Mrs. Jenny Patterson, a friend of his mother. In *Mrs. Warren's Profession* written (1893) it is hard to decide whether Mrs. Warren, the tough, mercenary brothel-owner, or her educated and 'enlightened' daughter Vivie is the more unpleasant character and the more threatening from a male's point of view. Shaw may have found models for the Warrens chiefly in his own imagination, but mothers are scarce commodities in his five novels and when the hero's mother *does* appear in *Cashel Byron's Profession,* she and her son find they have little in common. Mrs. Warren, too, is an absentee mother, and neither she nor Vivie is willing to give up her present way of life for the other's sake.

The only woman who is even mildly threatening in *You Never Can Tell,* however, is Mrs. Clandon: she seems almost

103

innocuous when compared with Wilde's Lady Bracknell. Her
invasion of England from abroad, backed by two daughters and
a son whose educations have been quite unconventional
reminds one of Lucinda Shaw's invasion of London from
Dublin accompanied by two daughters of whom one at least,
Lucy, was unconventional enough to go on the musical stage:
her son, whom she had more or less abandoned along with her
husband in Dublin, was to turn up years later and, according to
his own account, to sponge on her for a long time thereafter.
The treatment of the blue-stocking Mrs. Clandon in this light-
hearted play suggests that Shaw has ceased to fear his own
mother, even unconsciously, and has forgiven her for not being
able to love him. He has also, I think, forgiven her for her
inability to love his father. In one respect, however, Mrs.
Clandon's behaviour implies a rebuke to Mrs. Shaw. Unlike
George Carr Shaw, Mr. Crampton — whose surname is appropriate to his character but not to his status as the husband of
Mrs. Clandon — will be allowed to enjoy the company of his two
younger children as long as he consents to be their friend rather
than their ultra-conventional forbidding parent. After their
successive departures to London, Shaw's father never saw any
of his family again. As we shall see, the imperturbable juvenile
lead, Valentine the dentist, though partly resembling his
creator, requires no identification with the Shaw family. William
the waiter-and-*deus-ex-machina* whose stock phrase is 'You
never can tell', goes back at least to the Figaro of Beaumarchais
and perhaps ultimately to Aristophanes.

In accordance with a pattern of antithesis that occurs throughout Shaw's artistic career and was already to be observed in the
novels, his next play, *The Devil's Disciple* (also 1897), contains
what is arguably the nastiest woman he ever created — Mrs.
Dudgeon, the title character's mother. Shaw claimed that she is
'a replica of Mrs. Clennam' in Dickens's *Little Dorrit*, but to me
her cruelty is more memorable than that lady's. Her version or
perversion of Calvinism brings her no happiness: it merely
enables her to make others miserable. Her son Dick early made
up his mind that if this was Christianity, he was, to use Blake's
phrase, 'of the Devil's party'. His supposedly diabolical
morality, which makes him befriend his illegitimate cousin
Essie, is sharply contrasted in Act I with his mother's alleged
godliness. Mrs. Dudgeon keeps berating the orphan for the
father's sin and insisting that her place in society must therefore
always remain among the lowest of the low. Nevertheless, with

his usual fairness towards his characters, Shaw hints that much of Mrs. Dudgeon's bitterness springs from the thwarting of her love for her brother-in-law, Essie's natural father.

To his own dismay, Dick the diabolist — like Blanco the badman in *The Shewing-up of Blanco Posnet* (1909) — finds himself capable of a spontaneous act of self-sacrifice. When he is arrested as an American rebel by British troops who mistake him for Anthony Anderson, the local Presbyterian minister, he does not try to correct their error. Anderson's pretty young wife, Judith, thinks Dick is sacrificing himself for love of her. The play's first audiences, familiar with Dickens's *A Tale of Two Cities* and/or the Rev. Freeman Crofts Wills's adaptation of it for the stage, *The Only Way* (1899), probably shared her misunderstanding. Dick, they must have thought, could have no other possible motive, being a self-proclaimed atheist; Sidney Carton, though a genteel blackguard, at least believed in the God whom he disobeyed and therefore might offer up his life as an expiation of sin.

The third act must have bewildered such an audience, especially when Dick says to Judith:

What I did last night, I did in cold blood, caring not half so much for your husband, or ... for you ... as I do for myself. I had no motive and no interest: all I can tell you is that when it came to the point whether I would take my neck out of the noose and put another man's into it, I could not do it. I dont know why not: I see myself as a fool for my pains; but I could not and I cannot.

Dick is rescued from the gallows in the nick of time — after being condemned to death in an undeniably comic court-martial scene that prepares the audience for a happy ending. His rescuer is Anthony Anderson, now an American militia captain: he suggests that Dick should take over his abandoned pulpit. Institutionalised religion seems alien to Dick's temperament, but his last cry on the scaffold — when he still thinks he is about to die — 'Amen! my life for the world's future!' announces the acceptance of a vocation, be it religious or secular.

From the first, Shaw subtitled *The Devil's Disciple* 'A Melodrama in Three Acts'; it is, perhaps, all the more a melodrama because of the hero's escape, whereas *The Only Way* might claim to be a tragedy because Sidney Carton actually dies by the guillotine. To be a perfect example of its genre, Shaw's play should end with the hero embracing his beloved, but since Dick is really an anti-hero, the play ends instead with a handshake between him and Judith to seal his promise that he will never tell her husband of her momentary lapse.

The Devil's Disciple had its first production in New York, giving Shaw his first box-office success. One wonders whether the audiences, which must have included some Irish-Americans, mingled patriotic cheers and anti-British jeers with their laughter and applause. In Ireland, even today, the court-martial scene — in which the accused, certain that the verdict will go against him despite his innocence, baits his British captors and judges with all the wit and humour he can command — has a resonance quite different from what it must have possessed at its first London production in 1899. What's more, an Irish audience can still compare it with a perennial Dublin favourite that Shaw must have seen before leaving his native city, Dion Boucicault's *Arrah-na-Pogue, or The Wicklow Wedding* (1864). Because Boucicault, despite his mother's impeccable Anglo-Irish descent from the Darley and Guinness families, excelled as an actor in stage-Irish peasant roles, he made Shaun the Post, 'driver of the Mail Car between Hollywood and Rathdrum', the hero of his court-martial scene. Shaun, like Dick, has taken on the guilt of another, in this case Beamish Mac Coul ('The Mac Coul'), a fictional aristocratic leader of the 1798 Rising. When Beamish learns of Shaun's plight, he gives himself up to the British authorities: not only does he rescue Shaun, but he himself wins a full pardon. (Shaw's collateral ancestor Bagenal Harvey, a real-life rebel in '98, was not so lucky: the British hanged him.)[4] Shaun is delighted with one result of his trial: his beloved, Arrah Meelish (originally played by Mrs. Boucicault), reveals the true depth of her love for him in his danger; their interrupted wedding can resume as the play ends.

Besides borrowing most of his plot from *Arrah-na-Pogue*, Shaw steals one speech at least from the trial scene. When Shaun is asked whether he is guilty or not guilty, he replies, 'Sure, Major, I thought that was what we'd all come here to find out'. Similarly, when General Burgoyne asks, 'Any political views, Mr. Anderson?' Dick replies, 'I understand that that is just what we are here to find out'. In *The Dolmen Boucicault*, David Krause gives the best brief summary I know of Boucicault's career, besides pin-pointing Shaw's debt to *Arrah-na-Pogue* and his acquaintance with other Boucicault melodramas.[5] The only detail he overlooks is Shaw's debt to another facet of Boucicault's versatility. Although Krause lists *Used Up* (1844) as a collaboration between Boucicault and the comic actor Charles Mathews, 'adapted from *L'homme blasé*', he seems to have forgotten the passage from the preface to *Three Plays for Puritans* in which Shaw confesses that

... the stage tricks by which I gave the younger generation of playgoers an exquisite sense of quaint unexpectedness, had done duty years ago in Cool as a Cucumber, Used Up, and many forgotten farces and comedies ... in which the imperturbably impudent comedian ... was a stock figure. [6]

I was lucky enough to find a copy of *Used Up* in the University of California at Santa Barbara library (New York: Samuel French, n.d. [?1846/47]), in which Charles Mathews is given as sole author; the work, of which this is claimed to be the 'only published' edition, is described as a 'petit comedy'[sic] rather than a farce. In this and other vehicles for Mathews we find the prototype of Valentine and many another Shaw character, including the most imperturbably impudent of all — Shaw himself.

He was being impudent even as he wrote the words just quoted, twitting the New York critics for describing *The Devil's Disciple* as 'novel — original, as they put it — to the verge of audacious eccentricity'. A few lines before, he had pointed out that the play

... does not contain a single even passably novel incident. Every old patron of the Adelphi pit would ... recognize the reading of the will, the oppressed orphan finding a protector, the arrest, the heroic sacrifice, the court martial, the scaffold, the reprieve at the last moment, as he recognizes beefsteak pudding on the bill of fare at his restaurant. [7]

The Adelphi Theatre was the home of melodrama in London for decades and therefore a natural place for Boucicault to appear during his visits to England: for example, *The Colleen Bawn*, his adaptation of Gerald Griffin's novel *The Collegians*, enjoyed a long run there in 1860–61, with Mrs. Boucicault (Agnes Robertson) in the title role and Boucicault himself as Myles-na-Coppaleen. [8]

Shaw was being thoroughly unjust to his critics: of course there is originality in *The Devil's Disciple*, in *Arms and the Man*, in *The Man of Destiny*, all of which use the formulas of melodrama as temporary scaffolding, only to lay them in ruins sooner or later: *The Devil's Disciple* simply adheres to its formula a little longer than the others. Shaw repeated the trick just once more, in *Blanco Posnet*, which he subtitled 'A Sermon in Crude Melodrama'.

It is well known that Shaw wrote *The Man of Destiny* for Henry Irving, who kept an option on it for some time but never staged it. On the strength of a single line in this brilliant short play about Napoleon — obviously written for two star performers — I am convinced that Shaw envisaged Ellen Terry, Irving's usual leading lady, in the other big part, that of the Strange Lady. Note that her age is given as 'The right age, excellency'; this turns out to be not seventeen, as Napoleon suggests, but thirty. Ellen Terry was in fact forty-nine in 1896, just ripe to give up *ingénue* parts and begin playing thirty-year-olds. Shaw first laid eyes on Irving, playing the role of Digby Grant, father of the two pretty girls in the title roles of James Albery's comedy *Two Roses*, when the entire London production was brought to Dublin in May 1871, just before Irving began his thirty years' association with the Lyceum Theatre, London. The mature Shaw would have us believe that, although not quite fifteen at the time, he 'instinctively felt that a new drama inhered in this man ...'[9] In the 1890s he spend a lot of time trying to convince the great though unliterary actor — often using Ellen Terry as an intermediary — that he and Shaw together could still create such a drama. Irving was by then too old and too tired to take risks, but, ironically, a Dubliner of Shaw's own class, William Gorman Wills (1828–91), had supplied Irving with six roles in the years 1872–95, besides writing two plays for him, *Rienzi* and *King Arthur*, that were paid for but never produced. To the annoyance of Henry James, Irving played Mephistopheles in Wills's *Faust* rather than Goethe's; A.B. Walkley voiced similar complaints about Irving's Mephistopheles, Vanderdecken and Eugene Aram, and possibly hinted that a Don Quixote from Wills would also be a mistake. On the other hand, Walkley described Irving's Charles I and Dr. Primrose as 'two ... of his best things'. The first of these performances was in one of Wills's few original plays, *Charles I*, and the second in *Olivia* (based on an episode from *The Vicar of Wakefield*), a play which also gave Ellen Terry, in the title role, a better part than Shaw was ever to write for her, Candida and Lady Cicely Waynflete included.[10] No wonder Irving, with Bram Stoker also in his entourage, did not feel he needed another Dubliner, especially one who had never attended Trinity or any other college.

Throughout his life, but especially in these early plays, Shaw defied the Gospel warning by putting new wine in old bottles. Sometimes the wine burst the bottle, as we were warned on the highest authority that it would, so that for instance Act III of *Man and Superman*, when performed at all, is usually done as a separate play under the title *Don Juan in Hell*. The old bottle on this occasion was Da Ponte's libretto for *Don Giovanni*, which could not be persuaded to scale the heavens or descend into hell without the assistance of Mozart's music, cleverly smuggled by Shaw into the dream/vision of Act III.

Why, though, did Shaw, a self-proclaimed new dramatist, choose to put his heady wine into those particular old bottles: farce and melodrama and what one can only call 'costume dramas', for tragedies they are not? My first answer is a simple one: Shaw used these apparently obsolete formulas because they were the ones he knew best, and he knew them best because he had grown up on them in Dublin, where everything was behind the times according to London clocks; 'the theatre had hardly altered, except for its illumination by coal gas, since the eighteenth century'.[11] Besides being taken to the Christmas pantomime as a child, Shaw seems to have been a regular visitor to the Theatre Royal from his fifteenth year, when he first began earning money at Townshend's estate office, until he left Dublin at twenty. Because of the theatre programming of the time, he saw an incredibly large number of plays, though unfortunately they were usually performed very badly because of the stock-company system.

The duties of the resident company at the Royal were 'to support the stars who came to Dublin on their touring circuits, and to perform the Christmas pantomime and to keep the house open in the occasional weeks left unfilled by the stars'. As a background for his correspondence with Ellen Terry, published in 1931, Shaw felt the necessity to supply a general description of the old stock companies, so essential for the understanding of her career and, even more so, of Irving's. He insists, furthermore, that 'my own plays are written largely for the feats of acting [the stock companies] aimed at . . .'. This fascinating account, required reading for all Shavians, includes some personal reminiscences:

At my first visit to the theatre I saw on the same evening Tom Taylor's three-act drama Plot and Passion [1853] followed by a complete Christmas pantomime, with a couple of farces as *hors-d'oeuvre*. Tom Taylor's Joan of Arc [1871] had Massinger's New Way to Pay Old Debts as a curtain raiser. Under such circumstances serious character study was impossible ...[12]

These early experiences may have conditioned Shaw to make free use of stock characters in his own plays, but the touring star system permitted at least one characterisation in depth, that of the hero and/or heroine, in most plays.

'Of the English-speaking stars', continues Shaw, 'incomparably the greatest was Barry Sullivan, who was in his prime when I saw him in my teens, the last of the race of heroic figures which had dominated the stage since the palmy Siddons-Kemble days'. If he had grown up in London, Shaw could not have studied the art of this great Irish actor, who made a fortune by avoiding West End theatre rents and touring the provincial cities instead; he is buried in Dublin, with a noble statue over his grave.[13] Shaw also had an opportunity to study the grand style as interpreted by a woman, Adelaide Ristori (1822–1906), when she visited Dublin with her Italian stock company, which soon became, according to Shaw, 'even more unbearably stale than an English one'. Fortunately, the great male performer Tommaso Salvini played opposite her, giving Shaw an international standard with which to compare Sullivan.

There is a second, less obvious answer to my question about the choice of seemingly obsolete vehicles for new ideas — new to the theatre at any rate, as Shaw loved to point out, describing it as a far more conservative institution than the churches. In the preface to *Three Plays for Puritans* he insists that he does not profess to write better plays than Shakespeare, though many readers have misunderstood him to say the opposite:

The writing of practicable stage plays does not present an infinite scope to human talent; ... The summit of [this] art has been attained again and again. No man will ever write a better tragedy than Lear, a better comedy than [Molière's] Le Festin de Pierre or Peer Gynt, a better opera than Don Giovanni, a better music drama than The Niblung's Ring or, for the matter of that, better fashionable plays and melodramas than are now being turned out ... *It is the philosophy, the outlook on life that changes, not the craft of the playwright.*[14]

The counterpoint between the new ideas and the old techniques dazzled Shaw's early critics and audiences, giving them an impression of startling originality. Nowadays, when Shaw's ideas are seen as either not new or not true, his plays still hold the stage by virtue of their timeless plots and their unrivalled repertory of comic techniques.[15]

First unconsciously, then consciously, the young Dublin playgoer and opera addict learned to make use of a native critical talent and a capacious though not quite infallible memory to judge the living theatre and master traditional stage lore. At twenty he began to review opera and concerts for a London periodical, *The Hornet*, without making a fool of himself. By 1900, when the preface to *Three Plays for Puritans* was written, he had been the leading London music critic (on *The World*, 1890–94) and then the leading theatre critic (on *The Saturday Review*, 1895–98). He had crowned his critical campaign on behalf of Wagner's music with *The Perfect Wagnerite* (1898), just as he had begun his critical campaign for Ibsen's plays with the first version of *The Quintessence of Ibsenism* (1891).[16] On 22 May 1897 he published an article in the *Saturday Review* entitled, without hyperbole, 'Ibsen Triumphant'. In a month when Londoners had had the chance to see three plays by Ibsen — *John Gabriel Borkman*, *A Doll's House*, and *The Wild Duck* — it was surely safe to proclaim that Ibsen, who had already conquered so many other capitals, was finally in possession of insular, still partly Evangelical London.[17] Much of the credit for this triumph belonged to courageous actresses eager to play Ibsen's powerful women's parts, as well as to actors and theatre managers who also had to face public censure, but critics like Shaw and his friend William Archer fought valiantly too. Shaw was never more truly a champion of Ibsen than when reviewing the offerings of the London stage that were antithetical to the works of his idol. Take, for example, his critiques of *The Colleen Bawn* and *Olivia* in revival. Of the former he wrote, 'I have lived to see The Colleen Bawn with real water in it; and perhaps I shall live to see it some day with real Irishmen in it, though I doubt if that will heighten its popularity much'.[18] His review of *Olivia* contains a sort of hymn to Ellen Terry, still playing the *ingénue* lead at fifty, 'in appearance not discoverably a week older' than in 1885. (She had, in fact, created the role opposite Hermann Vezin at the Court Theatre in 1878, before she joined Irving at the Lyceum.) But the hymn soon turns into a scurrilous denunciation of Irving and Shakespeare:

... Olivia is by a very great deal the best nineteenth-century play in the Lyceum repertory; and it has never been better acted ... The third act should be seen by all those who know Ellen Terry only by her efforts to extract a precarious sustenance for her reputation from Shakespear:

it will teach them what an artist we have thrown to our national
Minotaur. When I think of the originality and modernity of the talent
she revealed twenty years ago, and of its remorseless waste ever since
in 'supporting' an actor who prefers The Iron Chest to Ibsen, my regard
for Sir Henry Irving cannot blind me to the fact that it would have been
better for us twenty-five years ago to have tied him up in a sack with
every existing copy of the works of Shakespear, and dropped him in
the crater of the nearest volcano. It really serves him right that his Vicar
is far surpassed by Mr. Hermann Vezin's.[19]

Is it any wonder that a playwright so gifted, so stage-struck, so
partisan, so knowledgeable about everything that happens
before and behind the curtain, should have made himself the
greatest master of the craft of comedy since Molière?

NOTES

1   Bernard Shaw, 'Postscript After Twentyfive Years', *Back to Methuselah*, rev.
    ed., The World's Classics. London: Oxford University Press, 1945, p.289:
    'I write such shameless potboilers as Pygmalion, Fanny's First Play, and
    You Never Can Tell, to oblige theatre managers or aspiring players ...'.
2   See Vivian Mercier, 'Shaw and the Anglo-Irish Comedy of Manners', *New
    Edinburgh Review*, no. 28 (March 1975), pp.22–24.
3   Bernard Shaw, 'Oscar Wilde', *Pen Portraits and Reviews, Collected Works*,
    Ayot St. Lawrence Edition, v. 29. New York: Wm. H. Wise, 1932,
    pp.301–02: *Our Theatres in The Nineties*, Standard Edition, 3v. London:
    Constable, 1932, I, 41–44.
4   This is a guess: Shaw's reference to his revolutionary ancestor fits no other
    historical figure. See *Complete Prefaces*, p.442: 'one of my grandfathers was
    an Orangeman; but then ... his uncle, I am proud to say, was hanged as
    a rebel'. Shaw's maternal grandfather was Walter Bagenal Gurly.
5   David Krause, 'The Theatre of Dion Boucicault: A Short View of His Life
    and Art', *The Dolmen Boucicault*, ed. Krause. Dublin: Dolmen Press, 1964,
    pp.9–47. For a list of Boucicault's plays, with dates of first production, see
    pp.248–53.
6   Bernard Shaw, *Complete Prefaces* (London: Paul Hamlyn, 1965), p.745. *Cool
    as a Cucumber* (1851), by William Blanchard Jerrold (1826–84), was also a
    vehicle for Charles Mathews: see George Rowell, *The Victorian Theatre: A
    Survey*. London: Oxford University Press, 1956, pp.65, 154. Boucicault's
    clumsy two-act comedy *Used Up* has for its hero Sir Charles Coldstream,
    Bart., who seems to be modelled after the Earl of Glenthorn, hero of Maria
    Edgeworth's novel *Ennui* (1809).
7   Shaw, *Complete Prefaces*, p.745.
8   *Dolmen Boucicault*, playbill reproduced on end-papers.
9   Shaw, *Complete Prefaces*, p.789.
10 Freeman Wills, *W.G. Wills: Dramatist and Painter*. London: Longmans,
    Green, 1898, *passim*. For James and Walkley, see *Victorian Dramatic
    Criticism*, ed. George Rowell. London: Methuen, 1971, pp.125–29, 134–37.
11 Shaw, *Complete Prefaces*, p.785.
12 Shaw, *Complete Prefaces*, p.786. Winton Tolles, *Tom Taylor and the Victorian*

Drama. New York: Columbia Univ. Press, 1940, gives careful summaries of *Plot and Passion*, pp.117–24, and *Jeanne Darc*, pp.236–38. The latter has little in common with Shaw's *Saint Joan*, except that 'It comprises a number of spectacular but loosely joined episodes ...'.

13 Shaw, *Complete Prefaces*, p.787; see also p.788: 'Had I passed my boyhood in London ...' For photographs of Sullivan and of his statue as Hamlet in Glasnevin Cemetery, see Christopher Fitz-Simon, *The Irish Theatre.* London: Thames & Hudson, 1983, p.104.

14 Shaw, *Complete Prefaces*, p.750; emphasis mine.

15 Shaw foresaw the loss of novelty but not the durability of the plays: see *Complete Prefaces*, p.746.

16 See however John O'Donovan, *Bernard Shaw*, Gill's Irish Lives. Dublin: Gill & Macmillan, 1983, p.77. O'Donovan asserts that the notion of Shaw as 'a lone fighter for the cause of Wagner in London ... is nonsense', and offers chapter and verse to prove his case.

17 *Our Theatres in the Nineties*, III, 122–44.

18 *Our Theatres ...*, II, 28; but see the whole review, pp.28–33.

19 *Our Theatres ...*, III, 37–38; but see the whole review, pp.34–40. The author of *The Iron Chest* (1796) was George Colman the Younger.

LENNOX ROBINSON: THE ABBEY'S ANTI-HERO

CHRISTOPHER MURRAY

I

So far as I am aware, Sir Peter Hall does not write plays. Diaries, yes; but not plays. If he did, would it be possible to conceive him as the decisive, formidable controller of the National Theatre whom the public has come to know? In February 1985, in response to cuts in the allocation of funds by the Arts Council of Great Britain, Hall could say, 'close the Cottesloe', and, lo, it could be closed. You don't fool around with a man like that. After he had given a lecture on directing plays I once asked him how he decided upon the meaning of a Pinter play, given the ambiguities. He had no trouble at all with the meaning, he assured me; and if he had, all he had to do was ring Harold.

In contrast, Lennox Robinson at the Abbey was a walking question mark. At the age of twenty-three he was faced with decisions of management he was quite incapable of handling. Unsure whether or not to close the Abbey on the death of King Edward VII, he sent a telegram to Lady Gregory at Coole, but receiving no reply before the matinee he went ahead with that performance and on receiving her reply advising closure thought it too late or illogical to cancel the evening performance, having played the matinee. The result was outrage on the part of Miss Horniman, who construed Robinson's as a political act and who called for his instant dismissal. Although Yeats and Lady Gregory supported Robinson and went to court when Miss Robinson withdrew her subsidy to the theatre the issue led to a major convulsion in the Abbey's history. Miss Horniman's withdrawal meant that the Abbey was on its own, for it was not until 1925 that it first received a government subsidy. Poor Robinson felt so miserable that he offered to do two jobs for one salary: secretary and manager. I doubt if he ever got over his sense of guilt that it was he who had deprived the Abbey of its sustaining subsidy. And Lady Gregory learned to despise him to a demoralizing degree.

The fact was that Robinson was too young and inexperienced when first appointed manager/producer* at the Abbey at the end of 1909. He had had one play staged there, *The Clancy Name* (1908), a piece of realism that set the tone for the generation of playwrights after Synge. But he had had little formal education and little exposure to the world of affairs. He was sent to London by the Abbey as nominal secretary to Shaw so that he could attend rehearsals under Granville-Barker and others, which he did for a month or so and then was plunged straight into directing at the Abbey. On two fronts his position was impossible: he had no business acumen and he had no authority. Intellectually and in personality he was the wrong choice. Or so it would appear.

The tours undertaken by the company to Britain and the United States in 1911–12 showed up his weaknesses. When he accompanied the players again on the third tour to America in 1914 Lady Gregory blamed him for mis-management, and he resigned from the Abbey. It was with some relief that he turned to another job, working for the Carnegie Trust as organizer of a scheme of public libraries in the south-east of Ireland. This gave him leisure to write his first really successful play, *The Whiteheaded Boy* (1916). He lived at this time at Cahirmoyle, County Limerick, on the estate of the O'Briens, with whom he became very friendly: he was to write a biography of the artist Dermod O'Brien later on (*Palette and Plough*, 1948). He was probably happier at this time than at any other in his career. But not even the Carnegie Trust provided a hiding place from the harsh realities of Irish life, if an employee insisted on being a writer, especially an outspoken one. The time came when Robinson published a short story which caused public controversy and was condemned in some quarters as blasphemous. Urged on by Yeats, Robinson refused to resign and was dismissed from his post in 1924. There was nothing for it then but the theatre, for better or worse.

In fact, Robinson was already back at the Abbey as manager by this time. Since 1919 his Carnegie work based him in Dublin and early in that year the Abbey found itself without a manager, after several years during which nobody proved either malleable

*Producer was the term then used for the director. The latter, because it is more familiar, is the term that will be used hereafter in this essay.

enough or strong enough to control a headstrong company. Yeats offered the position to Robinson. Robinson wanted to write, and needed a theatre for which to write; the Abbey needed a director, and he liked putting plays on stage: so he jumped at Yeats's offer. And Lady Gregory drew a long face. She tried, indeed, to stop the appointment, but Yeats had gone too far in his commitment to Robinson. He consoled her that Robinson would not now have to look after the account books, as he would be employed mainly to direct plays rather than to manage finances. Yet within a year Lady Gregory was trying to smooth the way for Sara Allgood to return to the Abbey as actress-manager and this would, apparently, mean Robinson's departure. As he always did before Lady Gregory, Robinson grovelled. 'Of course, I shouldn't like to leave the Abbey', he wrote to her, 'but I wouldn't much mind if it was the best thing for the Theatre, for really I've not much personal ambition but a great deal of ambition for the Theatre'.[1] She would have preferred him to fight, but he never did. In the event, he stayed on, and was given the assistance of Michael J. Dolan as manager in a few years. He was made a member of the Board of Directors in 1923, filling the place left vacant since the death of Synge.

Since both Yeats and Lady Gregory were tired by 1923 a lot of the day-to-day management of the Abbey was left to Robinson. There was a lot to be done to pull the theatre back from the brink of bankruptcy, following the hard years from 1919, during which political events in Dublin and the rest of Ireland kept the Abbey either closed by the curfew or sparsely attended when there was no curfew. In the nineteen twenties a new company was built up, a new group of playwrights emerged, in which O'Casey was only the most successful internationally, and a new, experimental theatre was opened, the Peacock, as the Abbey, subsidized by the Free State government, experienced a joyous rebirth. Robinson had a lot to do with this resurgence, because he put his heart and soul into the Abbey, but by the end of the decade he too was worn out. Frank O'Connor, whom Robinson helped in his career as librarian, provides a fascinating portrait of his older friend at this time in part three of *My Father's Son* (1968), and he makes clear that excessive drinking had made Robinson a danger to the theatre. By 1935 the Abbey was once again in dire financial straits, its poor standards the subject of editorials in the *Irish Times*.[2] According to O'Connor desperate remedies were called for, including a new Board of Directors, one of whom he was willing to be, and a new director of plays, who turned out to be Hugh Hunt. Robinson's position was humiliating, though the ageing Yeats did his best to protect him from the marauding pack. Yet after Hunt resigned in 1938 and O'Connor in 1939, following the death of Yeats, Robinson hung on and, in the face even of caricature on stage (in *The Money Doesn't Matter* in 1941), continued to write plays, to write his autobiography *Curtain Up* (1942), to edit Lady Gregory's *Journals* (1946) and to work on the official history of the theatre (*Ireland's Abbey Theatre*, 1951). He stayed with the Abbey, as a director, until his death in 1958.

But what was his achievement, it may well be asked, in view of the catalogue of faults laid at his door by his detractors in the nineteen thirties? Was the plain fact not simply that he was, as manager, an utter failure? And would this not mean, in turn, that his efficiency as director and even as playwright must be in question? It is when such questions are posed that one begins to realise how unpredictable the arts are, how unlike the world of business or of politics, however much these activities impinge. Because, somehow, out of or in spite of his manifest incompetence in some areas Robinson was able to be creative. He was not only creative in himself, as playwright, as editor both of his enemy's *Journals* and of the lectures delivered at the Abbey Festival of 1938 (*The Irish Theatre*, 1939), and as theatre historian, but also the cause of creativeness in others, whether actors and actresses or playwrights. In spite of glaring weaknesses, there was iron in Robinson, and courage and tenacity. He won the admiration of Ernest Blythe, who came in as managing director of the Abbey in 1941 and stayed until 1967.[3] Blythe was a tough Northerner, a former Minister for Finance and an able administrator. He was a man, certainly, who could have given Sir Peter Hall a run for his money. But Blythe was not a playwright, or a director, but a consummate administrator. Such men are viewed as either heroes or villains. Inasmuch as Blythe rescued the Abbey from almost certain collapse in 1941 and steered it through the difficult years after the theatre burned down in 1951, until the new Abbey was built and opened on the site of the old in 1966, he is a hero in Irish theatrical history. But inasmuch as he did all this at considerable expense to artistic standards he is to some, as to Peter Kavanagh in *The Story of the Abbey Theatre* (1950), a villain. Under Blythe's aegis, Kavanagh claimed, 'The Abbey Theatre board of directors was now packed against the forces of intellect, taste, imagination, and poetry' (p.182). Because he was possessed of all of these qualities just cited, Robinson deserves to be called the anti-hero of the Abbey Theatre: possessing them without the complementary managerial gifts of the kind Blythe had in abundance Robinson was liable, given also his self-deprecation, to be constantly under-estimated.

II

Three distinct phases may be discerned in Robinson's career as playwright, and with each of these, as Brinsley MacNamara has testified, he was a 'leader of trends in the Theatre'.[4] The first of these trends was that for grim realism, initiated with his one-act play *The Clancy Name* (1908). This was followed by *The Cross Roads* (1909) in two acts and a prologue, and *Harvest* (1910) in three acts. These were plays of Irish country life in which murder, brutality and the wrecking of dreams were prominent themes. The tone was pessimistic, the style uncompromisingly naturalistic. Other writers quickly followed this new mode, grimmer than anything seen before in the peasant drama of the Abbey repertory. These included T.C. Murray, R.J. Ray and St. John Ervine. 'We were very young and we shrank from nothing', says Robinson. 'We knew our Ibsen and the plays of the Lancashire school, we showed our people as robbers and murderers, guilty of arson, steeped in trickery and jobbery'.[5] But he also made clear years later, when writing the history of the Abbey, that these plays attempted to say something new about the Ireland after Synge's death (in 1909), in line with the atmosphere of the time. Thus, whereas the roots of this kind of drama can be traced back to Edward Martyn and George Moore, whose Ibsenist ideas Yeats disliked, the form it now took was less symbolist or lyrical than heretofore and much more analytic of Irish *mores*.

It happened that T.C. Murray was better at this form than Robinson: his *Birthright* (1910), *Maurice Harte* (1912), and the one-acts *Sovereign Love* (1913) and *Spring* (1918) indicate clearly, long before Murray's best play, *Autumn Fire* (1924), his superior insight into the darker areas of rural Irish experience. It is worthwhile considering why this is so. Murray himself, in a lecture at the Abbey Festival in 1938, said that it was Robinson who first showed him how to proceed: 'In their way of thought, their speech, their accent, the people that he created were the people I knew. From the field, the farmhouse, the shop, the wayside tavern, they seemed to have wandered on to his stage'. [6] But although Robinson sensed a corrupting influence in certain areas of rural living he couldn't assemble a coherent theory. At first he hit upon a real intuition, that the passion for respectability in provincial Irish life can be a tyrannizing force, leading to the extreme and ironic situation at the end of *The Clancy Name* where the mother prefers that her son should die rather than confess to a local murder. But then Robinson moved on to rather hazy theses. In *Cross Roads* a girl's choice of a loveless marriage so as to put into operation a theory of scientific farming brings tragedy on her head, and in *Harvest* all sorts of cases of degradation are traced to the over-education of farm people. These two latter plays ring false today. The fact of the matter is that Irish people do not live by theory or by a philosophy of life; they live, in the main, as if all the answers were provided by the Catholic Church. Robinson's Protestant notion of the individual's taking responsibility for his life simply is not true of Irish life. Liam de Paor has clarified this general point recently:

Tridentine Catholicism had a long and hard struggle in Ireland to supplant the medieval religion ... but by the end of the [eighteenth] century it was taking hold. The Enlightenment was its enemy. Its political, as distinct from religious, message to the people was to practise a farseeing prudence ... Long-term prudence required a quiet steady pressure for admission to the political nation; otherwise to wait patiently while the mills of God ground slowly. This, from the eighteenth century to the present day has been the main flow of the main current of articulate Catholic opinion and practice. [7]

In other words, Daniel Corkery was right, at least in the argument that the Protestant Anglo-Irish writer found great difficulty in understanding the soul and motivation of a peasantry overwhelmingly Catholic in religion. [8] Robinson tried to apply Ibsenist analysis to Irish provincial or peasant society, but, whereas Ibsen could, in *Pillars of Society*, trace social and moral corruption to a central figure such as Consul Bernick, Robinson could not. He could not point to any single feature of Irish life which was crippling the soul in its growth towards freedom. What he offered instead in these early plays was what the immature protestor will always offer, a sensational depiction of family misery attributed to bondage to some outworn or untenable theory. The plays are therefore contrived and artificial, in spite of the trappings of naturalism.

In his next phase Robinson ventured into politics as a way of clarifying his perceptions of Irish life. Here again he was grasping a nettle, which a subsequent writer, in this case O'Casey, was to turn far more effectively into a weapon with which to sting the bourgeoisie. Here again also Robinson had no clearly developed political theory which would answer his tragic interpretation of either current affairs or of history. O'Casey, after all, developed from being a republican to being a socialist, and underpinning his three great Dublin plays is the conviction that the rebellion of 1916 was a mistake, a betrayal of the vision of the Irish Citizen Army for a liberated working class. Accordingly, the cycle of violence, social chaos and family dissolution which is dramatized a-chronologically by O'Casey responds to an idea firm enough to demythologize the romantic conception of the 'fight for freedom'. Let audiences at *The Plough and the Stars* riot as they did, and had to if they were awake at all, the play retained its integrity through its coherent, ironic vision of recent history. Robinson was a nationalist, but a romantic one, an undying admirer of Yeats's *Cathleen ni Houlihan*. It would be unkind to say he resembled Uncle Pether in *The Plough*, but certainly he was rather a conventional patriot. Like so many, he found himself dismayed and disturbed by the events of 1916.

Before that, however, he wrote *Patriots* (1912), one of the best of his early plays. Robinson was justly proud of its structure and its use of taut dialogue, but conceded that 'the subject grew out of date in a few years'.[9] When James Nugent gets out of prison after serving eighteen years for political crimes he comes home to a family and a society changed in the meantime; where he is ready to start again and activate the dormant republican movement those around him have had enough and work to undermine his plans for a mass meeting. Nugent ends up broken in spirit by the apathy of the times. What may be inferred from this play on the political level is that Robinson despised the apathy of the people (compare Ibsen's *An Enemy of the People*), and the same point emerges from his Emmet play, *The Dreamers* (1915). Here it is the fecklessness of Emmet's supporters (shown in a pub scene in Act 2 that anticipates that of *The Plough*) that throws the whole noble enterprise of Emmet's attempt at rebellion into disarray and disrepute. As Emmet says, 'Kilwarden! the most righteous judge in Ireland slaughtered in the street like a pig. That's what I didn't understand — the suffering of the innocent — I shrank from no sacrifice myself'.[19] Commenting in his autobiography on 1916 and its aftermath Robinson said: 'England had won hands down, as she was bound to do, but it is wise to recollect that Ireland was fighting against her own mean, huckstering spirit'.[11] But after 1916 it was to be these same people, roused by Sinn Féin, that were to push forward towards the liberation of Ireland from England. How would this work out?

Robinson's biographer, Michael J. O'Neill, makes the point that a central subject in the early plays is the conflict 'of the dreamer and of the idealist with reality'.[12] But on the political level Robinson's problem was to define what 'reality' was. His only novel, *A Young Man from the South* (1917) is no help here, because it shows once again the dreamer involved in nationalism until violence opens his eyes to the anarchic nature of political conflict. In a Foreword, dated July 1916, Robinson says that if he were to revise (and not just rewrite) the book, as he was tempted to when the publisher's office was destroyed during Easter Week, his hero would have ended up in the GPO. He doesn't say what he would have been fighting for. Likewise in *Dark Days* (1918), four little stories of a republican nature, the Rising is seen as a watershed, but towards what is left vague. It is not until he wrote *The Lost Leader* (1918) that Robinson clarified this question, and now for the first time he came to terms with the negative implications of the struggle for freedom, so far as his own class was concerned. Here is how he described Major John White, J.P. in the play:

He and his two maiden sisters occupy the one big 'place' in the neighbourhood, when they die the heir, an Australian cousin, will sell the place, and COONEY *or his son will probably buy it. The* WHITES *will pass away, and the demesne of Castle White will become a grazing ranch. And with them will pass a tradition of hospitality and — though the present generation of* WHITES *is stupid — a tradition of culture. Castle White, with its formal pleasure grounds, its clipped yew hedges, its pictures, its spacious rooms, stood for something not ignoble in the life of the neighbourhood. But it might have stood for much more. Since the Union it has drawn itself more and more apart from the people; shorn little by little of its dignity it has made no effort to bridge the widening gulf, it has made no effort — even for its own sake — to understand its enemies. It is regarded now by* MR. COONEY *and his friends with a feeling almost of kindly contempt, and it will pass away unregretted. But because things might have been so different one mourns the extinction of the* WHITES, *one mourns it for the* COONEYS' *sake.*[13]

Here, rather than in the story which the play tells of Parnell alive and well in the west of Ireland after 1916, Robinson had the subject which could crystallize his otherwise romantic politics.

He dealt with this subject very fully and interestingly in *The Big House* (1926). By now Robinson realised that the Anglo-Irish were twice alienated, from Britain and from the Catholic majority. Yet this class, as he understood it, was Irish too. His biography of the member of a Sligo Anglo-Irish family, Bryan Cooper *(Bryan Cooper*, 1931), was to make this point very clearly, since Cooper became a *Teachta Dála* in the Free State government. But as early as August 1915, when he wrote the story 'An Irishwoman', later published in *Dark Days*, he saw that the first world war defined the first alienation. In that story an Anglo-Irish landlord, full of dreams to build up his estate, is drawn off to the war, where he dies, leaving a sister in charge at home. She finds herself unable to understand or sympathise with the cause for which he died, and feels 'with all this grief and loss no throb of kinship with England's Empire'.[14] *The Big House* takes it from there. The Alcock family of Ballydonal House in County Cork (Robinson's own territory) have lost one son in the first world war and with relief celebrate the armistice which should mean the safe return of their other son Ulick. When a telegram is brought announcing his death also the Alcocks are shattered but nevertheless their daughter Kate refuses to marry Captain Despard, a British soldier, and go to live with him in England, because, she asserts, her family is Irish and she wants to carry on Ulick's dream of maintaining the 'Big House' tradition in the community. During the Black-and-Tan war we see the Alcocks very much on the side of the native Irish, the Catholics, but by 1923, during the civil war Ballydonal House is on a cleft stick: favouring the Free State government it becomes the target of a reprisal attack by the Irregulars and is burned to the ground. Accepting defeat, the older Alcocks plan to leave for England, but Kate refuses to go. She stays to rebuild among the ruins, because she insists that she belongs: 'I was wrong, we were all wrong, in trying to find a common platform, in pretending we weren't different from every Pat and Mick in the village ... We must glory in our difference, be as proud of it as they are of theirs ... because we're what we are. Ireland is not more theirs than ours'.[15] But there was no concept of nationalism broad enough to accommodate Robinson's position. To the majority, the Anglo-Irish class was identified with Unionism, whereas nationalism had its basis in republicanism, and republicanism, to quote Liam de Paor again, 'remains antibourgeois'.[16] Robinson had a tragic theme here which he did not or could not express with the intensity necessary for the making of great tragedy. *The Big House* is riven with a determination to be fair to both sides. It goes far too gentle into that good night which was to sweep the Alcocks and their like into a Catholic state governed by the 1937 constitution.

Robinson had one more attempt at this theme in that very year, 1937. This was *Killycreggs in Twilight*, a story of the De Lury family faced with the collapse of its estate. But by now Robinson had learned to swim with the tide, and instead of rage he gives to his faded De Lury sisters a jaded acceptance of the inevitable 'twilight' of their way of life. The mood is Chekhovian, but perhaps like Brian Friel in a play that stands as counterpart to this one, *Aristocrats* (1979), Robinson is forging a new realism here, in accepting the law of change. In a key speech he makes Judith De Lury refer to *The Big House* as if to cancel out an older spirit of resistance:

There's no room in Ireland now for places like Killycreggs, for de Lurys and their like lounging and fishing and shooting. I wish we'd been burned out in the Troubles; I wish all our sort had been burned out. I wouldn't have behaved like that fool-girl in the play, *The Big House*. I would never have rebuilt Killycreggs, I'd have thanked God to be quit of it. [17]

Thus in his plays with a political background Robinson tried to reflect the changing moods of the times in which he wrote. His own romanticism, however, which had resulted in his revolt from the Unionist position held by his family in Cork, made it extremely difficult for him to believe otherwise than that 'minority' and 'majority' were terms which would disappear under the common name of Irishman once independence was achieved. Flawed though his achievement was in this dramatic area he did show how the theatre ought to be grappling with and interpreting history, a very important lesson for Irish playwrights.

The third phase of Robinson's playwriting career proved to be his most successful. This was as a writer of comedies. Paradoxically, less needs to be said about this phase than about others, for the work is so assured, so formally perfect, that it tends to make comment superfluous. The phase derived from that period of happy release from the burdens of Abbey management after 1914. It sometimes happens that when a writer ceases to try to make statements on one side of a question or another his work actually becomes stronger. The best comedies, at any rate, seem to derive from a holiday mood and incorporate the 'festive spirit'. So it is with Robinson. *The Whiteheaded Boy* was written in two weeks in 1916, *The Far-Off Hills* in three weeks in 1928, each of them following upon pretty rigorous work in serious drama. Each is a masterly comedy, unified in tone and atmosphere. Robinson claimed, in the Preface to *The Lost Leader*, that *The Whiteheaded Boy* was 'political from beginning to end', but nobody now believes this, nor is there any need to. The play marks a turning away from politics to study the lives and intrigues of provincial Irish people, not with the intense distaste and severity evident in Robinson's first phase but with detachment and amused tolerance. From the point of view of one of the people themselves (as the stage directions show) Robinson writes a comedy of manners, whimsical, ironic, good-tempered. He returns for his motivating force in society to that first observed in *The Clancy Name*, the passion for respectability. Now he observes in amusement the lengths to which a family will go to preserve its good name in the community, something that Denis Geoghegan, the whiteheaded boy himself, exploits to the full to his own advantage. The two young sisters are similarly 'planted' at the centre of *The Far-Off Hills*, suffering the fussy baby-sitting of Marian, their older sister, while they plot first to marry off their widowed father and then Marian herself, in spite of her avowed intention to enter a convent, the epitome of respectability. In *Drama at Inish* (1933) small-town society is turned upside down when it takes to heart the plays of Ibsen, Strindberg and others, as presented by a troupe of travelling players. The dangerous effects are stopped only when it is pointed out to the players that what they are doing is tantamount to uncovering in society what would be better left alone. As Annie puts it: 'Did you ever see a big stone in a field, Mr de la Mare? . . . You might be sitting by it, idle-like, some sunny afternoon, and then for no reason at all you'd turn it over. And what would you see? Worms. Little beetles that'd run this way and that, horrible little creepies that'd make your stomach turn, and you'd put the stone back as quick as you could, or you'd run away'.[18] Invariably in these comedies the stones are replaced and the unwelcome aspects of Irish life are, deliberately and self-consciously, covered over. The result is a type of satire alleviated by a strong affection for those satirized.

These comedies, and the many others which Robinson

penned, provided the model for Abbey playwrights to follow for a generation or more. They were well-crafted, for Robinson was an excellent exponent of the well-made play, and they paved the way for the comedies of George Shiels, Brinsley MacNamara and John McCann. Enormously popular, they proved invaluable to the box-office right up to the nineteen fifties, a matter which stern-minded critics sometimes interpret as connoting the superficiality of an author. But theatres cannot survive without box-office successes and in Robinson's case the comedies, for all that they cost him little effort in the making, represent his best artistic work. Another feature necessary to emphasise is their strong theatricality. The characterization is so varied and the scenes in the comedies so tellingly arranged that they offered from the start excellent playing roles to the Abbey company, a matter of considerable importance where a repertory theatre is concerned.

For Robinson, however, the comedies were not enough. He had ambitions to rise above the sort or material just described and to write plays that were international in style and appeal. It has to be borne in mind that from 1918 on he wanted the Abbey theatre to expand its repertory so as to include modern drama from other countries. Yeats, recalling the antipathy of Synge to just this idea some ten years earlier, argued against Robinson's suggestion. But Yeats agreed nonetheless to the idea of the Dublin Drama League which Robinson advanced as an alternative, and together the two men established this scheme for the playing at the Abbey on Sunday and Monday evenings of modern plays, mainly experimental in style, by the Dublin Drama League.[19] Beginning in 1919 the League, in which Robinson directed, acted, worked variously as secretary, vice-president and president, offered to Dublin audiences the best of modern plays from the continent and America.

This work has been documented by Brenna Katz Clarke and Harold Ferrar in *The Dublin Drama League 1919–1941* (1979), but while he was working with this group to complement the work of the Abbey Robinson also tried to expand his own plays, meant for the Abbey, in line with this internationalism. Occasionally, one of this new group of plays was rejected by the Abbey and staged by the League, for instance *Give a Dog* — (1929). Occasionally one played in London, for instance *All's Over, Then?* (1932), but without success. These were experimental plays, sophisticated in subject matter, daring in theme, at times daring in style, as was the use of expressionist techniques in *Ever the Twain* (1929). Taken together, this group of about six plays suggests an author straining every nerve to enter into discourse with his peers internationally, such as Eugene O'Neill, Noël Coward and Luigi Pirandello. The plays are frequently concerned with frustration, a crisis of identity or of the spirit which demands drastic, anti-social action, and so they contain a running away from marriage (*The Round Table*, 1922), a suicide (*Portrait*, 1925), or a murder (*All's Over, Then?*). *Give a Dog* — makes this theme of frustration bear particularly on the artist in society and so it may well have been expressive of Robinson's own state of mind, since he was rather stuck in a rut at the Abbey. None of these plays was really successful, and the last two mentioned were downright disasters. What they indicate, finally, is a lack of vision, or at best a drawing away from the implications of a horrific vision of life suggested by the material. 'Love seems such a terrible thing', the daughter Maggie comments in *All's Over, Then?* after her mother has tried to kill her; Maggie runs away with a man she does not love because she has seen what passion is like, and her mother commits suicide. Melodramatic though the scenario is it implies a fear of relationships very common in this group of plays, giving them the appearance of not quite stating what it was Robinson really wanted to say. If *Give a Dog* — is to be believed I infer that Robinson thought a yielding to the demonic was necessary for the renewal of the artist. Needless to say, you couldn't do this and stay on at the Abbey. So, with *Church Street* (1934) Robinson made peace with his urge towards experimentalism, and signalled that he recognized that his real, that is his theatrically viable, subject matter was not in cosmopolitan themes and settings but in the stuff of his popular comedies. Still, the example of his experiments was there for other writers to learn from, as George Shiels probably did in *The Passing Day* (1936) and Teresa Deevy in *Katie Roche* (1936).

III

To consider Robinson merely as writer would be entirely misleading. He was primarily a man of the theatre, whose work was not literary so much as texts for transfer on to a particular stage and intended for performance by specific actors and actresses whom he knew intimately. He is not so much an example, therefore, of the writer and the theatre as he is of the writer *in* the theatre. Whatever about his managerial skills, when it came to plays, their construction and their directing, Robinson was entirely at home. He was so steeped in the Abbey theatre that he may be identified with it in the nineteen twenties, thirties and forties. The little book he wrote, *Pictures in a Theatre* (1947), recently reprinted and updated by Micheál O hAodha (1983), displays him as virtually the curator of the Abbey's treasures, the guardian of its spirit and its intimate historian. This persona was created out of decades as director of plays and practitioner in the field. He is unique in this regard in the history of the Abbey Theatre, for no other playwright was so intimately bound up with production for so long as was Robinson. His influence was enormous, because not only was he the principal director of plays at the Abbey for almost thirty years but also a reader of new scripts, and adviser to new writers. His importance, accordingly, lies not just in the twenty-two plays which he wrote for the Abbey himself but in the ideas on drama and on production which he advocated and caused to be assumed into the tradition.

From his *Towards an Appreciation of the Theatre* (1945) it is clear that Robinson held a concept of integrated production as the criterion of artistic excellence. In this regard he was in line with the general development of modern theatre, ever since the pioneering work of Stanislavski and Craig.[20] Robinson saw as the supreme aim of the director the harmonization of text, acting, design and lighting. The director was essential to the creation of a unified effect: 'Without some such person in command the result is confusion' (p.25). The director should be unobtrusive, however, rather than dictatorial, Robinson believed, as such an attitude fostered greater creativeness in the actors. He gives a parody of this attitude in his novel, *A Young Man from the South* (pp.75–6): 'Presently Morrison drifted in, looking vague. He is an airified young man whom, personally, I dislike very much. ... He ran over a list of clothes vaguely, no one seemed to take much interest in the subject, the card players quarrelled in their corner, Gussy [Dossie Wright] was shouting for someone called Johnny [Seaghan Barlow], the beautifully dressed actress started again on her songs [for a concert elsewhere]. Morrison wandered out of the room'. This is supposed to be the greenroom at the Abbey during rehearsal. The narrator continues, 'the marvel was that out of all that vagueness and unpreparedness something very like a big success was achieved'. Of course Robinson is being impish here: 'vagueness' was often a criticism applied to himself (even

by Lady Gregory). But he did not really believe in the unprofes-
sional approach suggested in this passage. The following
passage from *Towards an Appreciation of the Theatre* gives a better
idea of his approach:

Much of the producer's [that is, the director's] work will have been
done before the first rehearsal. If he is able to do so he will make a scale-
model of each set with figurines — lead soldiers will do — to move from
position to position. He will mark each movement in his script, making
frequent diagrams illustrating the various groupings ... By splashing
with water-colour he will determine the colour of his walls, the carpets,
the furniture-coverings, he will decide on the style of the furniture, the
players' dresses, the type of pictures, the ornaments ... The more he
plots and plans, the more exact details are in his mind the better will
the players be pleased, for they hate to feel a fumbling, uncertain hand
directing them ... And the stage-carpenter and the property-man
should have their instructions in their hands at the first rehearsal; the
wardrobe mistress should know what is expected from her. There is a
mistaken belief that it is 'professional' to have a dress-rehearsal with
everything only half-ready, the doors not painted, 'of course, that's not
the table we are using', 'she's not going to wear that dress tomorrow
night', etc, etc. This is all wrong, this is the sign of a lazy producer ...
(pp.32–3).

The range of plays directed by Robinson was very great. Besides
his own plays, most but not all of which he directed, he directed
'a hundred plays by other authors', according to his own
estimate.[21] The figure is probably more than this, but in any
event it includes Irish poetic and experimental plays (Yeats,
Dunsany, Fitzmaurice), the plays of Goldsmith, Sheridan,
Wilde, Shaw, Ibsen, Strindberg, Hauptmann and O'Neill, as
well as new Irish plays from Colum's *Thomas Muskerry* (1910) to
Louis D'Alton's *The Spanish Soldier* (1940). This is excluding the
work he did for the Dublin Drama League. Since the Abbey was
a repertory company with a change of play at least every week,
and probably more often, in the years before Blythe took over
management, there probably wasn't time for a great deal of
directorial nicety; but this meant that Robinson had to be quick
and instinctive in setting and presenting a play. But a few
examples may serve to show this more clearly. The scenery he
designed for the opening of Yeats's *The Player Queen* (1919) was
praised as one of the most picturesque settings ever seen at the
Abbey, although the stage was too small adequately to make the
handling of the crowd scenes less than awkward.[22] Robinson
obviously did the best he could with a play he did not admire:

he had, in fact, enormous regard for Yeats as playwright, and directed eight of them at the Abbey, but he regarded *The Player Queen* as a failure: 'the play is full of colour and life, there is a most entertaining dance of the players dressed as beasts and birds but ... there is a philosophic idea behind the play which is never allowed to rear its head'. And so, 'in the end one feels cheated'.[23] He had a concept of authenticity in staging which extended to insisting on the simplest of lighting effects:

In [T.C. Murray's] *Birthright* the deathly fight between the brothers at the end should only be lit by two real candles. They give you the ominous distorted shadows on the walls, the semi-darkness when one candle is hurled to the floor, the utter darkness when the table is over-turned, and there is nothing but the sound of a scuffle and semi-articulate animal cries.[24]

That particular example shows how much feeling Robinson had for atmosphere on stage. As a final example Lady Gregory's version of *The Would-Be Gentleman* (1926) can be mentioned. Nervous of letting it be staged at the Abbey, because of the small stage and the smaller resources, Lady Gregory conceded that 'the skill of the producer overcame difficulties'.[25] Robinson gives some idea how he did this in his note to her text:

In a play like this — in a play full of colour and life and gay dresses — the setting should be as simple as possible and of some neutral colour. In the Abbey Theatre we used a grey curtained set with black swags, and black curtains at the back; and in the first act the only furniture was a large chair and a screen, both painted sealing-wax red. No change of scene is necessary for the second act, the large chair should be exchanged for three small ones and two small tables are needed. The table for the supper might be covered with a gold cloth, the other table — which must act as a side-table — with some duller cloth. It is well to have no properties except the absolutely essential ones, but to have all these individual and beautiful. One gold fruit-stand piled with highly-coloured fruit, some beautiful drinking-glasses, a coloured jug for wine will give an impression that a rich banquet is being prepared — an impression that fifty ill-assorted properties would never give (pp.358–9)

These details suggest that Robinson had a good visual sense of how a play should appear on the stage, although the actress Shelah Richards has said that he had not.[26] He had, indisputably, a concept of production that ordered all into beauty and significance. As he put it: 'Speed and tone — ah, there is where the great producer shows his mastery in his craft, not in trappings and fine scenery, not in gorgeous dresses, not in the cleverality he shows in handling some tricky bit of business, but by sensitive movement and grouping, by speeding up this sentence and retarding that, by suggesting to the player a nervousness at such a point, a truculence at some other moment, by going behind each speech and trying to catch its overtones, remembering the bearing, the significance, the relationship it has to other speeches later on in the play'.[27] In short, he brought his artistic impulse to bear on production, and thereby writer and director were indistinguishable.

Finally, Robinson's idea of a play must be mentioned, since this was what for a long time tended to govern the type of play accepted by the Abbey. It was a concept not too far removed from Yeats's, that is, it was classical, recognizing the primacy of plot and structure, the unity of action, and the integration of characters, theme and language in a unified whole. But Yeats favoured poetic drama almost exclusively, and hoped, up to the year 1919, that the Abbey might become the home of a new modern poetic drama. The development of the Abbey instead into a theatre where realism predominated was to Yeats a bitter disappointment.[28] Robinson, for his part, was largely responsible for this same victory of the 'Theatre of the head' of which Yeats complained. When O'Casey started to send in his plays to the Abbey the writing was truly on the wall. Yeats hated 'The Crimson in the Tricolour', and ended his severe reader's report thus: 'If Robinson wants to produce it let him do so by all means and be damned to him. My fashion has gone out'.[29] Robinson didn't, in fact, want to direct this play, but he did want to encourage O'Casey; so in forwarding Yeats's report (and rejection) he wrote to O'Casey:

Though I must agree with certain of these criticisms, I persist in finding the play very interesting. I have felt an attraction to all your work. If you still are interested in the subject of this play we might be able to make it over again and make a play of it. I think you have got the scenario — the shape of the play wrong, or if you have another play in your mind will you come and talk over the idea and we will work out a scenario together?[30]

O'Casey responded well to Robinson's letter and in time brought him the text of a new play, which became *The Shadow of a Gunman* (1923) and which launched O'Casey's playwriting career. In what follows I infer what Robinson had to teach O'Casey.

First, Robinson insisted that a play should be based on

experience in some way. Of *The Shadow of a Gunman* he said approvingly: 'The sentimentalities of his earlier dramatic efforts had vanished, he was writing of life as he knew it'.[31] Second, he insisted on a scenario and a tight organization of scenes. 'The play being mapped out in his mind the wise playwright will make an outline, a *précis* of his play running to, say, a thousand words . . . That outline may have to be done over and over again until it seems right. He should then proceed to plan the sequence of the scenes in his acts, treating his acts in the French manner, that is to say the entrance or exit of a character marks a new "scene" . . . And he will note what facts are to be conveyed in each scene.'[32] Third, he considered that what mattered in dramatic dialogue were speed and variety, as exemplified in the plays of Molière. Finally, he said that the playwright should, like a good card player, use at appropriate times suspense and surprise. Some of this rubbed off on O'Casey, as *Juno and the Paycock* (1924) shows: he had been urged (by M.J. Dolan) to read *The Whiteheaded Boy* in order to learn craftsmanship and it showed. In *Towards an Appreciation of the Theatre*, moreover, in order to illustrate a good opening to a play, Robinson analyses the start of *Juno* into seven scenes (pp.16–18).

Needless to say, there came a point when O'Casey had no more to learn from Robinson, and that probably happened with the writing of *The Plough and the Stars* (1926), which Robinson directed. Certainly, Robinson disliked *The Silver Tassie* (1929), and sided with Yeats about its rejection. This was enough for O'Casey, who never wrote another line for the Abbey afterwards. But if O'Casey's experimentalism tends to show up Robinson's ideas on playwriting as conventional it has to be said that by this stage O'Casey was rather overstepping the mark invisibly laid down for any writer in his relationship to any theatre. When he sent the script of *The Silver Tassie* to Robinson O'Casey also sent a cast list: he had actually cast the roles already![33] He had even gone so far as to ask Gabriel Fallon if he would take the role O'Casey had assigned to him (Simon Norton). Obviously, this kind of thing must irk any director, even if Robinson never said so. The feeling was inevitable that O'Casey was getting too big for his boots. The rejection of *The Silver Tassie* is something that must always be regretted, since it severed O'Casey's link with the collaborative theatre and drove him, as a playwright with a tendency to over-write, into difficulties which might well have been avoided had he always had to undergo the discipline of being an 'in-house' writer. But it is not inexplicable.

Besides O'Casey, a great number of Irish playwrights came under the influence of Robinson the play reader and advocate of the well-made play, including T.C. Murray, George Shiels, Denis Johnston (who learned more through Robinson's work with the Dublin Drama League than with the Abbey), Brinsley Mac-Namara, Teresa Deevy, Louis D'Alton and Paul Vincent Carroll. Teresa Deevy's comments in this regard are of value: 'He was always ready to listen to the author and to have the author beside him at rehearsal. . . . He never aimed to put his mark on the play (as some producers do) and therefore his mark was always on it.'[34] There is an element of genius in such tactfulness. Where talent existed he was aware of it and was able to bring it out. Ernest Blythe was struck by this ability in Robinson even when his health failed him at the end of his long career: 'He had a keen scent for talent and I never knew him to condemn as worthless a script in which it was afterwards generally felt there was merit'.[35]

An anti-hero is the modern version of the outmoded hero. He is a figure who far from being the sublime representation of human greatness magnificently in conflict with Fate is the inconsequential depiction of man's inadequacies in the face of tasks and situations beyond his competence to cope with. Lennox Robinson was such a modern figure, just as Yeats was not, being of the older more heroic tradition. In his role as manager of the Abbey Robinson may have cut a ridiculous figure. But sticking to the theatre as director and writer, as he did for over forty years, he achieved a dignity which a stormier personality might never have won. He loved the theatre with every fibre of his being, and the question of his own self-esteem was as nothing compared with the importance of creating new life on stage. He did this over and over again as director at the Abbey. He tried to do it for forty years in his own plays, in which he struggled to say something truthful and arresting about Irish life. In large measure, it must look to us now as if he failed as a writer to reach the first rank; no single play of his ranks with any by Synge or O'Casey. But in a few plays where the joy of life rose high enough in him to provide comic accounts of the absurdities and self-deceptions in Irish society he created plays that still delight audiences, as *Drama at Inish* delighted audiences first in the Peacock, then on the Abbey stage and later on tour, during 1983. The talk now is that *The White-headed Boy* is to be turned into a musical. Being the trooper he was, Lennox would hardly have objected. He might wonder, though, why his other plays are now so neglected. It is high time they were given another chance.

NOTES

1   Quoted by Robert Hogan and Richard Burnham, *The Modern Irish Drama, A Documentary History, V: The Art of the Amateur 1916–1920*, Mountrath: Dolmen Press; Atlantic Highlands: Humanities Press, 1984, p.267. Hereafter cited as *The Art of the Amateur*.

2   20 March and 26 March 1935. During the weeks preceding 20 March, Frank O'Connor and Sean O'Faolain severely criticized the Abbey in letters to the newspapers. Robinson replied in *The Irish Press*, 27 February.

3   See Blythe's lecture in *The Yeats We Knew*, ed. Francis MacManus. Cork: Mercier Press, 1965, p.64. Blythe obviously held O'Connor to blame for inciting Yeats against Robinson in 1935.

4   *Abbey Plays 1899–1948*. Dublin: Three Candles, n.d., p.17.

5   *Curtain Up: An Autobiography*. London: Michael Joseph, 1942, p.22.

6   'George Shiels, Brinsley MacNamara, etc.', in *The Irish Theatre*, ed. Lennox Robinson. London: Macmillan, 1939; repr. New York: Haskell House, 1971, p.124.

7   'The Rebel Mind: Republican and Loyalist', in *The Irish Mind: Exploring Intellectual Traditions*, ed. Richard Kearney. Dublin: Wolfhound Press; Atlantic Highlands: Humanities Press, 1985, p.165.

8   *Synge and Anglo-Irish Literature*. Dublin and Cork: Cork University Press, 1931; repr. Cork: Mercier Press, 1966, pp.79–80, 103–4. To leave out the spiritual side of the Irish character is, says Corkery, 'the Ascendancy convention' (p.104).

9   *Curtain Up*, p.43. Yet the discriminating critic Andrew Malone said: 'In thought, in dialogue and in construction *Patriots* is one of Lennox Robinson's best plays'. See his *The Irish Drama*. London: Constable, 1929, pp.178–9.

10 Lennox Robinson, *The Dreamers: A Play in Three Acts*. London and Dublin: Maunsel, 1915, p.57. This attitude can be compared with Denis Johnston's comment on Emmet, prefacing his own play about him, *The Old Lady Says 'No!'*: 'We all agree that it was a pity that some of his supporters had to murder one of the most liberal judges on the bench, Lord Kilwarden.' See 'Opus One', *The Dramatic Works of Denis Johnston*, Volume 1. Gerrards Cross: Colin Smythe, 1977, p.15. Johnston once told me, however, that he was not familiar with *The Dreamers*.

11 *Curtain Up*, p.104.

12 *Lennox Robinson*. New York: Twayne Publishers, 1964, repr., Grosset and Dunlap, 1964, p.76. Michael J. O'Neill's book, the definitive study on Robinson, is one to which I express my continuing indebtedness.

13 Lennox Robinson, *The Lost Leader: A Play in Three Acts*. Dublin: Thomas Kiersey, 1918, pp.67–8. This passage clearly anticipates the Old Man's attitude towards the Big House in Yeats's *Purgatory* (1938).

14 *Dark Days*. Dublin: Talbot Press; London: T. Fisher Unwin, 1918, p.9.

15 *The Big House*, in *Selected Plays of Lennox Robinson*, Irish Drama Selections 1. Gerrards Cross: Colin Smythe; Washington, D.C.: Catholic University of America Press, 1982, pp.195–6.

16 'The Rebel Mind: Republican and Loyalist', p.186.

17 *Killycreggs in Twilight & Other Plays*. London: Macmillan, 1939, p.83.

18 *Selected Plays of Lennox Robinson*, pp.251–2.

19 *Curtain Up*, p.122. Michael J. O'Neill, in *Lennox Robinson*, p.113, cites a letter from Robinson to James Stephens, dated 27 September 1918, in support of his contention that the Dublin Drama League was primarily

Robinson's brainchild. Robert Hogan and Richard Burnham, however, claim that Yeats was the prime mover: see *The Art of the Amateur*, pp.152–3.

20   See, for example, Edward Braun, *The Director and the Stage: From Naturalism to Grotowski*. London: Methuen, 1982.

21   Lennox Robinson, *Ireland's Abbey Theatre: A History 1899–1951*. London: Sidgwick & Jackson, 1951, p.85.

22   See Robert Hogan and Richard Burnham, *The Art of the Amateur*, p.216.

23   *Curtain Up*, p.65. From a practical point of view, Robinson discusses in detail the following plays by Yeats: *The Countess Cathleen, The Land of Heart's Desire, On Baile's Strand, Deirdre, The Player Queen, Four Plays for Dancers* and *Words upon the Window-pane*, pp.48–72.

24   *Towards an Appreciation of the Theatre*. Dublin: Metropolitan Publishing Co., 1945, p.36.

25   *The Translations and Adaptations of Lady Gregory and Her Collaborations with Douglas Hyde and W.B. Yeats Being the Fourth Volume of the Collected Plays*, ed. Ann Saddlemyer. Gerrards Cross: Colin Smythe, 1970, p.360.

26   Quoted by Michael J. O'Neill, *Lennox Robinson*, pp.71–2.

27   *Towards an Appreciation of the Theatre*, p.40.

28   W.B. Yeats, 'A People's Theatre: A Letter to Lady Gregory', in *Explorations*. London: Macmillan, 1962, pp.244–59. 'Yet we did not set out to create this sort of theatre, and its success has been to me a discouragement and a defeat' (p.250).

29   *The Letters of Sean O'Casey 1910–1941*, Volume 1, ed. David Krause. London: Cassell, 1975, p.103. The date given is 19 June 1922, about a year after O'Casey had submitted the script.

30   *Ibid*. The date of Robinson's letter is 28 September 1922.

31   *Curtain Up*, p.139.

32   *Towards an Appreciation of the Theatre*, p.16.

33   *The Letters of Sean O'Casey*, p.235. The date of this letter to Lennox Robinson is 5 April 1928.

34   Quoted by Michael J. O'Neill, *Lennox Robinson*, p.72.

35   *Ibid*., p.158.

METAPHOR AS DRAMATIC STRUCTURE IN PLAYS BY STEWART PARKER

ANDREW PARKIN

Stewart Parker first became widely known as author of *Spokesong*,[1] the play that earned him the *Evening Standard* award for most promising playwright of 1976. Since then Parker has written, among other works for radio, stage, and television,[2] the stage play *Catchpenny Twist*, first produced at the Peacock Theatre Dublin in 1977, and *The Kamikaze Ground Staff Reunion Dinner*,[3] a play first broadcast on BBC Radio 3 in December, 1979.

Spokesong gained mainly favourable reviews from theatre critics on both sides of the Atlantic. Parker gained much attention for his unusual and conspicuous tactic of presenting the 'troubles' in Northern Ireland only as background to his seemingly primary subjects, love, sibling rivalry, and the charms of the bicycle. A dissenting voice in the chorus of praise was that of Douglas Watt in the New York *Daily News* of 16 March 1979; despite, or perhaps because of, the proximity of St. Patrick's day, Watt attacked Parker for 'feyness' in using a bicycle shop in allegorical fashion. Gareth Lloyd Evans, in a brief notice in *Drama*, while appreciative of Parker's 'imaginative and caring use of words', could not see why he chose 'to express his play by tying it to the history of cycling (complete with actual antique specimens)'.[4] To understand why Parker did this, his dramatic method has to be more thoroughly explored than is possible in a brief review, and that is what this essay attempts to do.

From a reading of Parker's early play, *Iceberg*,[5] it would be possible to suppose that the promising young author could develop into a follower of German Expressionist theatre. The setting is the doomed *Titanic*. The main characters, Hugh and Danny, are shipyard workers in overalls, presented realistically. But they are backed by a chorus of musicians 'All of Whom

Appear in Evening Dress and White Face'.[6] The setting is a stylised arrangement of rostra '... at different levels, and connected by steps and ladders'. The luxury liner is merely suggested by a 'Centrally placed ... palm court arrangement', little tables bearing lamps, and 'At the highest point ... a life-boat davit and the stem of the life-boat which is suspended from it'.[7] This could suggest the kind of symbolic verse drama written by Auden and Isherwood in the portentous shadow of German Expressionism, or perhaps the influence of Piscator's early Volksbühne productions.[8] But that would be entirely wrong. *Iceberg* and Parker's later plays avoid the solemn philosophising, the stylised presentation of representative personages and enormous societal pressures, and the general earnestness of Expressionism. They also avoid, as they avoid post-war realism, the intensity of Piscator's political theatre, with its bold experimentalism, its movie projections, and its frank use of propaganda. Parker's early play, like his later work, is nearer to the native British tradition of music hall, with its mixture of comedians, song and dance routines, monologues, and sketches or skits. The Bandmaster in *Iceberg* is a master of ceremonies who, like many a North Country comic, jokes with the orchestra, though not with that air of sinister corruption flaunted by the MC in Bob Fosse's movie, *Cabaret*, derived, however tenuously, from between-the-wars Germany.

Iceberg, as might be expected of an early work, shows flashes of lively theatrical style, but is in sum disappointing. Parker does not sustain the very genuine interest established at the beginning of the play. Yet it foreshadows much of Parker's later technique. The play's situation is that the *Titanic* sails on her fatal maiden voyage carrying, among all the others, two Belfast workers, Hugh and Danny. A central irony is that they are, in fact, ghosts, having been killed in an accident during the building of the ship. The Bandmaster, in the character of Andrews, the vessel's architect, orders the two dead men around. The other musicians also double as the Tour Guide and passengers. The simplicity of this situation is complicated not by action so much as by language itself, especially its figurative effects. The ship is in itself a theatrical symbol of human hubris, specifically in the form of the doomed British Empire. This is quickly established through the Tour Guide's descriptions of the ship's interiors and antiques. Parker thus rapidly evokes the greatness and wealth of the British past. But the fact, sometimes unknown to those outside Ulster, that the *Titanic* was Belfast built, makes the set a physical metaphor of Northern Ireland. Dialogue makes this overt also when Andrews tells Hugh and Danny:

... we're ... representing the entire 14,000 men in the yard and beyond them the whole of Ulster. This ship is our proudest offering — to the Empire — and to the world — and I want it perfect in every detail ...[9]

This is further emphasised when the Lady Guide points out the William and Mary style of fittings and décor. This symbolism carries its own ironies within the overall irony of the ship's fate, as in the detail of the ornamental clock with female figures holding a crown above it to represent Honour and Glory crowning Time. The light humour of the Guide with a flock of tourists is inextricably linked with the bitter taste of lost hopes. Disaster is kept well in the background, but its shadow darkens the comic foreground. This is an abiding characteristic of Parker's style in *Spokesong* and *Catchpenny Twist*.

The ship of fools is, of course, an ancient image for the human condition; but Parker extends it beyond the stage set into the language of the play through apparently casual remarks, as in Danny's, 'Did you read about the Boat Race? Both their boats got swamped, they both sunk. There was nobody left to be the winner'.[10] This is apt as a metaphor of doomed Empire and also of the deadly vying of Protestants with Catholics in Northern Ireland. Danny's later remark, 'I've no desire to spend eternity living in a ship's lifeboat'[11] can be read as a reference to Ulster as a tiny bit of Britain tenuously attached to the sinking ship of Empire. The central metaphor is extended in other ways: the plight of the artist and entertainer in a failing society is evoked by segments of action, as when the Bandmaster rebukes the dispirited and nauseous band, 'All right, all right, it's all one in a hurricane. Just don't puke into the piano, that's all I ask'.[12] Extension and enrichment of the image can also be achieved through song, a constant device with Parker. Dr. O'Loughlin plays the piano and sings a concert party number in which he praises Tommy Andrews and his ship, proof against the elements. The heavy irony gets a touch of poignancy from the waving gestures of the chorus as they move off in slow motion wearing fixed smiles on their faces. That stage direction also owes more to the vaudeville and the cinema than to any hint of Expressionism.

Parker also extends the metaphor more obliquely by its link to traditional Irish themes. As the *Titanic* leaves Ireland Danny is inevitably reminded of Thomas Moore's song of exile, 'Tho' the last glimpse of Erin with sorrow I see',[13] but if to leave is painful, to stay could be worse; Hugh's comment in reply is hard and unsentimental:

The well-known death and exile merchant. What a country ... look at it ... the wild soft green of it ... stuffed full of itself. Full of its corpses. All it leaves you with is a pain in your bones.[14]

But Parker does not allow the audience to blur the distinctions between North and South in Ireland. The North has a massive industrial capacity, many skilled workers, and is part of the large English economy. Danny sums all this up in his defiant speech:

You don't need me to tell you the difference. Look at this boat, can you imagine them building it in Cork or somewhere?[15]

The episode ends with the Violinist stepping into role as Sir Humphrey Standish-Norton to sing 'England, Fair England', a piece every bit as patriotic and sentimental as the Tom Moore song, but not as simple and warm.

Parker even links Asquith's Home Rule efforts to the central image of the ship by having it headlined in the *Titanic*'s on-board news sheet, *The Atlantic Daily Bulletin*. The doomed ship metaphor also encompasses Belfast itself when Hugh suggests that in order to win the race for ever larger ocean liners, the shipyard will 'put a slipway' under the entire city and launch it, '... after the people have all been shot by the army — for refusing to obey orders and abandon ship'.[16] Ulster, of course, refused to join the Irish under home rule from Dublin. Thus the metaphorical method has multiple layers of suggestion: the plight of Ulstermen, seeing themselves as British, yet in danger of being legislated into union with the South, would be 'abondoning ship'; yet the absurdity of a floating Belfast is also clear. The ambivalence and ambiguity of metaphor makes it the most likely verbal device, together with its cousin, the pun, to capture the uncertainties, ambiguities, and absurdities of the situation in Ireland.

Parker's tendency to make everything a metaphor of Ireland, can, however, become tedious. When Hugh and Danny meet two girl passengers from the South, Rosaleen and Molly, the girls remain emblems, there being no space for their development as people. The themes of exile, home-sickness, and exploitation in the New York garment industry are too baldly and programmatically raised. Within the scope of a short play, Parker tries to cover too much. Similar criticisms apply to the brief episode in which the Bandmaster appears as the Stoker, and the imagery of the boiler room becomes an horrific image of hell. The episode is unprepared for and incongruous. In contrast, the further extension of the ship metaphor through the idioms of the language is, though less sensational than the hell imagery, a quietly effective way of making a point. When Andrews tells another character, 'You've got your Home Rule Bill launched anyway',[17] the homely idiom can suddenly extend beyond cliché back to the metaphor at the heart of the action, as Andrews goes on, '. . . she's only launched, I doubt you'll find that she'll never [sic] make it into active service'.[18] The dismal chain of Irish history stretching from the *Titanic* disaster to the present offers a sobering context in the minds of the audience for the friendly rivalry of the Northerner, Andrews, and the Southerner, O'Loughlin, who tries a note of warmth towards the end of the play: 'Here's to your ship, Tommy. I'm proud to be your countryman, even if you do disown me. Here's to your dream'.[19]

Hugh and Danny end the play by recalling the accident that killed them and congratulating their ghostly selves on having found an appropriate niche on the *Titanic*. At that moment the sound of the ship beginning to break up can be heard. In this respect, then, the play suggests the plight of Ulster, built upon the deaths of numbers of people, launched by the treaty, and now foundering on the iceberg of terrorism. The light-hearted tone, the jokes, and the fun that characterise Parker's style are set against the powerful metaphor of the ship that is essentially pessimistic. We all know what happened to the *Titanic*, and history cannot be reversed.

There are several elements in Parker's work that suggest the influence of the plays of W.B.Yeats. Parker studied Yeats as a dramatist during his time at Queen's University, Belfast. Yeats's early play, *The Shadowy Waters*, used a ship's deck as stage set, but here the analogy ends. But Parker, like Yeats, uses ghosts as characters, yet to totally different effect: the ghosts in Yeats's *The Dreaming of the Bones* and *The Only Jealousy of Emer* are figures from the far historical past or legend; Parker's ghosts are modern workmen. A closer analogy might be the ghosts of Yeats's *Purgatory*. True, Parker's Hugh and Danny are comic and realistic, more in the manner of Lord Dunsany, perhaps, than of Yeats. But in *Purgatory* the ghosts dwell in a ruined house, a central and dominant image of Ascendancy Ireland. It is the linking of characters to a central unifying image that Parker owes to Yeats, and this applies also to his use of the chorus figures. Yeats picked up this fertile idea of the central, unifying image from his reading of Japanese Noh plays:

I wonder am I fanciful in discovering in the plays themselves (few examples have as yet been translated and I may be misled by accident or the idiosyncrasy of some poet) a playing upon a single metaphor, as deliberate as the echoing rhythm of line in Chinese and Japanese painting. [20]

This 'rhythm of metaphor' as Yeats referred to it, seemed to him the perfect device for setting the scene, creating mood, and fuelling the verse of his brief dance plays. The image could appear in the chorus lyrics and provide the focus of the play's overriding emotion. The mask-like make-up of Yeatsian musicians in *At the Hawk's Well* fits the idea of the unifying image. Individual features are sacrificed for an overall decorative and aesthetic effect. Parker's use of the unifying image is tied to a very different dramatic and theatrical style. But the white face Musicians in *Iceberg* are given this alienating anonymity so that they function clearly as a chorus, and also to help them slip into other roles in an immediately acceptable way impossible to achieve by naturalistic means. In this they go beyond the function of the Yeats chorus. Parker also extends the use of the binding image to make it, as we have seen in *Iceberg*, always a metaphor of his subject, made physical in the stage setting, and pervading idiom, dialogue and characterisation.

It is worth jumping forward now in Parker's career to another short play with this rhythm of metaphor, *The Kamikaze Ground Staff Reunion Dinner*. Parker's touch is more certain, and he makes full use of the swift transitions that radio as a medium makes possible to extend the central image of the kamikaze tactic. Parker's characteristic blend of jaunty comedy with the lethal realities of politics and warfare, of laughter with pain, appears in the very title of the play, and in its opening monologue by the dentist, Makoto:

Yes, there's rather more to this little horror than I thought ... we were all stationed at Mabalacat Base in the Philippines together, you see. Open wide ... good ... yes, with the Special Attack Force ... you know, the Kamikazes ... *(The patient shrieks.)* [21]

The binding image of the suicide mission as a battle tactic provides the *raison d'être* of the play's action, the reunion of the ground staff. We are introduced to the characters through the sounds and conversations of their post-war civilian occupations: dentist, airline pilot, baker, taxi driver, and a financial consultant selling insurance. Parker's sense of humour and sharp ear for idiom pick up on phrases to reinforce the central image. In Shushin's bakery the week's production figures take 'a nose-dive' and Shimpu the cab driver, disgruntled with life, asks 'Don't you ever feel an impulse to cry out in protest, to smash it all right into the ground?'[22]

The tripartite structure of the play (introduction of characters; reunion party; airfield climax and resolution) keeps in constant mind the nostalgia among some, though not all the characters, for a warrior code now pushed aside but seen as superior to the disorder and squalor of the modern, post-atomic society. In losing the war, Tokkotai opines, Japan also lost discipline and respect for tradition. The nostalgic image of the heroic warrior code conflicts, however, with Kamiwashi's recollections of hastily trained youngsters, who '. . . were already half-dead with fright before they'd even cleared the ground'.[23] The outrage his view provokes fails to dispel Kamiwashi's realism and pragmatism. Comfortable in the post-war democracy, he calls the kamikaze mission 'a tactic of defeat'.[24] The conflict is between those who wish to rebuild the economy and subscribe to new trends in the free world, even if that means tolerating the democratic phenomena of mass protests, strikes, unruly students, and those others who seek to perpetuate the warrior code. When Tokkotai and Shimpu are about to carry out a kamikaze mission at the climax of the play, the target is the modern world of student communists, television, and mindless commercialism; their preferred weapon though is a modern, wide-bodied jet. The irony of the ending is that all they are able to commandeer is a bi-plane (technology more appropriate to their old-fashioned views) and that they accidentally crash into a mobile library moments after Tokkotai changes his mind about completing the suicide mission, having remembered that he wanted to attend his grandson's christening the following day. This Christian reference is one clue that the play is as much about Ireland as it is about Japan. Tokkotai's fellow veterans are convinced he completed the kamikaze mission. The press reports it as the accident it appeared to be.

In this play, four years later than *Iceberg*, Parker has jettisoned the chorus device and the over-eager symbolic characterisation of the earlier play. Dialogue is terser, racier, and funnier. The second term of the central image is less apparent than in *Iceberg*, but the kamikaze tactic is certainly applicable to the Irish situation. The Irish gunman is sometimes as fanatically patriotic as the kamikaze pilot, and suicidal in battle or hunger strike. He is bred on the heroic feats of the blood-soaked past. And he is often young and hastily trained. A grandiose mission will sometimes end in an absurd accident, as when a terrorist bomber blows himself up. Just as the Japanese warrior code was the product of an ancient civilization with a profound respect for stoic acts of courage, so, in the mythology of the Irish Renaissance and some of its literature, heroic patriots struggling to wrest Ireland from British rule were linked to the warriors of ancient times. Finally, in the atomic age when no one can afford to let local struggles get out of hand and escalate, the Romanticism of the Irish gunman, whether Catholic or Protestant, and that of the kamikaze pilot seem curiously akin, hopelessly old-fashioned, and disturbingly puritanical. They seem to belong more to the past, or the 'Third World' than to the European Common Market or Japan Incorporated. The commercial ethos of *Kamiwashi* naturally accords more closely with the direction of the majority of people in the Western commercial democracies than does the kamikaze code or that of the urban guerrilla.

The play in which the central metaphor is sustained most thoroughly and most amusingly is *Spokesong, or the Common Wheel.* Here the metaphor is developed as systematically and ingeniously as the 'conceit' was in Elizabethan poetry. Parker has found the theatrical form of the conceit by extending the central and unifying image into every aspect of the play including stage properties.[25] Chronologically, *Spokesong* falls between *Iceberg* and *The Kamikaze Ground Staff Reunion Dinner*.

Spokesong's dramatic conceit is the bicycle. It pervades the setting of the bicycle shop, the stage business, properties, songs, and the language of the play at all levels, using the pun, as in the title and subtitle, to enrich the connotations of the text at every opportunity. The notion of the two referents of a metaphor and a pun accords with the bicycle image itself, with its two wheels. And this image constantly reminds us that Ireland is an island with two peoples, two nations, two religions. The penny-farthing cycle, a property used in some productions of the play, is a ready visual aid to remembering the larger island of Great Britain with the smaller Ireland trailing behind, as was the case in the Victorian time frame that is part of the play's plotting. But the play is also set in the early seventies, so that the antique cycle also suggests modern Britain or modern Ireland with the smaller outpost of Ulster. The master of ceremonies figure, the Spokesman, rides a unicycle, suggesting the ideal of national unity, but one that depends upon skill and a delicate sense of balance as opposed to blundering violence. Indeed, the resonances produced by the metaphorical linking of unlikely material as the dramatic conceit builds account for a good deal of the charm and impact of the play.

Set in an old-fashioned cycle shop in Belfast, *Spokesong* exploits the second of the two facts known to every resident of the city. The first is that the *Titanic* was built there; the second that Dunlop, a Scottish veterinary surgeon, was living there when he invented the pneumatic tyre. The latter fact, together with the implications of the cycle image as detailed above, go some way to explaining why Parker uses the bicycle shop imagery. A third reason is that given by Parker and reported by Robert Berkvist in the *New York Times* piece already cited:

I had to make manageable the subject of contemporary Irish politics and the nature of the violence I've lived through in Belfast for the past 10 years ... And I wanted to do it in such a way that the audience would be taken completely by surprise, caught without its preconceptions. I decided that the way to do that was to write a play about the history of the bicycle — because that is the most unlikely way in the world to get into the subject of Northern Ireland.[26]

The conceit as a structural device locks the unmanageable and the unlikely together in a dramatic and theatrical chain that is the length of the play; the unlikeliness is essential for the originality that the conceit was often valued for in poetry, but it is also a means of breaking away from *preconceptions* — and sectarianism feeds on those.

Catherine Itzin describes *Spokesong* as '. . . a beautiful lyrical play combining a passionate and sentimental history of the bicycle with an equally passionate, but unsentimental tandem history of the troubles in Belfast'.[27] This lyricism is the prime quality and is achieved in the frequent songs, mostly original, but also including, inevitably, the old music hall favourite, 'A Bicycle Made for Two'. This, used as opening chorus, is a signal about structure as well as theme. Thematically, Ireland is a place where two peoples must learn to pedal in harmony. Structurally, the play has two plots in tandem: in contemporary Belfast Frank Stock runs his grandfather's cycle repair business, falls in love with teacher Daisy Bell, and succeeds in resisting the attempt of his adopted brother, who works as an English photo-journalist, to win Daisy and take her to England; secondly, through 'flashbacks', we trace the lives of Frank's grandfather, Francis Stock, racing cyclist on the first Dunlop pneumatic tyres, and his beloved Kitty Carberry, a 'new woman' of the 'nineties, who believes in votes for women, and, like Shaw's Vivie Warren, owns a ladies' cycle,[28] is educated, and has a head for business and orderly accounts. The play shifts between the living present and the life and times of the grandparents, including the period of Frank's youth, when he was raised by them after the death of both parents in an air raid. This structure demands the play shift between time frames and their appropriate vocabulary and speech patterns rather as a cyclist changes gear by moving the chain from one chainwheel to another.

The setting '... *should consist only of bare essentials, but the essentials should all be real'.*[29] This style allows for swift transitions between the three acting areas and between the styles of acting, mainly realistic, but also including the vaudeville style of the Trick Cyclist, and the performance of the musical numbers. The mixture makes for a fast pace in production, so long as the transitions work smoothly.

Parker's transitions are, in fact, achieved in a number of ways that are very effective. He has clearly learned from Thornton Wilder's *Our Town* and, nearer home, from the accomplished contemporary comic playwright, Peter Nichols. Nichols has a gift for presenting sad, even grim situations in a richly comic context.[30] After the opening chorus of *Spokesong*, the Trick Cyclist deftly switches into the mode of a public official for his monologue about a public enquiry concerning city redevelopment. This thread runs through the play, connecting the personal life of Frank Stock and his obsession with bicycles to the public life of the city, and through unofficial re-planning by means of bombs to the terrorist activity. Again there is a tandem effect. And the bicycle conceit accumulates connections like spokes radiating from the personal hub of the play's wheel (Frank and Daisy) to its public rim (the troubles in Northern Ireland). All transitions to the public enquiry scenes are quickly and fluently achieved by the Trick Cyclist's instant adoption of an official manner and the language of local government. The transitions draw attention to theatricality in itself, and we should not forget that the public enquiry is itself an image for theatre: plays on public themes have always been public enquiries in which theatre investigates matters of concern through the stage lives of its personae.

The Trick Cyclist, keeping the unifying image constantly before us, is a development of *Iceberg*'s Bandmaster, a vaudeville MC, a clown and a mime, a singer, a conjuror, a 'thirties cocktail lounge performer. Providing continuity, he becomes an evident emblem of the spirit of theatre and entertainment. He is the very creativity of the playwright and the actor. A quick change artist, he appears also as six extra characters (public official, clergyman, Kitty's father, Daisy's father, First World War Sergeant-Major, plainclothes policeman) and thus effects many of the rapid transitions between scenes. These and other transitions Parker also achieves by music and song, usually in such a way as to push the conceit forward; by means of stage business, such as the spinning of a cycle wheel together with lighting changes; by changes in style and language, as when the grandparents speak; by the action of cycling on or off stage; by the action of tossing official papers into the air in order to launch the closing chorus of Act I; and most arrestingly, by the offstage explosion that brings the troubles into the foreground in Act II.

In Act II our awareness of the themes arising from action and dialogue intensifies. One significant transition here is achieved by make-up: the grandparents appear as old for the first time. We feel the poignancy of their raising a child whose parents, as Kitty points out, might never have been killed by a German bomb, had Ireland been united. The transition back from this scene is Frank's comment upon it, an overtly thematic statement, uttered as if he ponders the significance of his past life, and the play itself, linking the gaiety of the scene in which he made love to Daisy's bicycle with the larger context: 'Love, war and the bicycle ... the gist of their lives ... mine too. My love, my war, my bicycle'.[31] Time, as a continuum of transitions, becomes part of the rhythm of metaphor by means of the repetitions of the Spokesong itself:

> Each cyclist's favourite folksong
> Song of the spokes, spokesong,
> Whisp'ring through the years
> Music that's good for the ears

Song of the spokes, spokesong,
Spinning along through the gears.[32]

The play on words suggests that folksong is a spokesong, or song that speaks for the people; it is also a spook song, song of the dead. Folk song addresses universals, speaks across generations.

Transitions that juxtapose time past and present create rich thematic cross references. The play of ghosts in a ghost-ridden cycle shop is framed by the tentative knocking at the door of a brash, 'seventies sensibility, Julian. But the ghosts themselves live in a transition period of history, in which older values (Francis) clash with newer, feminist ones (Kitty) already asserting themselves. From the ironic standpoint of the present, we know the conflict is not yet over, the story yet untold:

One day, Francis, Ireland will be a sovereign nation, and womanhood will be a sovereign estate. Not until that day will the ghosts of Parnell and Mrs. O'Shea be laid to rest.[33]

Parker's metaphor also astutely links the fate of Ireland to technological change. When the Trick Cyclist becomes Dr. Peacock (pride and sexual repression) it is clear to the modern audience that the new technology survived Victorian puritanic moral outrage that connected it with dangerous socialist ideas and disgraceful sexual liberation. By implication, the repressive prejudices of modern Ireland could be swept away in the rapid growth of modern technologies. Yet Parker switches straight from Peacock to Daisy, who tells us that school children in modern Belfast learn how to booby-trap vehicles. The implication is that repression spawns violence, and a new technology may simply be used for more violence. This undercutting shows that there are no easy solutions.

The introduction of Julian in Act I makes it apparent that modern technology may make it easier to perpetuate violence:

Julian: I'm recording the demise of Western society.
Frank: Is that a part-time or a full-time job?[34]

Again Parker undercuts, allowing no settled view or foregone conclusion, for Julian cannot conceal his disappointment that Belfast is not yet Golgotha. Parker thus raises themes but never leaves them cut and dried. In Act I he does this with the press's desire for newsworthy violence; with sibling rivalry; the war orphan and war baby; negative (war) and positive (inventions) versions of history; and the march of technologies. In Act II Parker continues with this undercutting technique. The bicycle, lauded in the opening music hall song as prophetic, sacred, free, and peaceful, then becomes an instrument of war, albeit an absurd one, in the amusing bicycle drill scene. The undercutting continues even as the realities of Ulster impinge. The bomb explodes in the street, yet the shop is minimally damaged. The Trick Cyclist's War Song has some of the Brechtian harshness, yet it retains the comic defiance of disaster known to the British in the war-time music hall. Douglas Watt's attack[35] on grounds of 'Feyness' simply misses the fact that cheeriness amid disaster is true to British and Irish sensibilities. But the pain lurks behind the smiles for those who know how to listen:

> I haven't lost your letter, ma
> I haven't lost my knife
> I haven't lost my rifle, ma —
> I've only lost my life[36]

When the Trick Cyclist appears as Daisy's intimidating father, the effect is understated, but all the more unnerving for being so. The sense of the bleakness of life in Belfast mounts in Act II, especially in the scene between Frank and Daisy when both express their horror at their own country:

Daisy: I found out the truth about this country at last ... Oh, there's a rich vein of humanity in it, no doubt. But it's not worth quarrying, Frank. It's too narrow and too damned shallow.
Frank: Every word's true. The place is poison.[37]

The scene outlining the grandparents' will demonstrates how the poison has been building up in the system. Leaving the lease of the shop to one brother, and the business to the other, in an attempt to do right by both, suggests the situation in Ulster where the land is claimed by Irish or British, and the business is run by Northern Irish. Julian sells the shop, just as the British could sell out to the Southern Irish, except that Julian sells to Daisy's Protestant father. Parker thus avoids simple allegory and preserves complexity. This complexity is further developed when Daisy reverses her decision to leave with Julian, undercutting his cynicism with her more honest realism; her reasoned, wary appraisal of the situation is the final stage in Parker's recycling of the arguments about Ulster:

Don't ask me how this hell-hole will ever redeem itself. All I know is, it'll only ever be done by taking account of the way people really are — all the people — in all their depravity as well as their sweet reason.[38]

Daisy emerges as the new landlord of the shop. The dead must be put to sleep. Parker's play suggests in the end that the future of Ireland depends on people's ability to do this, to pedal together, as it were, and the results may depend upon the women more than anyone else.

The tentative hope at the conclusion of *Spokesong* is undercut by *Catchpenny Twist*, a play first staged two years later. Parker still proceeds by means of song and dialogue, with a choric Vocal Trio who double as secondary characters. There is still the central binding image, the catchpenny twist of the title, but now the image does not become an all-pervading conceit; it is instead the answer to a riddle. The play's action is the charade which enacts clues to the riddle. Like metaphor, which has one foot in an experience and the other in a different but analogous one, the basic situation of the play '. . . tries to keep one foot in real life while the other steps into the realm of . . . well, nothing as grand as myth or allegory or even parable. I ended up employing the humble word "charade". It seemed to sum up the goings-on in my native city'.[39] What the play's action does is show the steps taken by the songwriters who are the play's main characters to lead them to the situation that spells catchpenny twist, or the commercial performer's moment of choice when he abandons integrity to reach success. For Roy and Martyn this is the moment they abandon their singer, Monagh, in favour of the protegées of Spalding, the record company boss. But the play also enacts the charade that spells the catchpenny twist of Nationalism. Marie, having involved Roy and Martyn in writing Nationalist ballads, brings them to the moment where politics must claim priority over their desire to be merely 'pop' music successes. They refuse to sell out to politics and reap the consequence that brings the climax in the catastrophe of Act II. Martyn opens a letter bomb. Instead of exploding out in the street, the bomb has now gone off right in our faces.

Parker deliberately makes his victims Protestant and Catholic alike. At the end of the play we are left with the senseless malice of the letter bomb, and the horror of men groping blinded by their own blood. A songwriting team, fragile image of national harmony, is destroyed. Daisy Bell decided to stay in Belfast; Parker now lives elsewhere.

NOTES

1   *Spokesong* was first produced for the Dublin Theatre Festival, 1975, and first published in *Plays and Players* Vol.24, No.3 (December, 1976) pp.43–50 and *Plays and Players* Vol.24, No.4 (January, 1977) pp.43–50. An act appeared in each issue.

2   A list of these may be found with a brief but not wholly accurate guide to his career in Frances C. Locher (ed.), *Contemporary Authors.* Detroit: Gale Research, 1982 Vol.103, p.386.

3   See Stewart Parker, *Catchpenny Twist, A Charade in Two Acts.* New York: Samuel French, 1984. See also Stewart Parker, *The Kamikaze Ground Staff Reunion Dinner* in *Best Radio Plays of 1980.* London: Eyre Methuen, 1981.

4   See *Drama* (Autumn, 1981) p.38.

5   Unpublished play, broadcast on BBC Radio, 1975. I refer to a version designed for a Dublin stage production of the play. Mr. Parker kindly supplied me with the typescript.

6   *Iceberg*, unpublished TS, list of characters on page following title page.

7   *Iceberg*, p.1.

8   See, for instance, Traugott Müller's set for *Segel am Horizont* in John Willett, *The Theatre of Erwin Piscator.* London: Eyre Methuen, 1978, p.59.

9   *Iceberg*, p.27.

10   *Iceberg*, p.8.

11   *Iceberg*, p.15.

12   *Iceberg*, p.10.

13   *Iceberg*, p.37.

14   *Iceberg*, p.37.

15   *Iceberg*, p.38.

16   *Iceberg*, p.42.

17   *Iceberg*, p.52.

18   *Iceberg*, p.52.

19   *Iceberg*, p.53.

20   W.B. Yeats in 'Introduction by William Butler Yeats to *Certain Noble Plays of Japan* by Pound & Fenollosa' in Ezra Pound and Ernest Fenollosa, *The Classic Noh Theatre of Japan* (1917; rpt. New York: New Directions, 1959) p.160, and for the brief phrase also quoted, p.161.

21   *Best Radio Plays of 1980.* London: Eyre Methuen, 1981, p.9.

22   *Best Radio Plays of 1980*, p.22.

23   *Best Radio Plays of 1980*, p.29.

24   *Best Radio Plays of 1980*, p.29.

25   Mr. Parker used the term in precisely this way in conversation with me about David Storey's *Home.* See also Robert Berkvist's piece on *Spokesong*, 'Play About Irish History', in *New York Times*, 11 March, 1979. As is well known, Shakespeare's plays abound in image clusters and have been called, somewhat implausibly, extended metaphors. Parker, however, has quite consciously taken the extended metaphor or conceit as a basic structural principle.

26   *New York Times*, 11 March, 1979.

27   See Catherine Itzin, 'Three New Plays', in *Plays and Players* Vol.24, No.3 (December, 1976) p.32.

28 Shaw's delight in bringing contemporary technology on stage is matched by Parker's use of actual cycles in *Spokesong*. Shaw has Vivie Warren's bicycle on stage in *Mrs. Warren's Profession*. The cycle as a symbol of the freedom it gives its owner seems to appeal to both writers. Daisy's cycle, Parker tells us, is rusty and ten years old, rather as Belfast is a bit of a wreck, after almost a decade of troubles, by the time *Spokesong* is staged.

29 *Spokesong*, Act I, in *Plays and Players* Vol.24, No.3 (December, 1976) p.43. Hereafter all references to this play will be cited giving its title, act number and page number only.

30 See for example Peter Nichols, *A Day in the Death of Joe Egg*. London: Faber and Faber, 1967.

31 *Spokesong*, II, 46.

32 *Spokesong*, I, 46.

33 *Spokesong*, I, 46.

34 *Spokesong*, I, 47.

35 See Douglas Watt, '*Spokesong* lets the air out of its tires', in *Daily News* (New York), 16 March, 1979.

36 *Spokesong*, II, 45.

37 *Spokesong*, II, 47.

38 *Spokesong*, II, 49.

39 Stewart Parker, 'Author's Notes' to *Catchpenny Twist*. New York: Samuel French, 1984, p.94.

YEATS AND THE NOH

MASARU SEKINE

Almost seventy years have elapsed since the publication of Fenollosa's translation of some of the Noh plays and the productions of Yeats's four plays for dancers.[1] During this time various scholars have tried to trace Yeats's interest in Noh and the influence of the ancient Japanese Noh theatre on his artistic works, but they have only shown the gaps between the two cultures; two similar and yet very different aesthetic approaches to the theatre. There are a few fundamental facts which have to be taken into account when these two types of theatre are compared; the social trends of the times when the Noh plays and Yeats's plays were written and the social functions of the theatres themselves, as well as current aesthetic and artistic values. Yeats's solitary meditation and search for ultimate beauty guided him from European arts through Arabic aesthetics to Asian ideals of nobility. Yeats is no more than a great poet who showed some interest in Noh as a possible break-through in his attempt to alter the techniques of the conventional European theatre and create new ones of his own. In his own view he failed to achieve his aims.

His devotion to the pursuit of ultimate truth and beauty in the form of poetry, and also his devotion to the ideals of nationalism in order to achieve the final independence of his country from England had blinded him, in other words, limited him as a playwright in his experiments in the theatre. Yeats had rejected conventional methods of realism on the stage and tried to establish a poetic theatre through his poetic plays. In the past history of the theatre poetry often made a strong appeal to audiences: in Greek plays, Roman plays, Elizabethan and Jacobean plays, dramatists used poetry as a most effective weapon to achieve climactic moments. They did not, however, avoid realism altogether. They tried to multiply it on the stage by the use of poetry, creating their most dramatic effects in the process.

151

Yeats, however, was different; he was a solitary poet who tried to re-create his own inner vision through the form of plays. Consequently the dialogues in his plays can be regarded, in effect, as his own speeches; he was uninhibitedly expressing himself as a poet in these plays.

The Noh theatre was established as a highly sophisticated form of drama around the late fourteenth century. The Noh had very strong support from the third Ashikaga Shogun, Yoshimitsu, and it had developed rapidly. Yoshimitsu saw Ze-Ami, the crucial figure in the Noh, when he himself was eighteen and the young actor twelve, at the performance given for *Kanjin*, a performance specially organised to raise funds for repairing temples. The young Shogun was charmed by this young actor and remained his patron all his life. Yoshimitsu's tastes in life and in the arts were aristocratic, and he had Nijo Yoshimoto, a poet and aristocrat of the highest rank, as his artistic advisor. Ze-Ami and his father Kan-Ami stood high in the favour of the Shogun and they were, in return, obliged to shape their drama to suit aristocratic patronage. The Noh theatre, then called *Sarugaku* (which had been a rather crude and realistic form of theatre) now began to take in the aesthetic achievement of *waka* poems, a form of poetry very popular among the aristocrats of the Heian and Kamakura periods. Ze-Ami was also influenced by the philosophy of Zen and other types of Buddhism. Such terms as *yugen*, *wabi* and *sabi* formed the young Noh actor's concept of theatrical beauty which was later described in terms of *hana* or flower:

... seeing actual flowers, one must understand the reason why everything in the *Noh* has come to be compared to *hana*.
All plants and trees flower at their appropriate season, and people appreciate their flowers because they are fresh and novel. *Noh* is the same as these flowers. One must try to strike an audience with the freshness of each play and each performance. All these flowers fall after a while; it is not their nature to last for a long time. When they open at the appropriate seasons, they strike people's eyes with their novelty and freshness. *Hana* in the *Noh*, one should understand, is the same freshness ... [2]

Ze-Ami's consistent concern, or indeed it may be more accurate to say obsession, was to achieve the highest level of theatrical art to satisfy his most powerful patron, Shogun Yoshimitsu. Despite the advice of his father, Kan-Ami, that he should keep in mind the equal importance of both public support and the patronage of celebrities Ze-Ami slighted the public, non-aristocratic element in his audiences by his pursuit of the subtle, gentle, sophisticated beauty of *hana:*

There is a crucial point. Sometimes the nobles arrive when the day's performances have already reached the middle or the last part of the programme, *ha* or *kyu*. Even though the Noh has reached this final stage of *kyu*, the minds of the nobles arriving late will be fresh and attuned to the first stage of *jo*. If a noble watches the last play of *kyu* with his mind attuned irrelevantly to *jo* he will not like the play at all.

With the atmosphere in the theatre changed, one cannot succeed, whatever one does. I wonder whether one should go back to the beginning of *jo*, but that doesn't answer the question. On such critical occasions, one should use one's intelligence, and perform gently and quietly a play of *kyu* with the mind, as if one were performing in the play of *jo*, the first play. [3]

We can see attitudes to the theatre in Yeats which are similar to those of Ze-Ami, despite the passage of five and a half centuries between them. Yeats says in: 'Certain Noble Plays of Japan' (1916), his Introduction to *The Classic Noh Theatre of Japan* (1916), translated by Fenollosa and edited by Ezra Pound, that his poetic drama also needs a limited cultured audience:

Let us press the popular arts on to a more complete realism, for that would be their honesty; and the commercial arts demoralise by their compromise, their incompleteness, their idealism without sincerity or elegance, their pretence that ignorance can understand beauty. In the studio and in the drawing room we can find a true theatre of beauty. [4]

Ze-Ami had improved the Noh, and made it a highly sophisticated form in order to satisfy the taste of the Shogun and other noblemen. To stand high in their favour meant greater prosperity and consequently better social standing for his troupe of actors. Sophistication, indeed, was pursued as a means of the troupe's and Ze-Ami's own survival. Yeats, on the other hand, devoted his life as a poet to a search for truth and beauty, but he did not aim to get some powerful king's or feudal lords' favour for his own sake. He had, of course, to earn a living from his writing but he had developed his own ideas before he presented his poetic works to anybody. He did not try to meet current fashions or traditions in his own artistic efforts. There is, however, a close resemblance in the attitudes of Ze-Ami and Yeats towards their audiences. They both almost disregarded the public's reaction to their work, and disregarded general popular reaction. In his Introduction to 'Certain Noble Plays of Japan' Yeats asserts that 'Realism is created for the common folk and was always their peculiar delight ... but the great speeches were written by poets who remembered their patron in the covered galleries'.[5] Yeats first came across the manuscript of Fenollosa's translation of Noh a few years before he wrote *At the Hawk's Well* (originally published in 1917), and he was almost instantly taken by this ancient aristocratic theatrical art of Japan, for it was the kind of drama he was seeking — a poetic as well as a noble drama.

Yeats's first attempt to write a play similar to those of the Noh, *At the Hawk's Well*, was first produced in 1916. He was assisted in its staging by a Japanese dancer, Michio Ito, who came to Europe to learn classical and modern European dance. Ito, however, did not know much about the Noh. Yeats's source of information was thus limited and he himself had never seen a performance of a Noh play not did he know anything of the history of the Noh. His desire to create a poetic drama, combined with his limited knowledge of Noh, led to his unique plays for dancers. As far as the first two of these poetic plays were concerned, they lacked dramatic life as a result of Yeats's complete denial of any stage realism.

His idea of using Irish folk tales and mythology as materials had some significance; in using them he increased both the nationalistic content and the poetic environment of his plays for dancers. Ze-Ami had also sought his material in mythological and historical events, choosing heroes for his plays from among those aristocratic warriors, those heroes who had died legendary deaths, such as actual figures from the history of the rise and fall of the Heike family. In the case of Yeats the time difference between the heroic age and himself was over a thousand years, while the time difference in Ze-Ami's case was only about two hundred years. In Ireland there were great changes during those thousand years. It was no longer ruled by the numerous kings of small kingdoms; ancient Irish tribal feudalism was destroyed and the whole country was ruled by outsiders in a regime ultimately based on military power. At Ze-Ami's time, however, although the Kamakura Shogunate was toppled by the Muromachi (Ashikaga) Shogunate, Samurai still ruled the country, and nothing much had changed. Thus when Ze-Ami's plays were performed within his lifetime they inevitably conveyed a greater sense of reality than Yeats's plays. When Fenollosa discovered the Noh about five centuries had elapsed since Ze-Ami's time. By then the Noh had lost its original realism, which had been modified by Ze-Ami and had latterly become increasingly ritualistic.

To revive these truly ancient heroes in the minds of Irish people with any sense of reality was much harder, and particularly as Yeats was using a poetic approach, denouncing conventional theatrical approaches. Also there was the very large time gap between Yeats himself and the older legendary heroes he was trying to recreate.[6]

Yeats and Ze-Ami both used poetry in writing their plays to strengthen their dramatic effects, by appealing to the emotions of their audiences. By this use of poetry both achieved a more effective approach to their audiences, sometimes surpassing the seeming reality produced in conventional theatres. To create poetic reality in this plays, Ze-Ami chose well-known characters from legend and history, and so did Yeats. Ze-Ami's Noh can be divided into five categories.[7] Apart from the first category, of religious plays, and the fifth, of miscellaneous plays, the second, third and fourth groups of plays deal with human emotions, as was obvious to the audience of the day, and is even obvious to us. So the presentation of the various emotions was of major concern to this leading Noh dramatist. As Ze-Ami had the third Shogun as his patron, he had to respond to his aristocratic taste. He had found the most effective and easy way of meeting the Shogun's requirements was to include well-known *waka* poems in his plays; these were associated with the main characters in the plays. He also wrote other parts of the plays' dialogues in a somewhat similar form of poetry. Japanese has hardly any accents or intonations, and Japanese poetry does not rhyme. *Waka* poems and other forms of poetry are composed by the syllables in a line, and a *waka* poem consists of five, seven, five, seven, seven syllables. A syllable very often is not a word but only a sound. Yeats, however, used his skill to give variety to his characters by writing speeches in different metres to distinguish them from one another. When both languages are compared, English is much more dramatic and suits the theatre better, as Japanese sounds very flat when it is spoken.

In the Noh theatre to cover this deficiency, the lack of variation in the poetic speeches in the plays, musical elements are freely included — in the form of musicians and chorus (*ji-utai*). There are either three or four musicians in the Noh theatre; a flute player, two drum players (*kotsuzumi* and *ootsuzumi*), and sometimes another drum player (*taiko*). The chorus for the Noh consists of eight Noh singers. The musicians and chorus combine to help to create a dramatic atmosphere and build up the tensions. Musicians in the Noh are called *hayashi-kata*, meaning musicians who cheer the players on the stage. They just play their instruments at intervals, with drum players' controlled shouts to measure the length of pause between their drum beats; they neither utter a word not move about, nor take part in the play directly. The chorus of the Noh is the same; they commentate and sometimes represent the *waki*, the actor in the supporting role, in conversations with the *shite*, the actor in the leading role, or even represent the *shite* in singing. The chorus in the Noh does not move; it is divorced from the action of the play, unlike the chorus in Greek tragedies and in Yeats's plays. In the Noh the chorus becomes significant when its members sing about the internal struggles or emotions of the hero, when the *shite* is enacting the scene. Yeats's use of a chorus in his plays is somewhere between that of Greek tragedy and the Noh. Yeats's chorus usually consisted of three persons who are characters in the plays, who move about on the stage and have their own speeches — it might be more accurate to say they speak on behalf of the poet. When they are not placed on the stage before the play begins they appear with their musical instruments — drum, gong, zither. They have both speaking and singing parts. They stay on the stage throughout the play, but they do not get involved in the action taking place on stage. Their role is to link the stage with the audience, just like that of the *waki* in the Noh, or the fools in Shakespearean plays. When the choruses in the Noh and in Yeats's plays sing, they produce totally different effects.

In Yeats's plays the chorus sings in an European way, like chanting in church choir singing, while in the Noh they groan rather than sing. The two major instruments used to provide the melodies also give completely different effects; the zither makes a soft melodious sound to attune the audience to Yeats's dreamy poetic world, while the sharp shriek of the Japanese flute (*fue*) shakes and disturbs its hearers, creating tension.

In Yeats's four plays for dancers, the musicians open the first scene of each play, singing as they unfold and fold the cloth. This unfolding and folding device for opening and closing the play seems very mediocre and amateurish to contemporary eyes. Despite the fact that these four plays were designed to be performed in a private parlour or in the drawing room of some aristocratic house, and thus were completely different from plays written for conventional theatres,[8] Yeats could not throw away the theatrical convention of a curtain rising and falling. He obviously felt that he must tell his audience the moment the play was going to start, to get them ready for it. The Noh, in that earlier time when it was performed in the private residences of patrons had had the same problems, but the seating of the musicians and the chorus had given the same effect as that produced by the raising of a curtain. In the Noh theatre there is a small curtain at the end of the bridge which links with the main stage. The main acting area of the square stage itself is exposed to the eyes of the audience with nothing to hide any of the characters except the corner pillars. In the Noh theatre usually the *waki* — the actor in a supporting role who is often a monk — opens the scene by introducing himself and revealing his intention to travel; and the play proper starts at the announcement of his arrival at his destination, often some historical site. The nature of the travelling song of the *waki* is pleasant and poetic, with a lot of reference to the surrounding natural scene and the season. This is unlike the effect produced by the introductory part, *At the Hawk's Well*, where the musicians stress the barren and desolate surrounding atmosphere.

As for the stage and stage devices, the Noh and Yeats's plays are very similar; neither is like the conventional European idea of a stage. Yeats's plays were first performed in the drawing room of a private house, because he had designed them to be performed for a limited number of people, a very select audience who were above the 'common realism of the theatre'. His stage directions do not suggest any use of stage properties except for a patterned screen. Poetic descriptions of the surrounding scenery is the only source on which the imaginations of the audience can create an appropriate scene in their minds. In the Noh theatre miniature-sized symbolic stage properties are used, such as a six foot tall semblance of a mountain, made of bamboo and cloth painted green (in which a person can hardly hide) or the skeleton of a boat made of bamboo. These Noh stage properties are also only hints for the audience through which they can create an image in their own minds. Yeats thought natural rather than artificial light was best for the productions of his plays:

... and we found it better to play by the light of a large chandelier. Indeed I think, so far as my present experience goes, that the most effective lighting is the lighting we are most accustomed to in our room.[9]

Similarly, in the Noh theatre today, coloured lights are not used, but only daylight or normal artifical lighting. This plain light, therefore, employs no tricks to give any illusions about the characters or the action. The Polish *avant-garde* theatre director of the 'sixties, Grotowski, also stressed the advantage of natural lighting in the theatre in his book *Toward a Poor Theatre* (New York,1969). Neither Noh plays not Yeats's plays need sidelights or spotlights or footlights, but this does demand much higher skills and techniques on the part of the actors. It takes at least ten years of hard intensive training to become a Noh actor and this training does not mean that the actor is first-class, but only a beginner, since it usually takes about thirty years to become an expert in this highly sophisticated ancient theatre.

Masks are employed in the plays of both Yeats and the Noh. Yeats appreciated masks because they could be more striking, more effective than ordinary heads and helped to make his plays more poetic. Thus all the characters, including the chorus, either wear masks or make their faces look like abstract masks in his plays. Yeats did not want an individual's facial expression to prevent his poetry being directly communicated to his audience. He wanted faces made impersonal and acting made less dynamic, even if this hindered the effectiveness of some of his stage presentation. In Noh plays masks are worn, usually by the *shite*, the lead, who performs the roles of women, gods, unnatural beings such as the ghost of some legendary or historic hero and other supernatural beings such as imaginary animals. Other characters who accompany the lead sometimes wear masks. The *waki* and his company do not wear masks. This division into characters who wear masks and those who do not gives a clue to the stage conventions of the Noh: that those who do not wear masks are characters who actually lived or may possibly still be living — and they are very often the intermediaries for the audience. Those who wear the masks are characters who are directly involved in the development of the plot of the play. In the Noh theatre even the lead sometimes appears without a mask if the play is classified as *sewamono* or *genzaimono*, both realistic plays. The musicians and chorus never wear masks. In the Noh theatre masks were used to avoid the creation of false images. There were no female Noh actors for centuries after the establishment of the Noh, and therefore the masks were necessary for Noh actors to perform female roles. The use of masks in the Noh is, then, to create a symbolic image, while Yeats's use of the masks was to reinforce the poetry of his plays.

Yeats had rejected conventional realistic dramaturgy, but he had a clear idea in his mind about how his plays should be produced; it is quite similar to that of the Noh in theory;

They will require a stronger feeling for beautiful and appropriate language than is found in the ordinary theatre. Gesture must become merely an accompaniment to speech, not its rival. Acting must be simplified, shedding everything that draws attention away from the sound of voice. Scene and costume, like the background to a portrait, must contribute to the total effect. [10]

Yeats, however, had not found an alternative system to replace conventional stage techniques so that his poetic drama could work fully on the stage. In the middle of his plays he inserted a piece of dancing, to show the culmination of the climax in order to avoid the banality of ordinary ways of performing a play. Towards the end of *The Dreaming of the Bones* the dance by Dermot and Dervorgilla has a relevant place in the action and thus contributes to the build-up of the climax or anti-climax. But in his first play for dancers, *At the Hawk's Well*, the dance by the guardian of the well has not so much relevance to the action, and it is hard to say that this insertion of a dance in the middle of the plot necessarily helps to strengthen the play. In the Noh there is usually a dance in a play, and its type varies according to the character and the nature of the play; it is usually used to express the accumulated emotion of the *shite*, and can last from five to twenty minutes. For a modern audience, however, the dance inserted into the action can seem totally irrelevant. When a dance brings the development of the plot to a standstill, it becomes less convincing, indeed very often seems unduly obtrusive.

Noh plays are, today, performed according to traditional existing stage directions for each play and no alterations are officially allowed. The stage directions give guidance to the *shite* as well as to the actors in the other supporting roles as to how moves and gestures should be made. The gestures are called *kata*, and Noh acting is a series of such fixed, stylised gestures. These fixed movements are highly symbolic and simple, and yet convey the intentions and emotions of the character. The formation of these symbolic gestures was achieved under the influence of Zen, through the paradoxical process of seeking maximum effect through minimum action. Such simple, symbolic gestures in the Noh have a strong effect on an audience and give them sufficient clues for their imaginations to create a deeper reality in their own perceptions and reactions than the seemingly realistic presentations created in the conventional theatre. Michio Ito, who was young, and an enthusiastic student of European dance, did not know enough about the Noh and its techniques to help Yeats find an alternative way of acting suited to his particular purposes in the performance of his dance plays. Productions of Yeats's plays, so far, lack in theatrical vitality. Noh, on the other hand, had finished its development and had no capacity for further improvement, while Yeats's plays still offer opportunities for new methods of direction and new methods of acting in future productions.

Yeats's plays have often been described as rituals but, as Richard Taylor says, they are not precisely this because they do not contain any obvious change in the nature of the main character:

It is often said that *At the Hawk's Well* is a ritual of initiation and that is true to a large extent, but it is difficult to say exactly what Cuchulain is being initiated into since he shows no real awareness or understanding of what his confrontation with the guardian of the well means.[11]

Not only in *At the Hawk's Well*, but also in *The Dreaming of the Bones* and *The Only Jealousy of Emer*, the leading characters do not change through the play. Each drama concludes when the lead character fails to obtain what he has been seeking. Cuchulain fails to obtain immortality; Emer fails to obtain Cuchulain's love; and Dermot and Dervorgilla fail to obtain forgiveness.

Most Noh plays, however, are religious rituals. The Noh is almost like the medieval miracle plays, created to encourage spiritual understanding. Its involvement with religion occurred very early in its development and the Noh theatre developed under the protection of the large temples and shrines, and was performed as an entertaining part of religious festivals, before it was sophisticated into a theatrical art by Ze-Ami around the end of the thirteenth century. There are also a few plays which deal with magical water for longevity and for various illness, such as *Kikujido* and *Yoro*. In the latter, a courtier is ordered by

Emperor Yuryaku to find out about a mysterious fountain in the Joshu region. There he meets an old man, the lead in the first part, who tells him about this mysterious water and takes him to the fountain. Then he explains its magical effects: it is both a cure for fatigue and medicine for longevity. In the second part, *Yoryu-Kannon-Bosatsu*, the guardian god of the mountain, appears and blesses the courtier and congratulates the Emperor for his righteous rule, hoping the peace of the country may last for ever. *Yoro* is a ritual play, in which divine power is demonstrated by the fountain water being given healing properties — and also by a blessing being given directly to the courtier, and, indirectly, to the audience. It also has a political message: by elevating the position of the Emperor to that of the god, and by asserting that peace will be maintained by the submission of the people to the power of the emperor. The intervention of the divine being makes *Yoro* a ritual play.

Yeats's *At the Hawk's Well*, on the other hand, included the guardian of the well among the characters of the play itself but did not focus so much on the magic water of the well or the mystery of its guardian. Young Cuchulain is at least equal to these two elements, the well and its guardian, or else he is given more importance than any other elements in the play. The water from the fountain is refused to both the old man and the young man. Cuchulain is led into an illusion by the guardian when the fountain produces some water, but he chooses to fight against the female warrior Aoife. Here we can certainly consider Cuchulain's awareness of what he is doomed to be, a heroic warrior. But the plot of this play convinces neither reader nor audience that this play should be considered as portraying the ritual of his initiation, since it is centred on the theme of immortality, sought by the young and old. Also Cuchulain has not changed at all throughout the play.

Yeats does not mention the Noh plays' influence on his second play for dancers, *The Jealousy of Emer*, though he admits his prior interest in 'the nature and history of woman's beauty which Robartes found in the *Speculum* of Gyraldus and in Arabia Deserta among the Judwalis'. [12] This play is not so much like a Noh play; obviously he did not intend to write this on any Noh model. He had, however, read a play about the jealousy of a woman in *Aoi-no-Ue*, one of the Noh plays Fenollosa translated, and he also knew another Noh play called *Kanawa*, in which a woman tries to get revenge on her unfaithful husband by herself becoming a devil. *Aoi-no-Ue* deals with the jealousy of the wife of Prince Hikaru Genji, whose jealousy does not turn her against her husband to seek revenge; her revenge is focussed instead on her rival, a mistress of the prince, whom she tries to kill by turning herself into a demon. But the prayers of a high powered monk intervene, and the vengeful mind of this jealous princess is pacified. Here the power of prayer and of God is stressed to conclude this ritual play. In Yeats's *The Only Jealousy of Emer*, Emer, wife of Cuchulain, gets really jealous when her last hope of winning back Cuchulain in his old age is threatened. Emer had controlled her emotions when Cuchulain had a young mistress, Eithne Inguba, as she believed that he would come back to her in his old age. When Emer asks Bricriu to bargain for Cuchulain's life, he asks her to 'ransom a less valued thing'.[13] This puts paid to her last hope of getting Cuchulain back. At its climactic moment, however, this play has unexpected developments, when the Woman of the Sidhe and Bricriu disagree about Cuchulain, and the Woman of the Sidhe gives him up. They each rush back to tell Manannan the king, to get him to punish the other. Cuchulain then wakes up and asks for Eithne Inguba, as Emer watches them.

In *The Only Jealousy of Emer* Yeats introduced two sets of people who live without much consistency in different realities. This leaves his play with a thwarted conclusion, and makes its content and plot unconvincing. As in *At the Hawk's Well*, dramatic conflict is thwarted; the bargaining of Emer and Bricriu is not concluded, and the Woman of the Sidhe does not conquer the spirit of Cuchulain — while Eithne Inguba, who was left out of the conflicts between the other characters, gets Cuchulain in the end. In the Noh, particularly in the dream plays, the ghosts of Samurai and other heroes usually appear in the first part in disguise and in the second part as a ghost. In the Noh there is, then, a clear distinction between the two worlds: between this world and the world of supernatural beings. In Yeats's mind, however, the world of the supernatural and the world of daily life, of human beings, were intermingled, especially in his concept of the Irish heroic age.

The Dreaming of the Bones is the most powerful play of all four plays for dancers, as its theme seems universal to Irish people and its action takes place in 1916, what was probably the most crucial event in the history of modern Ireland, the Easter Rising, occurring in that year. This play was first published in 1919, so it was written when the memory of the Easter Rising was still fresh and raw. The play is a moderate version of Yeats's earlier political play *Cathleen Ni Houlihan,* which had had a tremendous effect on Irish youth, and seems later to have made the poet regret encouraging unnecessary bloodshed. In *The Dreaming of the Bones* Yeats makes the Young Man represent all Irish people, and he works in the way a *waki* does in the Noh, from a structural point of view. The Young Man has escaped the fighting which took place in Dublin at Easter 1916 and wanders into a mountain. There he meets a strange couple, the ghosts of Dermot and Dervorgilla who had betrayed their country to the Normans in the twelfth century, and thus triggered off the subsequent incursions of the English into Ireland and their ruling over the country for over seven centuries. The couple wish the Young Man to utter a single sentence, to say that he will forgive them, for by this they will be freed from the curse with which they have been bound. But the Young Man refuses to forgive them, because he thinks the present occupation of the country by the English was initially caused by their self-interested love affair. It is clear that the Young Man is meant to represent Irish people in their resentment, anger, frustration, humiliation and belief that the couple should not be forgiven.

In the Noh, there are no equivalents to *The Dreaming of the Bones.* Because most of the plays are religious rituals, the closest examples we can find in the Noh are groups of plays called *genzai-mono* and *sewamono,* realistic plays. These plays are set in the present, and they deal with human emotions rather than political issues. Most of the plays, however, conclude with happy endings such as the reunion of a father and daughter in *Kagekiyo,* the rewards given to a faithful samurai by the Kamakura shogunate in *Hachinoki,* or a pardon granted to a religious aristocratic Samurai in *Morihisa. Shunkan,* however, is an exception. In this play Shunkan, involved in political intrigue, has been exiled to the island of Onigashima with two other colleagues. Shunkan is an atheist and laughs at the other two, who are religious men. After a while these two religious men are given their pardons and taken back by boat to Kyoto, while Shunkan is left on his own on the desolate island. The atheist is punished for his neglect of God and for his arrogance, despite his having been a monk. This is a reversed way of demonstrating the importance of religion. In the Noh divine intervention, in general, gives pardons and rewards to religious sufferers, and this makes the plays into spiritual rituals.

To Yeats, and Irish people in general, Dermot and Dervorgilla seem an unforgivable couple. The presentation of their suffering, their desperate begging for forgiveness and the rejection of their pleas make this play ritualistic, since hatred of English domination is widespread in Ireland. This hatred, indeed, seems to be rooted in Irish minds as strongly as their religion, and the presentation of this play leads Irish audiences to a remembrance of centuries-long humiliation, provoking nationalistic anger. The play was written almost immediately after the Easter Rising, but was not produced until 1931, a decade after Ireland gained independence from England.

With the exception of *The Dreaming of the Bones*, Yeats failed to provide consistent cohesive plots for his four plays for dancers. His poetry raced ahead of other theatrical elements, and these plays became projections of the poet's imagination before they were well sorted out as dramatic vehicles for it. These plays are indeed baroque creations, their musical and poetical elements mixed with dancing and acting without a dramaturgy controlling them to increase their total dramatic effect. Noh plays are a drama in which the story-telling element dominates the whole performance and is reinforced by the musical element and the dancing and acting. Consequently the stories of Noh have a consistency in their plots and usually contain a ritualistic element.

Yeats, however, had earlier written a more dramatically effective and a more moving play, *Deirdre*. This play is more complicated than any simple tragedy of a loving couple treated in the Noh, but it has elements which are closer to the Noh drama than those of his four plays for dancers. *Deirdre* is a short, intense play. It begins similarly to the four plays for dancers, with musicians' dialogues which provide a factual commentary on the play proper and thus build up the tension of the ensuing drama. Through a conversation between the musicians and Fergus, who takes an equivalent role to the *waki* in the Noh, they bring the audience to the core of the drama, the symbolic scene of Deirdre and Naoise playing chess, and their confrontation with Conchubar, the murdering of Naoise and Deirdre's following her lover by killing herself.

This legend or heroic tale was well-known among Irish people. The performance of this play is just like that of the Noh; it enacts a well-known story on stage, eliminating the unnecessary details which would be essential in the conventional theatre to establish convincing realism. Yeats changed his original source to create a more dramatic and tragic emphasis by having Deirdre kill herself immediately after the death of

Naoise. This condensation certainly increased the play's dynamic element, its emotional impact.

There are some obvious parallels, with the second, third and fourth groups of Noh plays which focussed on human emotions. As in *Deirdre*, the main characters of these Noh groupings are well-known legendary or historical persons. The Noh actors enact the most dramatic and climactic moments of these people's lives on the stage, with a reinforcement of the effect given by musical and dance elements. The acting is by no means realistic, but symbolic and stylised, with a minimum of movement. Each movement presents the essence of the emotional moods that the character is experiencing, and as this acting style is so symbolic and stylised, it almost becomes a moving sculpture which occasionally changes its poses. By rejecting realism in the Noh, Ze-Ami and his followers tried to express the heights and depths of emotional experience in their acting and also to universalise those emotions they sought to convey to their audience.

Yeats, then, had actually written what was the Irish equivalent of a Noh play in *Deirdre* before he knew about the Noh. Paradoxically, once he had learned about actual Noh plays by reading Fenollosa's translations, his conscious, deliberate attempts to create similar plays weakened his dramatic power. His four plays for dancers have nothing of, say Synge's energy; they lack true dramatic life, they lack a tough cohesive core.

NOTES

1 These are *At the Hawk's Well, The Only Jealousy of Emer, The Dreaming of the Bones* and *Calvary. The Dreaming of the Bones* and *The Only Jealousy of Emer* were first published in a Cuala Press edition in 1919; *At the Hawk's Well* was included in the Cuala Press edition of *The Wild Swans at Coole* (1917) and all four plays were published by Macmillan in *Four Plays for Dancers* (1921), *Calvary* making its first appearance in this volume.

2 Masaru Sekine, *Ze-Ami and His Theories of Noh Drama*. Gerrards Cross: Colin Smythe, 1985, p.144.

3 *Ibid.*, p.134.

4 Ernest Fenollosa and Ezra Pound, *The Classic Noh Theatre of Japan* (1916); reference is to reprinted version. New York; New Directions, 1959, p.156.

5 *Ibid.*, p.155.

6 Similarly in the case of *Calvary* (not discussed in this essay), we can see that Yeats's attitude to Christianity is not as accepting as is the attitude of Noh playwrights to religious beliefs, traditions and rituals. They seem closer to the religious aspects of their subjects; they do not question, do not re-interpret.

7	See the present writer's *Ze-Ami and His Theories of Noh Drama* (1985), pp.45–70.

8	Cf. W.B. Yeats, 'Note on "The Only Jealousy of Emer" ', *Four Plays for Dancers*. London: Macmillan, 1921, p.105: 'While writing these plays intended for some fifty people in a drawing-room or a studio, I have so rejoiced in my freedom from the stupidity of an ordinary audience ...'.

9.	W.B. Yeats, *Four Plays for Dancers*, p.3.

10.	A.N. Jeffares, and A.S. Knowland, *A Commentary on the Collected Plays of W.B. Yeats*. London: Macmillan, 1975, p.205.

11.	Richard Taylor, *A Reader's Guide to the Plays of W.B. Yeats*. London: Macmillan, 1984, p.58.

12.	W.B. Yeats, *Four Plays for Dancers*. 1921, p.105.

13.	*Ibid.*, p.36.

THE HUMOUR OF DEPRIVATION

JAMES SIMMONS

The prestige of criticism in the nineteenth and twentieth centuries was the triumph of the moral vision, of a belief in self-criticism, of the efficacy of guilt to produce virtue. Parallel to this was a desire to produce great burgeoning works of literature, like Shakespeare's plays, by people who felt they were a great deal cleverer than Shakespeare and could discover his secrets by analysis; but analysis produced only pastiche or experiment in drama, from Dryden to T.S. Eliot. The living dramatic work in that time was in rather narrow social comedies based on the real experience of the authors, and, perhaps, in the pantomime, melodrama, oratorio and ballet, forms that readily awoke a popular response; but are for one reason or another seldom considered in this context. I gesture towards this well-explored subject in order to set in context the achievement of Irish dramatists, Synge and O'Casey and others who are thought to have succeeded in producing poetic drama.

These poetic dramas are not in verse, which may imply that what we enjoy in Shakespeare was less the use of blank verse than other things, perhaps energy and reality. Criticism concentrated on analysing the use of language and defining the moral content in such a way as to suggest that new authors would not use language in a different way, and narrowing or misinterpreting the morality of the plays to support the critic's moral sense. In his prefaces J.M. Synge suggests other criteria. Here are a few essentials:

... when men lose their poetic feelings for ordinary life, and cannot write poetry of ordinary things, their exalted poetry is likely to lose its strength of exaltation ... It may almost be said that before verse can be human again it must learn to be brutal.[1]

Preface to *Poems and Translations*

... one must have reality, and one must have joy ... All art is

167

collaboration ... It is probable that when the Elizabethan dramatist took his ink-horn and sat down to his work he used many phrases that he had just heard, as he sat down at dinner, from his mother or his children .... I am glad to acknowledge how much I owe to the folk-imagination of these fine people ... from herds and fishermen ... from beggar-women and ballad-singers ... what was being said by the servant girls in the kitchen ... we have a popular imagination that is fiery and magnificent and tender ... rich joy ... what is superb and wild in reality ... [2]   Preface to *The Playboy of the Western World*

Much quoted as these passages are, we have still not exhausted their significance. Not that we want to turn Synge into an idol, for a phrase like 'folk imagination' can easily misguide a reader, as Synge himself may have been misguided, as Yeats certainly was when he failed to recognise in O'Casey's city-dwellers what he hailed in Synge's Aran islanders. Surely the key thing is that Synge went out among the people and listened, and this is where good playwrights since his time have found their richness: O'Casey, Shiels, Sam Thompson and our young contemporary dramatists in Northern Ireland.

It is still common for one of the audience to remark to a poet after a reading of new work, 'I'd like to see it on the page'. Academic critics confronted with a play on stage often have the same difficulty, and will come back the next day, having read the script, and tell you it wasn't as good as it looked or sounded. This long established technique of leisurely analysis doubts the reality, or respectability, of effects produced in performance; but that is the arena where music and drama have their main life, their socially effective life. Constant rereading and reflection is not what any author can expect, and where this is enforced at schools and universities it leads to the artificial, unhappy and negative experiences that have now made these institutions lose confidence in themselves. This came home to me very strongly a few weeks ago when I watched *The Beatin' Docket* (1985)[3] by Eddie Kerr in The Little Theatre in Derry. It was a new play by an author I had never heard of, performed by an amateur company; but the author was a Derry man, his subject was Derry, and part of my experience was listening to Derry people very much excited to hear their common discourse coming back at them from the stage.

One of my reactions was to resent all this laughter which felt at times like an incoherent and unhealthy willingness to laugh at mimicry and ignore implications; but we know from Gabriel Fallon's book[4] on O'Casey that this was what so excited

Dubliners with O'Casey in the first productions, and that the Dublin actors had a peculiar pride in interpreting characters close to home in their own dialect. Fallon uses the word 'rich' to describe the dialect. These are factors the literary critic doesn't know how to cope with in existing terms. Another confusion was produced by things I do know about, a lack of coherence in the director, an uncertainty of control in the actors; but incoherent directors are common on the professional stage, and all scripts are morally ambiguous. There is no correct way to present *King Lear* or *Macbeth*, although it is often possible to show that a given interpretation is in conflict with the script. But not only can the actors and the director be in conflict with the script, so can the audience. *The Beatin' Docket* is a mixture of farce, domestic drama and violence, like early O'Casey plays.[5] O'Casey called each of his first three plays 'a tragedy', and in each of them someone gets killed; but they aren't like anything that we usually call tragedy; audiences tend to laugh the whole way through, and this is what happened that night in Derry. Even when the young terrorist came on at the end with his gun and posed a threat to the lives of other characters, even when he himself was killed and lay bleeding on the stage, there was no abatement in the laughter. I was laughing too, with reservations. Here was 'ordinary life', it was 'brutal' and in a way it was 'superb and wild'.

This play, set in the Bogside, has the Hunger Strikes in the background in much the same way as *Juno and the Paycock* has the Civil War in the background. The neighbour's son in Long Kesh is thought to be joining in, the riots outside in the street are in protest, and in serious moments several of the characters say things like, 'If any of them boys die in Long Kesh then things will change'; but the recurring drama we see enacted before us is of sexual disillusion, three women bitter about their men folk and two men who reciprocate. Sexual feelings seem to have died out. The pregnant woman remembers conceiving in a brief and rare drunken copulation with her husband. Her father sneers at her mother:

Annie: What did I do? God, you're like a box of fireworks ... It
          doesn't take much to spark you off ...
Packie: It's a long time since you sparked anything off ...[6]

These sorts of put-down seem to be habitual; but in a more developed passage Packie remembers their happy early marriage when he claims to have taken the child for walks in her pram while Annie was at work in the factory. She reveals that she always knew he took the child into the local pub or bookie:

Annie:	... it was the same every week ... the same entrance ... you would be smelling like a brewery and the wain was covered in crisps and nuts ... baked into her face, her hair, her nappy ...[7]

This much-advertised, vital, working-class dialogue is very negative in its content. The basic unit of humour is someone saying something tender or ambitious or expansive and being put down by another: the speaker is either discovered in a lie or contradicted out of pure combativeness. In this play, apart from the sexual battles, the greatest cruelty is reserved for the young husband, Seamus, who aspires to be a singer/songwriter. He sings one song which is a rather sentimental account of a rambling Irishman who dreams of Derry as he drinks, fights and makes disillusioned love all over the continent of America:

Seamus:	That's not noise ... I'm composing a song ...
Packie:	Are you sure you don't mean decomposing ... it's dying a death ...
Seamus:	Ha, ha, ... (*sarcastically*) very funny ... a lot of people think I have great potential ...
Packie:	You have as much potential as a square wheel.[8]

His wife attacks him for singing old-fashioned Country and Western songs:

Seamus:	Jesus, what do you want me to do? Dye my hair purple and put a safety pin through my nose, and spit at the audience?
Mary:	You'd need a quare spit on you. Most of the audience is in other bars.
Annie:	That was cruel ...
Mary:	So's his music ...

The Derry audience, and the author in his preface, seemed to take all this as the warm humorous life of Derry. I laughed too; but I was worried that the humour of the down-trodden consisted of lacerating each other. Then I remembered that O'Casey's humour consists of the same sort of lacerations and put-downs, and perhaps even the best of Synge, too. In both authors the lyric outbursts are the least convincing part. One is almost glad to be rid of Christy Mahon. As old Michael says, 'By the will of God, we'll have peace now for our drinks. Will you draw the porter, Pegeen?'[10] But Pegeen is off in the corner making some sort of lament.

My literary, critical training made me very suspicious of this play for its lack of coherence. All the same, its vitality rebuked me in a way that Synge would have understood. Eddie Kerr obviously grew up among these people. His work was an act of 'collaboration', not achieved by selfconscious effort; but because he was one of the Derry poor. I may believe that I have learnt more about how plays work from my education than Eddie Kerr has from his (he lectures at a College of Education); but my sort of middle-class upbringing and early dedication to literature, on the Romantic pattern, has left me with much more introspection than experience of how other people behave. I was trained, as it were, in Synge's terms, to write the poetry of 'exaltation'; but watching this play, and other contemporary plays, by Martin Lynch and Graham Reid and Frank McGuinness, brought home to me the necessity of collaboration, that the privileged can be underprivileged or impotent if they sit in the study in front of their typewriter and books. One of the things that made Yeats into a serious poet was his work in the world. What is happening in the world is so much more than you can imagine, and you can't get at it through newspapers — not that this will stop me telling Eddie Kerr how he might have written a better play!

There has been something of a flowering of working class or popular drama in Northern Ireland in the last ten years, and this is particularly exciting for anyone who loves the stage and is frustrated or embarrassed to think that only 'the fur-coat brigade' goes to the theatre. O'Casey brought the common people of Dublin into the Abbey and so did George Shiels. In the 1960s in Belfast Sam Thompson did the same thing, and in recent years so did Martin Lynch with *Dockers*[11] (1981) and *The Interrogation of Ambrose Fogarty* (1982)[12]. This must be connected with certain television productions such as *The Boys from the Blackstuff* (1983) in England and Graham Reid's *Billy*[13] (1982) plays. These sorts of successes produce a double reaction which has a nice healing air about it, both giving a voice to people that have not spoken before and, by the power of the dramatist and the nature of his material opening the imagination of the rest of society to such voices. In this context you can suddenly feel very hopeful about the last thirty years, during which Pinter revealed the power and drama of submerged groups in England and the traditions of dramatic speech were altered so that the one voice of glamour and authority, the home-counties accent, became the voice for comic extras, and the regional accents, that had up to then only provided comic extras, became the fashionable voices: Albert Finney, Tom Courtenay, Robert Stephens, Sean Connery, Tom Bell ...; but having taken it as read that this flowering of working-class dramatists and actors was something to be celebrated, it was worrying to realise how much this colourful and energetic humour leans on mockery, the deflation of inspiration, the very tone and substance of those anonymous songs that rise from the ranks during war, parodying the patriotism of politicians and commercial songwriters. If the common experience is of failure, then anything hopeful or even serious is likely to seem pretentious.

My excitement over Kerr's play, that flowed so wittily on stage but looked a bit dead on the page, reminded me of one of Tyrone Guthrie's last great gifts to Ireland: a production of George Shiels's *Macook's Corner*[14] (1969), for which he assembled the finest Ulster actors. It would take a very experienced director to realise the potential dramatic power of this play, reading the script; but on stage it seemed as stylish and witty as the work of Oscar Wilde. Wilde's real power is often betrayed by productions that concentrate on period charm, on elaborate sets and diction and nostalgia, just as for many years productions of Irish plays seemed merely quaint, nostalgic. The best production of Wilde I ever saw was directed by another young Ulster playwright, Frank McGuinness. He used inexperienced actors and no set, so that you concentrated entirely on what was being said. *The Importance of Being Earnest* (1895) is the work of a young Irishman who sees through the conventions of this slightly mad but very prosperous society. Morality is stood on its head. The two young men are layabouts. What everyone remembers is the scathing voice of Lady Bracknell doubting the acceptability of a child entering society in a handbag; but she can accept such ancestry if enough money is involved. As far as that world is concerned every Irishman is born in a handbag. There is a similar atmosphere in *The Beaux' Stratagem* (1707) by the young Derry author, George Farquhar.

The poor, crippled Ballymoney playwright George Shiels deals with a much lower level of society; but he is dealing with the same world. In the country town there is a conventional puritan Christianity which gives the people their vocabulary and supposed ideals; but their behaviour reveals something entirely different, loveless, cynical greed; but the amoral gusto with which all the characters pursue money is invigorating. Macook is as proud of his ancestory and his home (mentioned in the Annals) as any aristocrat; but he is caught in the act of distilling illicit liquor and fined so heavily that his only hope of survival is to sell a plan of his still to an American bootlegger or swindle a neighbouring farmer out of his inheritance, by using his daughter. How central farce is to modern society! Shiels's black comedy prefigures Joe Orton. Macook is as self-righteous and implacable as Lady Bracknell, without the money and without the English sense of self-preservation. He cannot resist teasing the idiot son (whom he should placate) about his ninety-year-old father:

It's time he wasn't here. It's my opinion the Lord has forgotten him. You should take him up to the mountain and make him sit there till the Lord sees him, or you may have to shoot him yourself. [14]

The revelation of a pagan or bestial reality underneath the mask of piety and respectability is the key to most Irish comedy. Here it is in Synge, for instance:

Pegeen: Is it killed your father?
Christy: With the help of God I did, surely . . . [15]

and in O'Casey:

Boyle: I never heard him usin' a curse; I don't believe he was ever
            dhrunk in his life — sure he's not like a Christian at all!
Joxer: You're afther takin' the word out o' me mouth — afther all,
            a Christian's natural, but he's unnatural. [16]

The chief division in most of these plays is between the Uncle Tom characters, Shawn Keogh, Juno Boyle, and Annie Devlin (in *The Beatin' Docket*) who are slavish and respectable, taken in by church and state, and the characters who insist on living 'like the gentry' despite their circumstances: Captain Boyle, for instance, Macook, Christy Mahon, The Widow Quinn, Nora Burke (In Synge's *The Shadow of the Glen*) and Packie Devlin (in *The Beatin' Docket*). Synge is different from the others because he holds out the hope of transcendence, of lives being transformed by love and courage. Perhaps this is because he is not of the class about which he writes. There is a residual romanticism and longing to escape in Synge. It is often seen as a mystery in O'Casey's work that although in his own life he was an energetic trade unionist, the hope of workers improving their lot and changing society has no force in his early plays, and when it surfaces in *Red Roses for Me* and *The Star Turns Red* his writing has turned lush and sentimental.

Sam Thompson's *Over the Bridge* (1960)[17] is entirely a study of men at work, the importance and limitations of trade unions. It is set in the shipyards of industrial Belfast. This makes it crucially different from the other plays I have been discussing. Although they are haunted by the memory and prospect of unemployment, these men are relatively prosperous and have their hands on a lever of power, of self-preservation and self-respect. Having organised themselves they can sell their labour on decent terms. The shipowners need them when the market is good; but their power to bargain weakens when the market is bad. They are recognisably the same sort of people we have met in the other plays, pithy and combative in their speech. There is one Uncle Tom character, George Mitchell, who wants to be liked by the management and works all the overtime he can get to make money for himself and his ambitious wife. There is no representative of the other Captain Boyle category because the scene of the action is the place of work. The play is not about the heroic struggles involved in establishing a union, although it is haunted by the figure of Davy Mitchell, an old idealist who has sacrificed himself for the benefit of his brother workers in the past and troubles them now when they want to enjoy their security and prosperity. He comes to the centre of the stage only at the moment of crisis when a Catholic worker insists, against all commonsensical advice, on going to his workbench in defiance of a Protestant mob, incensed because the I.R.A. may have planted a bomb and there is a deep feeling that Catholics are involved. The trade union leaders are powerless to control the mob, although the union is anti-sectarian. These things have happened in the past and the only way out is for Catholic workers to stay off work till the bad feelings die down. Peter O'Boyle is too proud or stubborn to take this easy way out. He goes to his bench and Davy Mitchell goes with him, one to be maimed, one to die.

Before this powerful incident Rabbie White, who goes 'by the book' rather than the spirit, dominates the stage. He is cynical, fluent, ingenious, excellent at put-downs; but different from all the similar characters previously discussed because his life is given a coherent shape by his union duties and his job. As the play opens we watch him in the work room signing a hymn, and then we realise he is filling in his football coupon:

Rabbie: (*to himself*) Perm two groups of four from six groups of four. Fifteen lines at tuppence a line. Half a crown staked ... (*he sings*) 'The night is dark, and I am far from home. Lead thou me on ...'. (p.19)

We watch Rabbie coping with a slightly pompous boss, curbing George Mitchell's greed for overtime, guiding the young shop-steward Warren Baxter. This is not a farce, not even a comedy; but there is a good deal of rough wit in the interchanges. The darker side intrudes when a good worker loses his job because his religious fanaticism makes him anti-union.

It should interest outsiders to know the plot of this play; but the history of its production raises yet another interesting issue. There was pressure put on the board of the Group Theatre not to stage the play. The ostensible objection was that a play about bigotry might cause trouble; but the suspicion was that some sort of censorship was being exercised. The controversy broke up the Group Theatre and a break-away group, led by James Ellis, eventually put the play on in 1960 at the Empire Theatre, an unheard of venue for a local play (The Group is a tiny theatre). Partly because of the controversy, Thompson's connections with the shipyards and the popular radio serial that he wrote, the theatre was filled with people who normally never saw live drama. It ran for a very long time and was then transferred to Dublin for a successful run, and next on to London where it was taken off after a few nights. It might have a better run now since London has become familiar with the Ulster problem and England has its own racial riots; but whether or not (and I can see an old-fashioned element in the play), it was exactly the play Belfast needed. It rejuvenated the notion of Ulster drama, of the local theatre, of the possibilities of the drama of commitment. It showed that Catholics and Protestants could be brought together and have a mirror held up to their bigotry. We felt the seriousness of the play on our pulses. That does not make me reluctant to subject the text to critical analysis (to which it stands up very well) and to try to place it in some larger context, but my critical judgement would be insignificant beside the important effects felt by a whole city, which cannot be gainsaid.

Twenty years later Martin Lynch had a similar success (but no controversy) with his plays, *Dockers* and *The Interrogation of Ambrose Fogarty*. I am excited by good plays that bring people into the theatre, less so by good plays that only attract a specialist audience. Lynch's work has most of the qualities for which Synge was looking; but I would like to draw special attention to a scene in the second play. Society has changed since Thompson's day. The young hero, Fogarty, is from the slums of West Belfast; but he has spent two years at University and is a thoughtful socialist. The interrogation is painfully and fairly presented. Fogarty is innocent of any connection with the I.R.A. but the police are seen to be in a very difficult situation, trying to get convictions in a city where witnesses are either afraid to tell the truth or sympathetic to the terrorists. The interrogators have a hunch Fogarty is guilty, but no evidence. They humiliate him and beat him up; but they are not the Gestapo. They share the police station with men of integrity who are not afraid to report irregularities. When Fogarty does not 'confess' after the statutory number of hours in detention, he is set free. The system is corrupt, but not altogether out of touch with justice.

This is well enough done, and worth doing; but where the play reaches great heights is in the interrogation of a secondary character, Willie Lagan, a half-witted Country and Western singer, so in love with show business that even threats and blows cannot break through to him. The people who stood up best to conditions in the concentrations camps were Communists and Methodists, people of firm convictions not dependent on their place in society. Lagan is a sort of parody of this. He is a compulsive joke-teller, and in the context where we have just witnessed pain and humiliation he forces a series of quite funny jokes on his interrogators. He has more conviction than they have:

Willie: (*He forces a handshake on* Peter *and* Jackie) Magic. Magic. Every one a gem ... (*another fit of laughter*).

When they threaten him he presumes that is a joke too and says so.

Peter: Are you finished yet, Willie?
Willie: Yes, yes, finito.
Peter: Ready to answer a few questions?
Willie: Yes, yes. Fire away. Hold on, hold on. What's the star prize? A car, a car? No. No. A year's supply of dummy-tits? (*Laughs*) Right. Fingers on the buzzers.
(Jackie *bangs* Willie's *fingers*.)
Sore, sore. (p.61)

This is very funny; but you'd need to have a very sharp sense of theatre to realise the power of it, reading the script. I was lucky enough to see the part performed by one of our best young actors, Ian McElhinney. You could set the performance beside J.F. McCormick playing Joxer, or Olivier playing Archie Rice.

The interrogation of a clown obviously has metaphysical dimensions. You can see the interrogators exposed to themselves in their grotesqueness, much more than they are exposed by the thoughtful answers of Ambrose Fogarty. Willie's vulgar energy is greater than theirs, and when they hurt him, 'Sore, sore', simply registers pain without horror or respect. The torturer has to break into the world of the victim to achieve his ends. Courage and faith may resist; but so can apparently shoddy faith, if it is held intensely enough. When they offer him a bribe for information he is indignant at the low rate:

Willie: If I brought that to the Regional Secretary of the Northern Ireland Touts' and Informants' Union, they'd laugh at me. No way, twenty pounds a week! Touts' Union wouldn't wear that, wouldn't wear it. (pp.62-3)

One night a member of the audience stood up, sounding remarkably like Willie Lagan and pointed to the stage, shouting, 'See him? That's me'; the liveliest evidence of Lynch's collaboration with his people. It is strange, though, how education emasculates. Ambrose is poor; but he is a self-improver, like Mary Boyle, and you can hear this in the gentility of his speech, his introversion and rationality. If he had finished his degree at the university he would probably be teaching in England; but even if he has chosen to stay in the slums, education has taken the edge off his tongue. Perhaps education really is a weapon of the ruling classes.

This confrontation between Willie Lagan and the special branch detectives holds the key to my apparently random reflections. O'Casey's chief ploy in his two great plays is to confront the powerful and educated with the clowns. This may have been part of his inheritance from Shakespeare. A clown should be powerless, ingenious, energetic, uneducated, irrepressible, with a sense of life and humour rather than principles or a theory. The poor peasants and the working class, as they appear in all these plays from Synge to Martin Lynch, have these qualities and perform this function.

NOTES

1 J.M. Synge, *The Plays and Poems,* ed. T.R. Henn. London: Methuen, 1963, p.288.
2 *Ibid.,* p.174.
3 Eddie Kerr, *The Beatin' Docket:* unpublished ms.
4 Gabriel Fallon, *Sean O'Casey: The Man I Knew.* London: Routledge & Kegan Paul, 1965.
5 Sean O'Casey, *Three Plays.* London: Macmillan, Papermac, 1966.
6 Eddie Kerr, *op.cit.,* p.6.
7 Eddie Kerr, *op.cit.,* p.21.
8 Eddie Kerr, *op.cit.,* p.19.
9 Eddie Kerr, *op.cit.,* p.18.
10 J.M. Synge, *op.cit.,* p.229.
11 Martin Lynch, *Dockers.* Belfast: Farset Co-operative Press, 1982.
12 Martin Lynch, *The Interrogation of Ambrose Fogarty.* Belfast: Blackstaff Press, 1982.
13 Graham Reid, *Billy: Three Plays for Television.* London: Faber and Faber, 1984.
14 George Shiels, *Macook's Corner:* unpublished ms. (Ballymoney Public Library), p.7.
15 J.M. Synge, *op.cit.,* p.183.
16 Sean O'Casey, *op.cit.,* p.22.
17 Sam Thompson, *Over the Bridge,* ed. Stewart Parker. Dublin: Gill & Macmillan, 1970.

WHAT IS *THE PLAYER QUEEN* ALL ABOUT?

SUMIKO SUGIYAMA

I

Critical discussion of *The Player Queen*, after all the attempts by its commentators to come to grips with it, seems to revert to the original question which puzzled the audience of the play when it was first produced in 1919: 'after the performance everyone was asking one another in the foyer what it was all about. No one knew and everybody assumed it to be high art'.[1] Apart from the assessment of its artistic value over which we can hardly expect Yeats's critics and scholars, unlike its first audience, to come to an agreement, the same question, well over half a century after that first performance, still seems to linger; no one, in fact, seems to know exactly what *The Player Queen* is all about. Does this mean that the play is another Yeatsian riddle that draws us into infinite temptations to solve it only to baffle them all? This paper is another attempt to answer that question, or rather what Yeats intended it to be all about. Now that more than eleven hundred surviving folios of prepublication manuscripts and typecripts of *The Player Queen*, selected, arranged, transcribed and edited by Curtis Bradford into nine scenarios and as many as thirty-two drafts,[2] are brought to light, the question seems not only to be worth asking but also the one possible way now left to approach that initial question: what is *The Player Queen* all about?

Although *The Writing of The Player Queen* does not sustain the myth that Yeats suggested — of an unsuccessful verse tragedy reborn, through Ezra Pound's midwifery, into a brilliant farce, it does show that there is a radical change between an earlier version of the play which comprises, in Bradford's editorial, all the scenarios and the first seventeen drafts (a version which Yeats worked on from 1907/8 up to 1910 and abandoned) and a

179

later version to which he returned in 1915 with a fresh orientation, bringing it to its present form virtually in 1917. What divides the two seems to centre around the new dispensation theme which is either totally missing from the earlier stage of the original version or vaguely hinted at in some of its later drafts, while it came, to all appearances, with the bringing in of the unicorn, to dominate the play as it now stands. The difference seems even more radical than the shift from the play's tragic to comic mode that is not as dramatically sudden as Yeats led us to believe but towards which he is moving as early as in Draft 11.[3] *The Player Queen* was originally not at all as it is, nor did Yeats intend it to be as it now stands, when he conceived it in 1907/8; all that talk about 'the coming of a new dispensation' and 'the new Adam', and so on was 'superimposed' on what had been there 'late in the process'[4] of its making. The question raised, then, must be preceded by another: what was *The Player Queen* originally all about, or what did Yeats originally intend it to be?

We have Yeats's own remarks uttered here and there in his prose writing that *The Player Queen* was a dramatisation of his doctrine of the mask or, at the time of 1907/8, of 'the thought I have set forth in *Per Amica Silentia Lunae*' which in his own words[5] 'was coming into my head'. That 'thought', not the new dispensation, was the original nucleus around which he tried to construct a play, getting himself involved in such hard struggling that he piled up draft after draft, and all in vain. Yeats certainly did not distort the facts. *The Writing of The Player Queen* does show the author, at its very initial stage, tentatively 'studying the effect of role-playing on character, the effect of the mask on the face beneath it', as he studied it in the character of the principal actress of a group of strolling players, first called only the Player Queen and in the meantime given her name Decima.[6] To demonstrate that 'the mask can have more power than the face it conceals', Yeats has the Player Queen 'change places with the real Queen'[7] — a device which we still see constituting the main plot of the play in its finished form, though whether it continues to carry the same message as it did is yet to be seen.

Here must be raised a question: Why *must* Yeats demonstrate the 'thought' about the mask which became most central to him by the incident of the heroine becoming queen and not, for instance, by the hero becoming king? The question is not as trivial, even nonsensical, as it might look, but seems crucial to the understanding of the play, especially of what Decima represents, even symbolises, in terms of the doctrine of the mask. Over this play, anyone might agree with John Rees Moore who calls it 'a curious play', so 'crowded with odds and ends from the Yeats workshop'.[8] His remark suggests a strategy to be employed in this paper: it does not concern itself much — as some studies do, with those 'odds and ends' which, after all, do not seem to make up a coherent whole — but sticks to what is essential in the play, to the heroine of its title (who, no one can doubt, presides over its action both in the original and finished form) and to the main plot of the play she represents.

Having raised what seems the crucial question about *The Player Queen*, I want to focus on 'The Mask', a song originally written for the play and included in *The Green Helmet*. It is commonly assumed that the lyrics, written for and sung in Yeats's plays, carry this central, often symbolic message, or create the dominant tone or mood in which the action takes place. 'The Mask', as the title automatically suggests, ought to be central in, even symbolic of the play, especially the heroine of its title. The weight that the song bears in the whole play is demonstrated in the device of Decima making her first appearance on the stage from her hiding place singing that song, before it is replaced by 'the song of the mad singing daughter of a harlot' when it takes on a radical reorientation.[9] Although it is often pointed out that 'The Mask' — the first place Yeats used the word 'prominently'[10] in verse — is a kind of key to his subsequent development both as a poet and as a man, its importance in the play, surprisingly enough, has not been given the attention it should deserve. Fortunately, Scenario 9 has its version, its first extant version, in prose, which is worth quoting in full since it keeps the original *dramatic* context in which Yeats conceived the song:

My beloved sang to me why do you wear that golden mask and eyes of emerald. I would know what you are, I would see your face. Put away that burning mask, I cannot see it without trouble. As I sang to my beloved if I put away my mask your heart would no longer beat, beat violently. One has calm when one knows what people are.

Ah, you would not sigh for me any longer; I wish for the praise of your sighs. That is why I will always wear my burning golden mask, with the eyes of emerald. Then my beloved sang to me, I do not even know if you are a friend or an enemy.[11]

The version quoted above reveals that 'The Mask', and the play as well, originated in what might be called 'a love story': something to which the finished form of the poem affords no clue. It might be narrated as follows: the passion of her 'beloved' who *was* passionately in love with her (the physical evidence being his violently beating heart and love-lorn sighs) has burnt out — 'Ah, you would not sigh for me *any longer*'. She has a curious reaction for a woman who has found herself in such a situation: she has put on, and is determined, as she announces to her beloved, to continue to wear the 'burning golden mask' — apparently to restore and keep to herself his old violent passion as it was: 'That is why I *will always* wear . . .'.

This is a very curious situation. Before allowing our curiosity to explore it, certain points must be made clear. First, considering the biographical elements out of which Yeats began to create many of his works and which their earlier drafts often retain, the first extant version of 'The Mask' indicates that the doctrine of the Mask must have been originated in some affair close to the poet's heart. Second, in the play the song is supposed to be written of Decima by Septimus, her beloved throughout the first version and married to her later. This enables us to assume that the woman and her beloved in the song correspond to the heroine and the hero of the play respectively. Third, the woman wearing the mask in the song obviously coincides with Decima attaining the mask, or becoming the queen in the play. From this it follows that Decima's role as the queen resulted from her having lost Septimus's love and her having the same wish as that of her counterpart in 'The Mask'.

The rather curious situations that emerge from the analysis of the earlier version of 'The Mask' all point to the focal figure of the play and her identity: who and what is the Player Queen whom we can identify with the woman in 'The Mask'. The question revolves upon the point of whether Decima bears 'traces of the features of Maud Gonne', or is one of Yeats's Muses. The view put forward by Helen Vendler[12] is challenged by Harold Bloom who would have none of 'the esoteric meaning' of the play 'the indefatigable Wilson' has given us and sees 'a greater danger' in reading it as an aesthetic allegory in Helen Vendler's manner.[13] Certainly it is hard for Harold Bloom — and for any of us, for that matter — to find 'overt connections to Yeats's love for Maud Gonne'[14] in the play as it now stands. As early, however, as his *The Man and the Masks* (1949), Richard Ellmann, who had access to some earlier drafts of *The*

Player Queen, saw Yeats speculating about his failure to win Maud Gonne in his creation of two antithetical lovers, Yellow Martin and Peter[15]; or, in the words of Decima's speech that Ellmann quoted from one of these drafts — 'Let me become all your dreams ...' — Bloom himself sees 'Yeats's deepest personal dream, of Maud Gonne as an apocalyptic Image of his own fulfilled desire'.[16] With all the extant drafts of the play now brought into view, those connections, too overt to be misunderstood, are all there, especially in the original version. It is, in fact, crowded, to restate John Rees Moore, with 'odds and ends' from that love. They give rise to an assumption that Yeats began to write *The Player Queen* with the whole history of his relation to Maud Gonne, from his first meeting with her in 1889 to 1907/8, pressing in upon him. *The Player Queen* cannot be otherwise interpreted; if approached that way, on the other hand, the play is not so confusing nor incoherent, at least in the author's intention, as has been so often pointed out.

'We are wrong in reading Yeats', Bloom warns us, 'ever to forget for long his characterisation of himself as a young man':[17] a young man who 'had gathered from the Romantic poets an ideal of perfect love' — 'I would love one woman all my life' — and who 'was twenty-three years old when the troubling of my life began'.[18] In discussing *The Player Queen* we are wrong to forget this for even a moment. The play in its original version returns to that love and to that troubling, which created what might be called the first-day obsession. On that fatal first day, Maud Gonne, tall and beautiful, filtered through the young poet's eye preoccupied with 'romantic doctrine [which had] reached its extreme development', presented herself as an Image, a symbol: 'she seemed a classical impersonation of the Spring ...'.[19] Then and there, she enslaved the poet; she was queen of his life and work, both in her queenly beauty and in her queenly mastery, cruel and despotic, over him. A young poet who wrote those beautiful love poems inspired by her — 'your image that blossoms a rose in the deeps of my heart'[20] — was a young man who was under such 'great personal strain and sorrow' that, towards the end of the century, was 'never before or since so miserable' in his life, 'tortured by sexual desire and disappointed love'.[21] The poet's own confession offers good grounds for Helen Vendler's view that Yeats in his description of his Muse — the Image-Muse, she aptly calls her since Helen, Yeats's most typical Muse figure, is 'at once the inspirer of epic and the image celebrated in the epic' — is 'simply describing Maud Gonne (or rather his idea of Maud Gonne)'. Professor Vendler remarks 'that the cruel and absorbing nature of the Image, its despotic claim on the poet, are symbolised in the image of Helen and of women like her'.[22] To achieve song, the Image-Muse exacts an endless sacrifice from her worshipper. As early as the eighteen-nineties, Yeats must have been aware of this cruel fate of the poet. It is well expressed, though not with such detached savage intensity as in some of his last plays, or in 'The Binding of the Hair', one of the stories included in the 1897 version of *The Secret Rose*. The story is 'overstuffed to the point of self-parody',[23] self-parody of the poet's relation to his beloved, who at once inspires and is celebrated in his work, for instance in the legendary figures of the bard Aodh and Queen Dectira with whom he is deeply in love. The story, narrated in that highly hushed tone of the nineties, comes to its savage ending, in which Aodh's severed head, hanging from the bush, sings a song to praise the queen:

> You need but lift a pearl-pale hand,
> And bind up your long hair and sigh;
> And all men's hearts must burn and beat ...[24]

The prose version of 'The Mask' echoes those words, *sigh, burn,* and *beat,* which are typical of Yeats's lyrics written during this period. His relationship with Maud Gonne during the nineties — a successful decade for him as a poet but the most unhappy period in his whole life — came abruptly to an end. Maud Gonne, without giving him an inkling of it, married John MacBride in 1903. The Muse deserted the poet; and he ceased to sing. Now, in 1907/8, Yeats had the 'thought' about the mask coming into his head and set himself to put it in a play, entitling it *The Player Queen*: a crucial work begun at a crucial time which led him not only gradually to recover the lyrical power he greatly feared he had lost but also to grow out of being a *poète maudit* into the poet of his later work. The writing of *The Player Queen* (virtually finished in 1917), the formation of the doctrine of the mask (given its first full expression in *Per Amica Silentia Lunae* in 1917) and his rebirth or re-making (which took place decisively in *Responsibilities* in 1914), all these spanned the same years and, obviously, were closely inter-related.

What then does the incident of Decima becoming the queen represent, even symbolise, in terms of the doctrine of the mask? Did not Yeats in that dramatic device try to restore to her old throne his Muse who had fallen from it by committing an act which, in the poet's view, amounted to virtual suicide? Or, if we recall 'the cruel and absorbing nature' of the Image-Muse and her 'despotic claim on the poet' (those characteristics with which Decima is amply endowed) we might restate the situation this way: possessed and obsessed by her, the poet had to free himself from her persecution by restoring her to the throne, her proper place, but one he was by then not unwilling to concede to her. Here we can ask why the Muse can only be restored with the mask, the 'burning golden mask, with the eyes of emerald', covering 'what's behind', or her real face. Maud Gonne with whom Yeats had been blindly, infatuatedly in love, was much more his idea of her — a reservoir of his dreams, a symbol of beauty, or whatever she may be called — than a woman of flesh and bone. Her marriage to 'a drunken, vainglorious lout',[25] must have made him realise something of her real, 'human' character. The lady to whom the poet had offered his devotion as his queen or a goddess turned out, after all, to be 'human', if not to say a bitch.[26] In the 'writhings and twistings over the question of her marriage'[27] in his mind, Yeats must have come to some realisation of the disparity lying between her real face and his conception, or the Image, of Maud Gonne — 'she seemed a classical impersonation of the Spring ...'. The finished version of 'The Mask' must be read in this context.

> 'It was the mask engaged your mind,
> And after set your heart to beat,
> Not what's behind'.

It *was* 'the mask', the Image, that engaged the poet's mind.

Now, what would the poet do with the duality he discovered in his beloved? As Ellmann remarks, Maud Gonne's rejection of his love had come too late for him to mollify its shock, as most men do, 'in the pattern of other experiences'. Even more important, the whole affair had been so 'closely connected with the enterprise of writing verse',[28] that Yeats, after several years' silence, was in a crucial position where his whole poetic world, lacking its presiding spirit, would collapse if he could not find some way to break through this deadlock. Furthermore, the Image lived, as it was to live to the end of his life, as vividly and powerfully as on that first day, still absorbing the whole devotion and adoration of the poet who was in dire need to rehabilitate himself, to have his heart 'beat, beat violently' — if not to hunger for love-lorn sighs any longer — by recovering the source of his inspiration. In *The King of the Great Clock Tower*, the stroller says: 'she is not so tall as I had thought, not so white and red, but what does it matter . . . ?'; it was the 'image in my head' mattered.[29] Yeats might have said the same thing. All these circumstances, the poet's inner need and drive, moved him to build up an artefact, an aesthetic myth in which he would restore his Muse to her old throne and let her play the role of queen, preside over his poetic world as she used to.

The development of the plot in the original version then, as is to be seen, is not only the extension of the situation presented in the prose version of 'The Mask', but also comes pat, too pat to the view developed above. Although minor details ceaselessly change from draft to draft, the main plot is fairly consistent. The principal actress of a group of strolling players is to play Noah's wife in a biblical play to be given by the troop to honour the occasion of the Queen's appearance to her people for the first time. She, on this very occasion, has 'made up her mind' not to play the part she has played hundreds of times. She wants to and must play the part which makes her feel 'very passionate, very noble, very intense',[30] instead of Noah's wife — 'an old, toothless, peaky-chinned, drop-nosed harridan',[31] as she describes it, echoing a good satirical vein which Yeats had developed. The great part turns out — in Draft 7 and carried through — to be the queen's part in 'The Queen of Babylon', Septimus's youthful play that the Player Queen has found.[32] Intent on 'that and nothing else',[33] she has disappeared. All this, reported by other characters, prepares the scene in which Decima puts out her head from her hiding place and sings that song, 'The Mask'. This leads to her discovery by Nona. Her confrontation either with Nona or with Septimus that follows centres on the two claims she makes tirelessly: one to her queen's part and the other to Septimus's love, both of which are, as it were, two sides of a coin in her assertion that if he loves her truly he will give her a great part. Her fierce jealousy which preys on Nona is another expression of this.

From the preceding development of the plot several vital points emerge. The first is Yeats's characterisation of Decima. She is a beautiful girl, though her beauty is assumed rather than elaborated on in the play. Decima, wild and wayward — 'flighty', Septimus calls her in the finished version — is blamed by Nona for causing such troubles, especially putting Septimus, actor-manager to the troop, into difficulties. Decima's 'cruelty', under the torture of which her beloved is driven to Nona for 'comfort', is innate in her character, the essential part, as it

were, of her relation to Septimus. This is made clear in the
author's description of her as 'one of those people who torture
those they love'.[34] It is brought into sharp focus in the exchange
between the two women:

Friend: Why do you torture Yellow Martin so?
Player Queen: Because I love him and want him to be always thinking
                about me.[35]

There is little doubt that Decima is endowed with 'beauty' and
'cruelty', the two requisites of Yeats's Muse. If her identity is
clear, then the nature of her relation to Septimus is almost self-
evident. Since there is little disagreement among critics over this
point even in the play as we read it now, it seems to be
redundant to dwell on it further.[36]

The 'beautiful and cruel' Decima wants to and must play the
queen's part in the youthful play by Septimus that she has
found. 'I must burn or shine', she says, 'I must be Herodias, or
Maeve, or the Queen of Sheba . . .',[37] a speech which rings with
variations, on the names of queens, through the original version
and which even echoes into Drafts 18 and 19, the first two later
drafts. Finally she attains to the role, though it resolves into an
unexpected happy ending in some earlier drafts. After Decima's
identity and the nature of her relation to Septimus have been
made clear, this tell-tale device needs no further explanation.
The significant point is Septimus's obsession with 'the first day'
when he met Decima for the first time and, then and there, fell
in love with her. In Draft 8, Yeats adds his note which reads:
'Might not Martin have written the Babylon play when first in
love with P. Queen?'[38] The following speech by Decima is even
more significant. It comes from Draft 29, virtually a completed
draft, which Yeats finished in the spring of 1917.[39] This suggests
that the heroine's character there stands as it stood in the
original version. In the speech Decima must play the queen's
part, because she 'look[s] beautiful and everybody admires
[her]'. She then adds:

Septimus says to himself 'I am married to a phoenix'. Every new eye
that sees me is like his eye on the day we met for the first time and
when he hears a murmur run along the benches, he loves me as well
as on that first day.[40]

After such disclosing devices and speeches, there is no surprise
in Decima's assertion that she in playing the role of queen is

embodying her beloved's dreams. 'Your dream had made me queen', she says in a downright way. Draft 12 has that significant speech Decima makes, the one quoted by Ellmann which has already been mentioned:

Let me become all your dreams. I will make them walk about the world in solid bone and flesh. People looking at them will become all fire themselves. They will change; there will be a last judgement in their souls, a burning and dissolving. Perhaps the whole age may change. Perhaps the whole age may learn ...[41]

Standing on this ground, Decima makes another assertion that her queen's part is bound up with Septimus's love for her. Surprisingly enough, it creates melodramatic scenes in which she accuses Septimus, attributing his reluctance to give her the queen's part to his betrayal of her. By placing Nona between them, Yeats wrote scenes which richly deserve the name melodrama. Since this is the most curious feature in the original version which was not allowed to get into the farce the play became, it is worth further examination. The following exchanges are all from Draft 8. They are, as usual, quarrelling over Decima's queen's part and Septimus's love for her.

Player Queen: ... Who believes in any but another's dream? I would set yours up before all eyes ... Martin, Martin, I was never so much yours, for now that I have lost your love I have your dreams.
Martin: I would I could understand you.
Player Queen: Love me truly and you will understand, ...
Martin: I have never cared for any but you. It was your teeming brain made you think me false.

His protestation does not convince Decima until:

O, I shall sift your soul. I shall draw my fingers through it; I shall know what is there. I shall shake it through a sieve and see what the wind leaves.

To prove the truth of what he says Decima demands a love test: Septimus is to put Nona in chains and leave her in a dungeon of the castle. He refuses to commit such a cruel act and Decima hurls her shrill jealousy at them:

Go, go, go, free; be lovers. Go to your marriage, but you'll find little pleasure there, because I'll be a ghost and haunt. In the depth of the night let her but spread her arms and call you to her, and I'll see it and put my face to hers until she screams.[42]

Threatened by the assault of the rebels, Septimus and Nona flee. Decima thinks that she has been betrayed and determines to confront death either by killing herself or by being killed by the rebels — another form of suicide. Her determination is circumvented by the turn of things — her changing places with the real Queen, whose appearance is timely — which results in raising her to the throne. The incident either stands as it is, or is followed by an unexpected happy ending, with Decima's reunion with Septimus who, after all, turns out to be true to her and with her final announcement: 'I shall be Noah's wife'. How the play ends depends upon Septimus's love for Decima; his betrayal, or her imagining it, leads to her crowning, while his truth, though hardly convincing after all that has happened, resolves into a happy ending. Yeats makes no exception to it.

To sort out what has been discussed and find the issue or issues at stake, the late Professor Curtis Bradford is worth quoting here. Of the title heroine of the play, he remarked that 'fatal Decima', as contrasted with 'domestic Nona'

is conceived of initially as a hyper romantic, a would-be Iseult or Deirdre, anxious to cast Septimus as Tristram or Naoise, but above all a believer with Yeats that life should somehow partake of the enhancement of art.

He attributes the failure of the original version to 'the implications of the fact' Yeats came to see, 'that his play threatened to collapse into melodrama'; so he 'shifted to prose and the comic mode'.[43] Although he did not seem to be aware of it, Bradford's remark raised what seems a central issue: why such a highly artistic belief, demonstrated in terms of the doctrine of the mask (certainly a belief shared by Yeats, if not by Decima whose romantic roles are the embodiments of her beloved's dreams) led, or misled, the poet into writing melodrama that verged on bathos. This seemed a most unsuitable vehicle to bring such a highly artistic belief to dramatic life, and the last kind of thing Yeats was likely to write, though he was to write draft after draft, wasting 'three summers and some part of each winter' before he 'had banished the ghost, and turned what I had meant for tragedy into a farce'.[44] Tearing up 'hundreds of pages'[45] — besides more than 1,100 folios that survive — Yeats had to free himself from *The Player Queen*, 'the ghost' as he called it. Although the identity of the ghost, is obvious, the above remark by Yeats offers us a vital clue about the ghostly, spectral nature of *The Player Queen*, or the Player

Queen herself. As Ellmann observes, at Maud Gonne's marriage Yeats, 'instead of condemning her, condemned himself', 'took all the blame out of all sense and reason',[46] as he let the speaker of 'The Cold Heaven' say. Does not the line read: he turned a deaf ear to all the blame his sense and reason were attributing to his beloved? The blame he bore on his conscience, submerged into his psyche, became a spectre, a ghost taking the form of his beloved's ghost that haunted and afflicted his conscience. It continued to lay claim on his love and to accuse him of his betrayal — 'I would have him think of me all day and all night'.[47] Yeats, of course, had violated, or had been driven by his beloved's cruelty to violate his own 'ideal of perfect love', having had affairs with 'Diana Vernon' (Mrs. Shakespear) — who is shadowed in the character of Nona — and with other women by 1907/8. The psychic effects that Maud Gonne's marriage created in the poet's mind account for the question so far unanswered: what made Yeats write those melodramatic scenes in which Decima's fierce jealousy, reminding us of the 'furious' character of Yeats's Muse, goes as far as to make her say, 'I will be a ghost and haunt . . .'. Decima here is hinting at the suicide she might commit to spite Septimus. In some earlier drafts — and in the finished form — she does, in fact, almost kill herself, and this is only prevented by the Queen's timely appearance. Decima confronts death before she is crowned. The restoration, or the resurrection, of the Muse to her old throne only takes place after her undergoing a kind of ritualistic death; the ritual takes the form of suicide because the Muse, in the eye of the poet, committed a suicidal act.[48]

So far the play has been discussed from the view of Decima as one of Yeats's Muses. Objections to it can easily be anticipated. Harold Bloom, for instance, challenges Helen Vendler's reading of *The Player Queen* as an aesthetic allegory because Decima is 'hardly the Muse herself', though she 'may be the muse of Septimus'.[49] Decima in the original version is indeed 'hardly the Muse herself'. As A.S. Knowland points out, Decima has her 'self' divided into 'the human Decima' and 'the symbolic Decima',[50] or her face and her mask. It is only when, after undergoing a ritualistic death, she attains to the throne that she can be really called the Muse; at that moment she might say — 'I will always wear my burning golden mask, with the eyes of emerald'.[51]

The main plot of the finished play stands as it did and carries the same symbolic message as before. Decima's Muse-like character is cryptically but revealingly demonstrated in a crucial exchange between her and Nona:

Nona: You think that you have his every thought because you are a devil.
Decima: Because I am a devil I have his every thought. You know how his own song runs. The man speaks first — [*singing*]
        Put off that mask of burning gold
        With emerald eyes, ... [52]

'The Mask', moved here and no longer in its full form, still serves as a key to the heroine of the play and her relation to Septimus; hence to the symbolic meaning that her attaining to the mask, or her becoming the queen, bears in the whole play.

II

In 1915 Yeats returned to the writing of *The Player Queen* which he had abandoned in 1910. Around the same time he introduced in it the unicorn motif which, during the span of another seven years, slowly but steadily enlarged until it came to constitute, to all appearances, an independent plot to be super-imposed on what had been a play about the heroine becoming the queen. Since the meaning of this new plot obviously hinges upon the symbolic meaning of this fabulous beast — a favourite symbol of Yeats — the evolution of the unicorn motif in the whole process of *The Writing of The Player Queen* will now be traced. In spite of its dominance in the finished play, the first allusions to the unicorn are brief and tentative. Draft 19, dated 1915, has two speeches alluding to the unicorn: the first that have any real significance in the play. Septimus compares Decima to a unicorn, calling her 'beautiful but flighty like the unicorn'. And the Prime Minister says in reference to the mob, 'I am their only substitute for a unicorn'.[53] Yeats adds, in draft after draft, various other allusions to the unicorn which centre around the Queen or the poet-hero Septimus, until he makes the final additions in the Macmillan text of 1922. One of these is the crucial speech by Septimus announcing

the end of the Christian Era, the coming of a New Dispensation, that of the New Adam, that of the Unicorn; but alas, he is chaste, he hesitates, he hesitates.[54]

That 'Yeats lived among unicorns, so to speak'[55] is by now a well-known story. Many unicorn icons with which he was familiar and which obviously lent themselves to the recurrence of the unicorn symbol in his work are catalogued, together with their reproductions, by Giorgio Melchiori; a few are added by Curtis Bradford, also with their reproductions.[56] I leave to these scholars discussion of the origin, both visual and esoteric, of the image of the unicorn in Yeats's mind and of how it became a favourite symbol in his work. Instead, I focus on the year 1915, when the first section of his autobiography, *Reveries over Childhood and Youth,* appeared with its frontispiece representing a unicorn descending from the starry heaven with the motto MONOCERIS DE ASTRIS — 'the Unicorn from the Stars', the title of the third grade of the Order of the Golden Dawn, of which Yeats was a member, and the title, too, of one of his plays. He had commissioned Sturge Moore to decorate the frontispiece of all his books published by the Cuala Press, the printing press run by his sister Elizabeth Yeats. By 1915 the unicorn had become for the poet, in Melchiori's description, 'a distinguishing personal symbol, a sort of private seal, a hall-mark on his work',[57] always associated with violent destruction and ruin through some mysterious power from above.

In the same year Yeats put this most cherished symbol of his in *The Player Queen* and after 1917 (when the plot concerned with Decima's ascent to the throne had been virtually completed) his efforts were almost solely directed to enlarging this unicorn myth. It surrounds Septimus, the poet-hero of the play, so much so that it can almost be called his property.[58] And his speeches referring to it are all concerned with his vision of the union of the beast with a mortal woman. The allusion to it is more overt in earlier drafts than in the finished play: 'Oh, that the unicorn would engender upon some woman another race'.[59] It is still to be seen whether or not 'beyond the Prime Minister there is a more apocalyptic marriage looming for Decima',[60] but there is no denying that this unicorn bears an identical likeness to Yeats's whole series of supernatural animals that beget their progeny upon a mortal woman; going back to 'that clean hawk' that begot Cuchulain in *On Baile's Strand,* anticipating the Swan in 'Leda and the Swan' and the Great Herne in *The Herne's Egg.*

'Ego Dominus Tuus', Yeats's poetical development of the doctrine of the mask, was included as a prologue to *Per Amica Silentia Lunae*; this poem was written in 1915, the same year that the unicorn had come into *The Player Queen.* In the poem 'Ille', the Yeats figure, calls to 'the mysterious one' who shall

look most like me, being indeed my double,
and prove of all imaginable things
The most unlike, being my anti-self.

These lines — and the poem in general — turn out the best
definition of how the unicorn is related to the Swan, of 'Leda
and the Swan'. The unicorn does 'look most like the Swan,
being indeed its double, and prove[s] of all imaginable things
the most unlike, being its anti-self'. This may seem to parody
one of Yeats's most esoteric poetic passages but what is most
puzzling about the unicorn is the extreme antinomies — chastity
and the act of lust — through which Septimus's vision presents
it. This is all the more embarrassing because the unicorn is a
traditional symbol of chastity, and Yeats, and Septimus, first
follow that tradition. Hearing citizens and countrymen
exchanging monstrous rumours about the Queen coupling with
the great white unicorn 'in the lonely hours of the night',
Septimus is quick, though slow in his physical reaction, to
protest against such a slander upon the unicorn: 'it is chaste, . . .
it is the most chaste of all the beast in the world'; and 'its
chastity is equal to its beauty'. But the same man, soon after
that, charges the beast on the same ground, 'because of
chastity', raging extravagantly

I shall die railing upon the beast because, owing to a pedantic scruple
or some congenial chill of the blood, he will not become the new
Adam.[61]

At this point the reader may well be tempted, in exasperation,
to dismiss (as Harold Bloom does)[62] Septimus's vision as a
raving fantasy concocted in his reeling drunken brain. But we
cannot but notice there an extreme application of the doctrine of
the mask: the unicorn, chastity itself, attains its opposite, its
mask, if it can cast, as Septimus wishes, 'a pedantic scruple' or
'some congenial chill of the blood' and be brute enough 'to
beget upon some woman a new mankind', the new Adam.
Septimus announces that he will 'journey to a cavern in Africa
and sing into the ear of the Unicorn epithalamions until he,
unable to endure any longer his desirous heart, becomes the
new Adam'.[63] On that day the unicorn, metamorphosed into
the Swan, will make its descent to the earth. The unicorn, thus,
forms the exact anti-self to the Swan, 'most like it' and 'most
unlike'. What looked like a parodic re-writing of the lines from
'Ego Dominus Tuus' is really a definition of the antithetical
relation existing between the beast and the bird.

How, then, is the unicorn related to Septimus? 'The unicorn is both an image and beast', he says. He also claims that 'Man is nothing till he is united to an image': an idea which can be taken to be most central to *The Player Queen* in its final form. To put the question of how Septimus is united to the unicorn, 'both an image and beast' is to find the answer hinted at in that re-writing of the lines from 'Ego Dominus Tuus'. Through the unicorn motif, Yeats is searching out the poet's own mask in much the same way through his dramatic device of the heroine becoming the queen, he has had Decima — a Maud Gonne figure — discover and attain her mask. This play was, as Yeats has often stated in his prose, an attempt to dramatise the thought which became his doctrine of the mask.

It has often been pointed out that *The Player Queen* deserves careful study because its 'official' theme, the doctrine of the mask, is so clearly central to Yeats. This is especially true of *The Writing of The Player Queen*, because it covers a most crucial period in Yeats's poetic life during which he remade himself from the *poète-maudit* of *The Rose* and *The Wind among the Reeds* into the poet of *Responsibilities*, at once a decisive departure from his earlier work and a stepping stone for further evolution of his poetic career. It has been believed that the transformation had much on the one hand to do with Maud Gonne's rejection of his love for her and, on the other, with his forming his doctrine of the mask. But no satisfactory explanation of how these two factors were inter-related to each other has been given by any critic. The mask worn by the lady in 'The Mask', which exactly corresponds to the mask Decima attains in the play, is Maud Gonne's mask — her Image — as set off against her real face to which Yeats had been totally blind, and which only her marriage forced him to realise; 'It was the mask engaged your mind ...'. Instead of his 'imagined image' the poet found 'a real image'[64] there: a painful experience, a shock, to which Yeats was to return again and again in his later work. The germinal idea of the doctrine of the mask derived from this split between mask and face in Maud Gonne, not from some urge on the part of the poet to unify the opposites in himself. In Draft 12 of *The Player Queen*, Yeats characterises Septimus as 'Over sincere. In love with Player Queen, but ... incapable of wearing of a mask'.[65] If Yeats's idea of the mask originated in his own mask, it is hard to understand why the poet-hero is given such a characterisation in a play whose theme, the author announced, was the doctrine of the mask. It is equally difficult to see why the plot centring around Septimus was super-imposed very late in the process of the writing of the play, while the device of Decima's ascent to the throne was in it from the very beginning. The poet's wearing of the mask was necessitated by his discovery of the difference between his beloved's mask and her real face.

Yeats gave various definitions of the mask in various places in his writings. In the 'Introduction' to *The Resurrection,* he makes a rather curious comment on *The Player Queen,* saying that what he put in *The Player Queen* was 'the thought that a man always tried to become his opposite, to become what he would *abhor* if he did not desire it'.[66] Since Yeats means that to become one's opposite, to wear the mask, was to try to become what one would abhor if one did not desire it, the mask was a means of unifying desire and abhorrence, two directly opposing forces, into some harmony. But the question arises of why a man always tried to become what he abhorred; why did he abhor what he desired? These extreme antinomies, the conflict between two elements directly opposed to each other, prompt us to speculate about what the poet's own mask really was — ultimately what was his doctrine of the mask. They also return us to the extreme antinomies in the unicorn and how Septimus can be united to the beast.

The unicorn, chastity itself, through its consummation of an act of lust attains its opposite — its mask — and so, the message of the play seems to assert, achieves a full realisation of its whole being, the unity of being. For there cannot be a beast that lacks the impulse of lust, the root of generation, and it suffers from a state of half-being while he hesitates; hesitation caused by some 'pedantic scruple' or 'some congenial chill of the blood' or whatever the reason is — 'alas, he is chaste, he hesitates, he hesitates'. Yeats projected his own mask on to the unicorn. The extreme antinomies, chastity and lust, were the image of his earlier poetic self and that of what he must always try to become henceforward, both in his life and work, so as to overcome the inadequacy of his earlier poetry.

That Yeats's youthful poems of the 'nineties are 'singularly chaste'[67] is a matter beyond dispute. As 'his attitude towards Maud Gonne had a great deal to do with the state of mind that generated'[68] those works, it reflected his enforced platonic relation to her, 'a *belle dame sans merci*': 'unctuous celibacy', Yeats called it, recalling his earlier years later in life. In those poems Maud Gonne was his ideal, to be worshipped from afar

by a poet-lover full of 'reverence and fear',[69] and Yeats assumed
the role of a knight ever at his queen's service, making 'his
passion unrecognizable by subduing and obfuscating it'.[70] But,
quite understandably, sex was the greatest problem of his
youth, as he candidly confessed in later life. The poet who
stitched and knitted his 'dreams' into beautiful poems for his
beloved was 'tortured by sexual desire and had been for many
years'.[71] His *Memoirs* and *Autobiographies* tell us how: 'being in
love, and in no way lucky in that love', he 'had grown
exceedingly puritanical', until he set up an 'ideal' of 'ascetics of
passion' who 'kept their hearts pure for love . . . as other men
for God, for Mary and for Saints'.[72] That whole world he had
built up with such tender care for the sake of love, or more for
the sake of his 'ideal of perfect love' — the temple of an ascetic
aesthete with his beloved for the image to be worshipped —
suddenly collapsed with her marriage.

Giorgio Melchiori observes that in the second decade of this
century a shift of stress occurred in Yeats's poetry; the stress,
until about 1916, remained constantly on destruction, while
around that time a new theme of birth entered, 'with ever
greater insistence on the idea of the act of generation', matched
with 'an extraordinary frankness and vigour' in the poet's
approach to physical passion culminating in the Leda sonnet
and later in the Crazy Jane poems and other late works.
Melchiori points out that it is in *The Player Queen* that Yeats for
the first time mentions and insists on the act of generation 'as
the necessary cause of decadence and renewal'. Melchiori also
argues that the union of Leda and the Swan, for instance, in
which Yeats envisioned a cosmic moment of destruction and
renewal is 'but a projection onto a cosmic plane of his intuition
of what happens in the soul and mind of man' — in essence, the
process of poetic creation. Such a view can now be taken to be
a critical commonplace in the discussion of Yeats. Melchiori
attributes the direct force that caused this shift of stress to the
Easter Rising of 1916, calling it 'the Token of a New Birth'[73] —
'All changed, changed utterly: A terrible beauty is born'. That
dramatic event, an eternal human drama enacted on a cosmic,
mythic plane in Yeats's vision, sparked in him a sudden flash
of intuition, a sensing the shape of things to come, which was
to be given a most dramatic expression in 'The Second Coming'
of 1919. But the unicorn came into *The Player Queen* in 1915, a
year before the Rising. Although Yeats mentioned its union
with a mortal woman for the first time in a draft, dated 1917, he

must have associated the beast with a certain idea, which he was to develop around it. If not, it is hard to explain why he introduced the motif in the play at all.[74] Melchiori's view hardly explains why Yeats came, at this particular stage of his life, to project the process of poetic creation on to the 'sexual' union of a beast and a mortal woman. The Easter Rising, a political event, hardly suggested such a union to the poet. Here it seems very significant that Yeats first mentions it in *The Player Queen*: a work which deals with his relation to Maud Gonne. This justifies a view that the initial stimuli behind Yeats's shift of stress did not come from outside, not from any public event, but from the poet's own love affair, from his heart which was, after all, always 'closely connected with the enterprise of writing verse'.[75]

It is hard to say exactly when, but certainly by the time he introduced the unicorn motif into *The Player Queen*, Yeats must have come to a realisation that 'the energy impelling all creation' is 'desire'[76] or, to put it in more concrete terms, his desire to be united with his beloved. The changed fortune of his relation to Maud Gonne may have brought home this stark reality to the poet. His reconciliation with her took place five years after her marriage, in 1908. Ellmann, breaking the long-believed myth of their life-long platonic relationship, tells us that Yeats and Maud Gonne 'were lovers'[77] around that time. He quotes an entry Yeats made in his journals:

What end will it all have — I fear for her and for myself — she has all myself. I was never more deeply in love, but my desires, always strong, must go elsewhere if I would escape their poison. ...[78]

The affair was brief and Yeats's celibacy continued, with sporadic interludes, until his marriage in 1917. 'For Yeats, at least', Ellmann comments on the incident, 'this autumnal flowering of a springtime passion had an importance out of proportion to its brevity'.[79] It certainly did. Yeats was able to overcome something, if not all, of the inhibited feeling he had always had about Maud Gonne, and he could now gaze more frankly into his inner state than ever before, and with a frankness which was ever increasing. What he confronted face to face there were those 'desires, always strong' which, as he must have keenly realised, had much to do with his creative activity: the psychological drama between his desires and his battle 'to escape their poison'. The true nature of Yeats's supernatural animals and his relation to them can be seen in *The Herne's Egg*:

> ... boys take common snow, and make
> *An image of god or bird or beast*
> To feed their sensuality:
> Ovid had a literal mind,
> And though he sang it neither knew
> *What lonely lust dragged down the gold*
> That crept on Danae's lap, nor knew
> What rose gainst the moony feathers
> When Leda lay upon the grass. [80]

'Common snow' again refers to 'a real image' which boys — or rather the boy — in this verse take, believing it to be their 'imagined image'; These lines hardly need any further exegetical comment beyond the words of Septimus 'the unicorn is both an image and beast'. 'Man is nothing till he is united to an image'. Helen Vendler remarks convincingly that the conjunction of man and woman in Yeats has always 'to do with creation'. It either takes the form of the union of a supernatural animal with a mortal woman, or that of the poet and the Muse in *The King of the Great Clock Tower* and in its rewriting, *A Full Moon in March* — 'aesthetic allegories' in Bloom's words. But it seems wrong to identify Leda and Attracta with the poet figure. The poet cannot be 'alternately male and female'. [81] He is always male. How can the Swan — a traditional emblem of the poet, and Yeats's recurrent symbol of poetic inspiration — be the Muse in the 'Leda' sonnet? The same is true of the Great Herne in *The Herne's Egg*. These supernatural animals offer good cases for Freudian theories of sublimation.

The question, however, of why a man abhors what he desires recurs — Yeats's long-drawn, unnatural celibacy during which he imposed upon himself an ideal of the 'ascetics of passion' and prided himself upon it, all the while desperately desiring to be united with his beloved, left an indelible mark on his psyche: the split between carnal and spiritual love. It gave rise — to say the least — to an 'uneasy relation between spirit and flesh', [82] as in the later triangle relation between poet, mistress, and lady in 'The Three Bushes', or in the earlier Septimus-Nona-Decima triangle in *The Player Queen*. It created in Yeats a sense of carnal love as something belonging to a lowly level of human existence and, as such, a thing abominable and detestable; the act of lust was 'beastly'. Crazy Jane in her series of poems is a *persona* through which the poet explores, with infinite repulsion and attraction, the duality of love with an emphasis on the urges of the body. In 'The Last Confession' a woman (who seems like Crazy Jane), makes her curt comment on her 'traffic' with men: 'beast gave beast as much'. The 'beast' in man formed part of the 'beastly' side of Yeats's supernatural animals — a beast is still a beast if it belongs to the divine — or into such a lowly, foul figure as the Swineherd (a disguise for the poet) soiled by the dung of swine in *A Full Moon in March*.

With this splitting of spiritual from carnal love in Yeats, that painfully shocking discovery of the difference between the mask and the true face in Maud Gonne must have devastated the poet's psyche; the lady the poet had worshipped as a goddess turned out to be 'common snow' or a 'bitch'. The 'bitch' element in woman developed in turn into the harlot-like behaviour of Yeats's Muse who, in his description, resembles 'women who creep out at night and give themselves to unknown sailors and return to talk of Chinese porcelain'; her 'virginity renew[ing] itself like the moon'.[83] And in *A Full Moon in March*, the Queen, 'proud and stiff', for all her denial, does 'stretch and yawn' — a sign of sexual awakening — at the approach of the Swineherd and finally descends 'for desecration and the lover's night'. Yeats's intense and painful preoccupation with this carnal side of love[84] finally expresses itself in the excremental and bestial images so dominant in some of his late works, such as the Crazy Jane series of poems and those two 'aesthetic allegories'. And they are in *The Writing of The Player Queen* also.[85]

Nona, Decima's rival for Septimus's love, is called simply 'Friend' or 'The Friend' for a long time in *The Writing of The Player Queen*. Unable to endure the 'torture' of his 'beautiful and cruel wife', Septimus finds 'comfort' in her 'kindness'. Nona is set off against Decima who, because of her 'devilish' cruelty, 'would become more beautiful in his eye' and so can be the source of his poetic inspiration. In the first extant version in prose of 'The Mask', the man implores his beloved to put off her mask, because 'I do not even know if you are a friend or an enemy'.[86] In the finished text of the poem, he also says, 'I would but find what's there,/Love or deceit'. If the Mask — the Image — holds infinite allure and attraction for the poet, his sense of 'what's behind' cannot but make him react with repulsion, because, despite the Biblical teaching, it is impossible to love one's enemy and his or her deceit. For all the repulsion and abhorrence on the part of the poet, however, the desire she kindles in him drives, or 'spurs', him on to his act of creation. In *The King of the Great Clock Tower*, the first lyric sung in it evokes, from *The Wanderings of Oisin*, the tableau of a hound pursuing a hornless deer, and a young man following a lady with an apple of gold. It is evoked from the otherworld of Tir-na-nog not because, as Helen Vendler thinks, it suggests that 'time is both irrelevant and inimical to poetry'[87] but because Yeats found in that tableau a symbol of 'the desire of the man which is for the woman, and the desire of the woman which is for the desire of the man'.[88] And that was the basic pattern he found in his relation to Maud Gonne: a pattern 'emblematical of eternal pursuit'[89] and eternal frustration, with vision coming between 'like terrible lightning' which is the moment of poetic creation — in essence, an eternal cycle of the poet's act of creation. And in 'The Mask', the debate is closed with these final words: 'What matter, so there is but fire/In you, in me?'

Yeats's keen sense of the duality of love ultimately leads to the antithesis of Self and Soul in his later poetry, the Soul representing, in his own words, the circuit 'which carries us into God', while the Self is that 'which carries us into man'[90] or, in other words, all that Yeats attributed to 'the heart' — 'blood and mire', 'the foul rag-and-bone shop of the heart'. How absurdly parodic a version she may be, the Queen whose wish is to 'resemble Holy Saint Octema in everything' represents the Soul. 'Love is the beginning of all sin', she says; love, 'a fearful passion', 'halooing on a troop, anger and lust and shame and sacrilege', still makes people 'do anything', because there is 'so much sweetness in it'. That is what she has most 'feared of all things' and it has led her to shut herself in the convent.[91] It is not very hard to hear in these speeches by the Queen the claim of the Soul in 'A Dialogue of Self and Soul' who urges the Self, absorbed and drawn by 'Sato's ancient blade' 'emblematical of love and war', to 'scorn the earth' and be delivered from 'the crime of death and birth'. However strong the pull of the Soul might be in him, Yeats made his choice, choosing 'perfection of the work', refusing a 'heavenly mansion' and 'raging in the dark'. He compared the way of the poet to the way of the warrior, as opposed to the way of the saint — not unreasonably because the poet, caught between two opposing forces, wages a war which is to be fought out in his own mind. The poet does 'make, out of the quarrel with himself, poetry'. The antithetical discipline he imposes upon himself in assuming the mask — 'a man always tried to become ...' — is all the more urgently called for because in this one-man battle — a battle he wages against himself — great is the temptation to retreat (to the protecting shelter that 'the friend' is ready to offer to him) to shun the 'conflict' with 'the enemy' and all the ignoble complications involved in it. But if he shrinks from the battle, he cannot but lapse into the absurdly inadequate way of life that the 'saintly' Queen represents; or even into the man in the episode of a countryman, who 'refused to get out of his bed at five-and-twenty', saying 'life is a vale of tears', until 'they carried him out to the churchyard' forty and four years later. This man is obviously Yeats's extravagant parody of what he might have become. 'Life is a vale of tears': that was what he himself might have said when Maud Gonne deserted him for 'a drunken, vainglorious lout'.

The unicorn can be the poet's anti-self, but another problematic issue must be faced, that of the coming of a new dispensation which the descent of the unicorn brings in. But it is now clear that an apocalyptic moment is synonymous with the consummation of an act of poetic creation in Yeats. *The Player Queen* offers us a clue as to why and how Yeats came to envision the process of poetic creation in that cosmic moment of destruction and renewal. In *Per Amica Silentia Lunae* Yeats calls 'happy art' 'a hollow image of fulfilled desire', while 'when its lineaments express the poverty or the exasperation that sets its maker to the work, we call it tragic art'.[92] Though hardly a satisfactory one in universal terms, Yeats's definition of 'tragic' and 'tragedy', it can be assumed, always echoes the tragic resonances of that tragic event, Maud Gonne's marriage, which threw his life into a disaster as great as some second 'Tragical History of Noah's Deluge' — the title of the play which the troop is going to perform in the Queen's presence, with Septimus in Noah's role. This is not an overstatement because the world without Maud Gonne, his 'queen', was equal to a state lacking the queen — as in the case of the country in *The Player Queen*. Such a state in its turn, as is always the case with Yeats, is an image of the whole world thrown into chaos and anarchy like that which once took over the world at the Flood.

Yeats's doctrine of the mask is his grand aesthetic myth in which he perpetually enacts a drama where the poet, masked as the Swan or as the Swineherd, woos his Muse[93] — or his Image-Muse in Vendler's terms — and finally succeeds in being united with her, at a price amounting to the severing of his head; a symbolic sign of their union being the 'kiss' between them, which is also symbolic of the consummation of his act of poetic creation.

This doctrine saved the Image, and saved the poet's life from falling irrevocable ruin and disaster, as well as accommodating in it the Freudian theory of sublimation. In Draft 20 of *The Player Queen*, Yeats makes Decima mention that symbolic 'kiss', which anticipates the two 'aesthetic allegories' written in his old age:

> he [Septimus] must win me everyday anew;
> And he'd no fear to pay for every kiss
> So great a price, that love being bought anew
> Day after day, night after night for years
> Would stay forever as when his eyes first looked on mine.[94]

In the play, the poet's act of creation perpetually re-enacts what once happened to the world at the Flood. For if the desertion of his Muse wreaked upon the poet a havoc as great as that of the Flood, the restoration of her to her old throne equalled the restoration that the whole world underwent after the Flood. Yeats, in his vision of that cosmic moment of destruction and recreation, was simply describing his own experience of what took place in his soul and mind at Maud Gonne's rejection of his love for her and his reconciliation with her. This is not an overstatement. The earlier draft of 'Reconciliation', a poem occasioned by that event, hints at what the restoration of Maud Gonne to his world meant to the poet:

> ... but now
> That you have come again, ...
> We've so remade the world ...
> Find all the living world you took away ...
> The world's alive again ...[95]

A similar reference is also found in *The Writing of The Player Queen*: 'Now I know that you love. All's well again, and the world made afresh'.[96] The references are fragmentary, but a remark Yeats made in *A Vision* reinforces the idea they suggest. He says that 'the creation itself had been but a restoration', periodically recurring in the month of March — the month when 'Love began to prevail over Discord' — whose presiding spirits were the 'world-restorers' — the Messiah, the Spirit that moved upon the water, and Noah on Mount Ararat.[97] And we know that Septimus is going to play Noah's role in 'The Tragical History of Noah's Deluge'. One of the most crucial autobiographical passages reveals what poetic creation really meant for Yeats. In it, he writes: 'supreme masters of tragedy', represented for him by Dante who had his Beatrice 'snatched away' by fate,

> would not, when they speak through their art, change their luck; yet they are mirrored in all the suffering of desire. The two halves of their nature are so completely joined that they seem to labour for their objects, and yet to desire whatever happens, being at the same instant predistinate and free, creation's very self. We gaze at such men in awe, because we gaze not at a work of art, but at the re-creation of the man through that art, the birth of a new species of man.[98]

What sounds like an apocalyptic speech by Septimus — '... the coming of a New Dispensation, that of the New Adam, that of the Unicorn' — really means nothing other than 'the re-creation of the man through that art, the birth of a new species of man', the New Adam.

In spite of Bloom's wholesale dismissal of Septimus's vision of the unicorn, we can no longer doubt its authenticity. Nor do we have much difficulty in finding the reason for Septimus's banishment. He is to be banished not because the poet 'has become obsolete'[99] nor because he is 'a Pistolian rhetorician and not a poet'[100] but because the stance he has adopted has become obsolete and has to undergo a transformation like that his maker has undergone during the process of writing of *The Player Queen*. Septimus hints at committing mass-suicide in the high table lands of Africa; he and the unicorn 'shall both be killed' because 'if we cannot fill him with desire he deserves death'.[101] The killing by the hand of the poet himself of this most cherished symbol only meant his giving a death sentence to his earlier poetic self, to whom the unicorn belonged: the *poète maudit* or the prophet-poet like Martin Hearn in *The Unicorn from the Stars* who is parodied by Septimus in *The Player Queen*. In earlier drafts he is called Yellow Martin; Martin with the colour of the decadents added to him. After *The Player Queen*, Yeats's references to the unicorn are very few. But the beast, reincarnated in the Swan, is to enact a drama exactly as Septimus envisioned it. And we may be all too willing to join the poet and say in unison with him:

Man is nothing till he is united to an image.[102]

NOTES

1 Quoted in A.S. Knowland, *W.B. Yeats: Dramatist of Vision*. Gerrards Cross: Colin Smythe, 1983, p.61.
2 See W.B. Yeats, *The Writing of The Player Queen*, ed. Curtis Bradford. Dekalb: Northern Illinois University Press, 1977. This essay follows Bradford's editorial and his dating of each draft throughout.
3 *Ibid.*, p.111.
4 *Ibid.*, p.461.
5 *The Variorum Edition of The Plays of W.B. Yeats*, ed. Russell K. Alspach. New York: Macmillan, 1979, p.761.
6 Scenario 1: *The Writing of the Player Queen*, p.21.
7 Scenario 2: *Ibid.*, pp.22-2.
8 John Rees Moore, 'The Janus Face: Yeats's *Player Queen*', *Sewanee Review*, 76, 4, Autumn 1968, p.613.
9 Draft 17, the last draft of the first version, contains the song placed near the end of the play: *The Writing of the Player Queen*, p.264.
10 Richard Ellmann, *Yeats: The Man and the Masks*. London: Faber, 1969, p.174.
11 Scenario 9: *The Writing of the Player Queen*, p.30.
12 Helen Vendler, *Yeats's Vision and the Later Plays*. Cambridge: Harvard University Press, 1963, p.134.
13 Harold Bloom, *Yeats*. Oxford: Oxford University Press, 1978, p.329.
14 *Ibid.*, p.333.
15 Richard Ellmann, *op.cit.*, p.171. Septimus is called Yellow Martin in several drafts.
16 *Ibid.*, p.176; Harold Bloom, *op.cit.*, p.333.
17 *Ibid.*, p.338.
18 W.B. Yeats, *Memoirs*, ed. Denis Donoghue. London: Macmillan, 1972, pp.32, 40.
19 W.B. Yeats, *Autobiographies*. London: Macmillan, 1970, pp.399, 123.
20 'The Lover Teils of the Rose in His Heart'.
21 W.B. Yeats, *Memoirs*, p.125.
22 Helen Vendler, *op.cit.*, pp.36, 38, 37.
23 *Uncollected Prose by W.B. Yeats*, vol.1, ed. John P. Frayne. London: Macmillan, 1976, p.390.
24 This 'song of the head' is 'He Gives His Beloved Certain Rhymes' in *The Wind among the Reeds*.
25 'Easter 1916'.
26 A harlot-like behaviour of Yeats's Muse is to be recalled.
27 Richard Ellmann, *op. cit.*, p.168.
28 *Ibid.*, pp.168, 165.
29 *The Variorum Edition of the Plays of W.B. Yeats*, pp.996, 995.
30 Scenario 3: *The Writing of the Player Queen*, p.23.
31 Draft 21, though with a slight difference: *Ibid.*, p.320.
32 Draft 2 already refers to 'a boyish thing, about a wild, impossible romantic queen ...': *Ibid.*, p.36.
33 Draft 8: *Ibid.*, p.80.
34 Scenario 3: *Ibid.*, p.25.
35 Draft 13: *Ibid.*, p.170. The similar exchange is repeated in several drafts.
36 It can be documented amply from *The Writing of the Player Queen*: for instance, 'She was singing that song about Jack and Jill that she always sings when she has had a triumph over Martin' (*Ibid.*, 82); 'I'd have him

think of me all day and all the night until the scared moon fled Before his desperate thoughts, and the male sun Sprang out of bed' (*Ibid.*, p.213): 'What is this heartbreak but the fiery nest . . . where life, the holy phoenix, comes from life?' (*Ibid.*, p.216).

37 Draft 6 and carried through: *Ibid.*, p.48.
38 Draft 8: *Ibid.*, p.91.
39 *Ibid.*, p.396.
40 *Ibid.*, p.378.
41 Drafts 7 and 17: *Ibid.*, pp.72, 132.
42 *Ibid.*, pp.91–3.
43 *Ibid.*, pp.454–5.
44 *The Variorum Edition of the Plays of W.B. Yeats*, p.933.
45 W.B. Yeats, *Mythologies*. London: Macmillan, 1971, p.334.
46 Richard Ellmann, *op.cit.*, p.169.
47 The words by Decima are repeated time and again throughout *The Writing of the Player Queen*.
48 The death seems to take the form of 'death by water'. Septimus much fears that Decima might have drowned herself while she has disappeared. The biblical play to be performed is 'The Tragic—al History of Noah's Deluge'. The mask of the 'drowned' sister of Noah — who does not exist in the Bible — is 'saved' to serve as the mask with which Decima covers her face at the end of the play in the finished form. Furthermore, the drowned 'figure in a shroud' in 'His Dream', the first poem in *The Green Helmet*, is resurrected into the Helen-Maud Gonne figure in 'A Woman Homer Sung', that follows in this collection. Is it because of the purifying, regenerative power of the element, or some biographical element involved in it?
49 Harold Bloom, *op.cit.*, p.329.
50 A.S. Knowland, *op.cit.*, p.70.
51 As for the group of characters surrounding the Queen, 'foil' is the word to apply to them. The Queen is the exact converse of Decima. The collecting of tax-money and the citizens' indignation which makes them rise against the Queen are all devices to bring the plot up to a point where Decima changes places with the Queen.
52 *The Collected Plays of W.B. Yeats*. London: Macmillan, 1967, p.411. If we roll the word 'devil' on our tongue — devil, daemon, daimon — we come to that mysterious figure the Daimon.
53 Draft 19: *The Writing of The Player Queen*, pp.283, 286.
54 *Ibid.*, p.421.
55 *Ibid.*, p.428.
56 Giorgio Melchiori, *The Whole Mystery of Art*. 1960; rpt. Westport: Greenwood, 1979, pp.35–72; *The Writing of The Player Queen*, pp.426–46.
57 Giorgio Melchiori, *op.cit.*, p.54.
58 The unicorn allusions associated with the Queen, in their parodic humour carried to the point of monstrous bestiality, are not to be taken very seriously.
59 Draft 26: *The Writing of The Player Queen*, p.350.
60 Harold Bloom, *op.cit.*, p.330.
61 Draft 28: *The Writing of The Player Queen*, p.359.
62 Harold Bloom, *op.cit.*, p.329.
63 Draft 30: *The Writing of The Player Queen*, p.407.
64 'Solomon and the Witch'.

65 *The Writing of The Player Queen*, p.121.
66 *The Variorum Edition of the Plays of W.B. Yeats*, p.933.
67 Giorgio Melchiori, *op.cit.*, p.64.
68 Richard Ellmann, *op.cit.*, p.165.
69 W.B. Yeats, *Memoirs*, pp.72, 127.
70 Richard Ellmann, *op.cit.*, p.165.
71 W.B. Yeats, *Memoirs*, p.71.
72 W.B. Yeats, *Autobiographies*, pp.334–5.
73 Giorgio Melchiori, *op.cit.*, pp.56–66.
74 Cf. The Prime Minister's speech which is one of the first allusions to the unicorn: 'I am their only substitute for a unicorn'.
75 Richard Ellmann, *op.cit.*, p.165.
76 Helen Vendler, *op.cit.*, p.48.
77 Richard Ellmann, *The Man and the Masks*. Oxford: Oxford University Press, 1979, xxvi.
78 Richard Ellmann, *The Man and the Masks*, 1969, p.192.
79 Richard Ellmann, *The Man and the Masks*, 1979, p.xxvii.
80 *The Collected Plays of W.B. Yeats*, p.649.
81 Helen Vendler, *op.cit.*, pp.153, 146.
82 *Ibid.*, p.131.
83 W.B. Yeats, *A Vision*. London: Macmillan, 1969, p.24.
84 The 'beast' in man mirrors the 'bitch' in woman, or vice versa. That is why Decima and the unicorn are described as 'consubstantial': both are 'beautiful but flighty' and both 'terrible' when they love.
85 Cf. A Song by Decima in Draft 21: *The Writing of The Player Queen*, p.334: 'I will not now that I discover/That the dung is to the fly/What my beauty's to a lover? Fall into the dumps and cry? But rather say I've luck enough/If some strong beast will be my love'.
86 Scenario 9: *Ibid.*, p.30.
87 Helen Vendler, *op.cit.*, p.142.
88 *The Variorum Edition of the Plays of W.B. Yeats*, p.843.
89 W.B. Yeats, *Explorations*. London: Macmillan, 1962, p.392.
90 *Ibid.*, p.307.
91 Drafts 21, 17 and 29: *The Writing of The Player Queen*, pp.342, 262, 391.
92 W.B. Yeats, *Mythologies*, p.329.
93 Leda and Attracta are surrogates for the Muse.
94 *The Writing of The Player Queen*, p.324.
95 W.B. Yeats, *Memoirs*, pp.172–3.
96 Draft 16: *The Writing of The Player Queen*, p.233.
97 W.B. Yeats, *A Vision*, p.249.
98 W.B. Yeats, *Autobiographies*, p.273.
99 Helen Vendler, *op.cit.*, p.125.
100 Harold Bloom, *op.cit.*, p.330.
101 Draft 28 and 1922 text: *The Writing of The Player Queen*, pp.358, 421–2.
102 Harold Bloom raises two questions about *The Player Queen*: one is 'why Yeats was ready to change it to farce; another, what then is Yeatsian high seriousness if the doctrine of the Mask cannot be pondered for a long time without a saving irony?' They are, as he says, really worth asking about the play (*op.cit.*,pp.328–9). For an answer two inter-related factors can be suggested: one is the origin of the doctrine of the mask itself and the other Yeats's relationship with Maud Gonne which was to be carried on to the end of his life. The whole myth, named the doctrine of the mask, having

originated in such circumstances as have been described in this essay, was always precariously poised between tragedy and farce in Yeats's mind. This is particularly so because his affair with Maud Gonne in 1909 decisively dragged 'the goddess' down to earth, and he was to live always face to face with 'the living face' behind the mask of Maud Gonne; the disparity between drawing further and further apart, until he came to discover in her 'a bad, head-strong, cruel woman' and her 'foolish, smiling face'. These descriptions are among the last additions Yeats put in the play in 1934 *(The Writing of The Player Queen,* p.450). The process of his discovery of her 'real image' was parallelled with his increasing sense of farce underlying the whole artifice and his attendant destructive ironies about the whole affair.

THE EMERGENCE OF MODERN ANGLO-IRISH DRAMA: YEATS AND SYNGE

ROBERT WELCH

What was Yeats's idea of drama? Despite the fact that he went through several phases in his own career as a dramatist his notion of what drama was remained remarkably consistent. His essay on 'First Principles' in *Samhain: 1904* states that drama is what 'all the arts are upon a last analysis'. By this Yeats meant that in drama we get life purified into form so that everything extraneous drops away from the action, the gesture, the speech, and we are presented with life, essentially.

Symbolist extremism? Intolerance of the daily round? Such accusations as these might be levelled at Yeats's theory of drama, but it is worth considering seriously, to see how far it will take us, and to what extent his notions are borne out in a number of central plays in the early Anglo-Irish dramatic movement.

Yeats writes, again in the essay on 'First Principles':

In Ireland, where the tide of life is rising, we turn, not to picture-making, but to the imagination of personality — to drama, gesture.

He was dismissive about the kind of poetry that he described as 'picture-making', which comes about when the tide of life is low. Keats was an example of this kind of poetry and the poem of Keats he cites is the 'Ode on a Grecian Urn'. These pictures 'make us sorrowful', he says, because 'we share the poet's separation from what he describes'. It is a forlorn and alienated poetry full of wistfulness and frustration. The other kind of poetry, however, is grounded in involvement with life and is in love with life. It is at the root of drama, because drama presents for us our human life in all its moving complexity, and our

208

perception of its form is linked to our own experience as individuals who are part of society and yet apart from it. Drama presents us with a sense of ourselves at one with the rest of humanity and yet also different from it.

All the arts, Yeats said, are drama upon a 'last analysis' and part of what he meant has to do with the way drama confirms our sense of ourselves in society by representing actions that correspond to our own actions, movements and stories. But it also confirms us, simultaneously, in our apartness from society by representing those actions and movements on a stage or some area set apart. The area that is set apart, whether proscenium arch, a corner of a room made significant by the unfolding of a cloth, or just simply a clear space in the middle of some forest, reminds us that our doings are ludicrous, terrible and strange. The actor who arises to tell a story speaks to our paradox: our being involved with life; our being apart from it.

Drama — all art, in Yeats's view — is our way of speaking to ourselves about that central paradox. Again, if we continue to take this view seriously, we see that to Yeats's mind, art, including drama, is not a means of delectation for the privileged or the exhausted but a very central part of human activity — *the* central part, Yeats would argue. Only art, drama, speaks to us about how things really are in the relationship between the human mind and the networks of being from which it arises. It is saving speech.

In drama, in this sense, we see life taking a new form, not out of organic matter, but through the codes of our speech, and gestures, and through the co-ordination of them with our material objects. All becomes elaborately coded. In this activity meaning increases because the drama enacts a growing network of ever more complicated relationships between its elements, our responses to them and our responses to our responses. Plot is all about the discoveries of networks of relationships in a formal organisation that is a thing of life, but also inorganic. In drama, in art, Yeats would argue, we grow in meaning, because in drama life takes a form that it has not taken before. The networks of relationship that the plot unfolds are the equivalent of rhyme in verse: things accord; we experience their harmony; we know it to be like that in life, and the reason we know it to be like that is because of art and its dramatic unfolding of those networks.

Drama, then, in Yeats's view, is intimately linked with life and with the forms of life. 'Picture-making' is what happens when we lose faith in our ability 'to bring forth a second nature', in Sir Philip Sidney's phrase, 'which makes the much-loved world more lovely'. It is more lovely because we see in the second nature which is art or drama the networks of relationship with which life is instinct. Later on, in his 'In Memory of Major Robert Gregory', Yeats compared Gregory to Sidney because he had the capacity to select and organise things in such a way as to make their formal relationships evident and telling. He could, Yeats says, have counselled him and his wife on how to arrange all the 'lovely intricacies of a house' when they were getting the Tower ready because he was a hearty 'welcomer', someone for whom form was easy because of a secret discipline of attentiveness and delight. No 'picture-maker', Gregory's eye was delighted by what it saw because it perceived relationship between exterior life and the 'gazing heart'. An artist, Gregory had the power of drama and gesture: in him 'the tide of life was rising' and his contact with that gave him the ability to make a second nature of unity and form.

Yeats's poem on Major Robert Gregory shows how consistent and traditional Yeats's thinking is: he links his ideas of artistic and dramatic form with that deep though undemonstrative exponent of humanist thought, Sir Philip Sidney. But we need to return to the essay on 'First Principles' and to consider again some other phrases from the passage quoted earlier:

In Ireland, where the tide of life is rising . . .

For Yeats the art of drama was an art of conference with life. Life in Ireland had never, for a variety of reasons, achieved full dramatic expression. His aim was to create a second nature for Ireland, in the drama, whereby Irish people might become conscious of the life in them. Yeats's theatre is a radical one, totally dedicated to a renovation of perceptions. It is not nationalist, though it is, Yeats would argue, national.

If the tide of life was rising in Ireland, then drama was the means whereby that life could achieve its most direct expression. Since the death of Parnell, Yeats had worked to bring about a cultural renaissance in Ireland. Along with Douglas Hyde, Lady Gregory and George Moore, he thought that the way lay open to redirect national energies away from the strife of politics into art and culture. There were many aspects to this work, but Yeats and A.E. (George Russell) shared the view that the evocation of certain images based upon Irish mythology would have the effect of reactivating old codes, old sources of power, once again. These images would beget other images; the past would act upon the present; the present would be transformed by the establishment of a network of relationships with the past. Ireland would enter into a second nature. The drama would be the most effective way of making these manifold connections, because drama is at once social and individual. It acts as a cohesive force in a social fabric, but it does so while emphasising the individuality of the spectator, his sense of his strangeness and difference.

Ireland, so unfortunate in so many respects, was fortunate in one outstanding circumstance: it retained, still, at the end of the nineteenth century, something of a pre-industrial, pre-modern connection with folk-belief, rituals and practices. For many, even in the cities, a world where nature and men were interanimated in systems of relationship was not completely dead. Ireland, underdeveloped, impoverished, forgotten (think of the said neglected acres of Moore's *The Untilled Field*) was a place ready for mystery. A cynic might even say that one way of dealing with boggy intractable acres is to convert them into the bottomlessness of symbol and legend and make them emblems of the deeps of the mind.

Again Yeats is ahead of us. Another of his basic ideas is that all real art (and we have seen that for him art *is* drama) must have some element of tragedy in it. It is this that gives art its exultant joy. Art is tragic because it is in defiance of all that exterior fate snatches away. The more that is snatched away the greater the potential for the joyful laughter of tragedy:

> There's more enterprise
> In walking naked.
> ('A Coat')

Again we come back to Ireland, a country from which much had been snatched away, a country with great resources of exultant joy, with a long memory, with a great deal of semi-legendary mythological material all waiting to be networked into the second nature of a Yeatsian relevatory art. Because for Yeats, as for Blake, and Spenser before him, art was revelatory. Imagination was linked to salvation. Through imagination the second nature could be activated; the networks of relationship that art reveals in life for life, could be set humming. The harmony that rhyme exemplifies in verse could be set going between myth and reality, images and experience, theatre and street, paragraph and speech, period and parliament. Yeats was seeking a coherent dramatic art that would exult joyfully in despite of the misfortunes of Ireland in the nineteenth century. Nationalist art? No, but national.

This is how we might come to a reading of *Cathleen ni Houlihan* (1902). The play is dedicated to Lady Gregory, one of the great women of Irish literature. This is appropriate because Lady Gregory brought Yeats back to the countryside by going on walks with him when he stayed at her house in Coole; they were collecting folklore together, and this had a profound and lasting effect on Yeats, for it re-introduced him to something he had missed since his childhood, contact with ordinary country people. Also, that they were collecting folklore was a bonus, in that the landscape and the people were being linked in the system of codes and relationships upon which folklore depends: if you pluck ribgrass, which is good for lumps, and the wind changes, there is a danger you will lose your mind. Folklore reads the countryside as a living code, and the country people to whom Lady Gregory introduced Yeats knew this language.

Cathleen ni Houlihan presents the world of Ireland embodied in a single figure, the old lady who appears on the day the French land at Killala in 1798. Michael Gillane is to be married next day, but instead goes off to join the French, having been drawn into rebellion by the talk of the old woman, who is Cathleen ni Houlihan. The play, in a masterly way, sketches in sufficient detail so we gain a sense of small agricultural world, preoccupied by money concerns and by plans for the future. The old woman comes in and for a time does not disrupt the naturalistic circumstantiality. Michael's father and mother think the old woman is astray in her wits when she says that the strangers have taken her 'four beautiful green fields'. Gradually her real nature is unfolded and Michael falls under her spell. She intones the names of those who have died for love of her:

There was a red man of the O'Donnells from the North, and the man of the O'Sullivan's from the South, and there was one Brian that lost his life at Clontarf by the sea, and there were a great many in the West
. . .

At the end of the playlet, when Michael leaves with her, Michael's brother Patrick is asked if he has seen an old woman going down the path:

Patrick: I did not, but I saw a young girl, and she had the walk of a
        queen.

In its small way this play is a masterpiece. The naturalistic,
homely convention is held right up to the point at which the old
woman begins to intone the names of Ireland's dead. At that
point the audience realises she is other. At that point, too, all the
old identifications of Ireland with a female figure, stretching
right back to the goddess of sovereignty herself in Celtic
mythology, are reactivated and *because* the naturalistic
convention has been so definitely established the old networks
of emotion are given locality and actuality. The language of the
play is spare and lively, and recognisably the English of the Irish
country people. Patrick, turning around from the window
where he has been listening to the sounds of cheering from the
town explains the tumult vividly but inaccurately:

> They are cheering again down in the town.
> Maybe they are landing horses from Enniscrone.
> They do be cheering when the horses take the water well.

The real reason for the cheering, of course, is the roar of
acclamation the revolutionary French receive from the Irish, and
so the action of the play is linked to insurrection.

Revolution, the Irish countryside, the old goddess of
sovereignty who presides over life and death, the talk of country
people, songs and poetry, sacrifice: these are the elements that
are encoded in the network of relationships that this play
presents. It is entirely coherent; it is meant to be and is an
interaction between past and present. Such images as are
presented here beget other images and a sense of the richness
of Irish culture, in its capacity for self-reference and for
significant unity, is conveyed. The kinds of emotion with which
Yeats artfully plays are raw and fierce but they are orchestrated
into a formal arrangement that is simple, profound and direct.

In 'Man and the Echo' in *Last Poems* Yeats asked himself

> Did that play of mine send out
> Certain men the English shot?

The answer to that question, is, one supposes, very probably.
But, though it may seem callous to say so, that consideration
was not any business of the artist in Yeats. What he had to try
to represent was the 'tide of life' which was rising in Ireland,

and that would include things that might have incidental bad effects. What matters about *Cathleen ni Houlihan* is not what moralised political attitude we may adopt towards it, but the way in which it co-ordinates passion, imagery, legend and historical association.

Cathleen ni Houlihan is still a disturbing play, so strong a charge of life does it carry. The same can be said about J.M. Synge's masterpiece *The Playboy of the Western World*, first produced at the Abbey Theatre in 1907.

> And that enquiring man John Synge comes next,
> That dying chose the living world for text . . .

So Yeats wrote of Synge in 'In Memory of Major Robert Gregory'. Yeats is linking Synge with Gregory, and both with his ideal of that to which the artist should aspire, to be 'life's epitome'. Synge, in Yeats's view, had the 'discipline' necessary to be an artist, to be someone capable of making a world which would be complete in its variety, a 'second nature' in Sidney's phrase. The 'living world' became his text, which he enquired into, elaborated, and interpreted in his work.

It is the quality of interpreted life, of life opened up, that strikes us in the *Playboy*. Time and again, in reading the *Playboy* one is struck by the uncanny way in which Synge has carried into his text the way Irish country people speak, talk and think. In my own, limited, experience I have heard West Cork people come out with locutions just as strange, feelings just as wild and terrifying, as anything in the *Playboy*. This is not a world that Synge has invented out of nothing.

In the *Playboy* we recognise the life presented to us as arising out of modes of speech and patterns of behaviour which are Irish, but the way in which they are presented to us, in the elaborate and brilliant language, makes us think about them even as we recognise them, makes us feel them strange despite our closeness to them. In a sense the riots the *Playboy* caused were a true reaction to the play's method and technique.

A Dublin audience, seeing the *Playboy*, in 1907, would realise that this was how they themselves were, or how they had been not long since. Practically everyone in that Dublin audience of 1907 would have had a relative or would have known someone living in the traditional, and, to an urban way of thinking, in the backward, way of life Synge's play re-enacts. Synge was enquiring into exactly what they were attempting to escape from into a modern world of new suburbia, where the old ways and the old codes and the old language could become a fit object of sentimental attention, but nonetheless dead. This is one of the themes of Joyce's short story 'The Dead'. The last thing most of them would have wanted was an epitome of Western life as Synge gave it.

The trouble with the *Playboy* was that Synge's play is an extraordinarily accurate reflection of Western Irish life, unsentimental, undignified, unmediated by any considerations other than the creation of that world in and for itself. His craft is so sure, his technique so perfect, his involvement with his material so total that the play becomes an entirely convincing world. All the parts interlock. Formally it is a masterpiece.

Take the language. Synge's language is vivid. It is based upon the English speech of the Irish country people of his time, with constructions and grammatical patterns taken from Irish. But the English speech of the Irish country people is itself dependent upon the grammatical and syntactical forms of Irish. The syntactical strangeness of the speech, its distance from standard English usage draws our attention to it as a thing in itself: it is 'foregrounded' in the Formalist use of that term. But the people of the play, like Irish country people, take their language seriously. In the following exchange Christy tells Pegeen, her father and his cronies that he's killed his da. Just before this Christy has been saying that his soul is damned and that he only has hanging to look forward to. Watch the way the language draws attention to itself: words like 'speaking' and 'saying' are re-iterated; and when Christy tells them what he has done Pegeen repeats what he says with an Anglo-Irish usage of the copula, that derives from Irish, and has the effect of making the players and audience think again about what Christy has said:

Pegeen   (*with a sign to the men to be quiet*): You're only saying it. You did nothing at all. A soft lad the like of you wouldn't slit the windpipe of a screeching sow.
Christy   (*offended*): You're not speaking the truth.
Pegeen   (*in mock rage*): Not speaking the truth is it? Would you have me knock the head of you with the butt of the broom?
Christy   (*twisting round on her with a sharp cry of horror*): Don't strike me. I killed my poor father, Tuesday was a week, for doing the like of that.
Pegeen   (*with blank amazement*): Is it killed your father?

In itself Pegeen's phrase is insignificant, but in the context the

Irishism 'Is it . . .' (*'An é gur mharáis t-athair?'*) followed by the verb 'killed', has the effect of drawing to our attention the emphatic way Irish people use speech and the strangeness of the act described. Also advanced here, in the play of the language, is the whole notion of the relationship between an actual thing and its 'likeness', which is a major theme of the play and one totally involved with the use of language and rhetoric: 'A soft lad *the like of you* wouldn't slit the windpipe of a screeching sow', and: 'I killed my poor father, Tuesday was a week, for doing *the like* of that'.

Through the story Christy tells and re-tells of his killing his father and in the way that story is received he discovers a new self, one that he can hardly recognise, so 'unlike' his old self is it. He looks at his likeness in the looking-glass at the beginning of Act II and remembers the old piece of glass he and his father had down in Kerry:

Christy: Didn't I know rightly I was handsome, though it was the divil's own mirror we had beyond, would twist a squint across an angel's brow; and I'll be growing fine from this day, the way I'll have a soft lovely skin on me and won't be the like of the clumsy young fellows do be ploughing all times in the earth and dung.

It is through his story, his language, that Christy's self is reborn 'fine'. The medium of the play, to which Synge pays such close attention, is the mode of Christy's transformation into a new likeness. The *Playboy* plays with possibility and in doing so opens up a world which is formally orchestrated and one in which language is continually made strange. The story Christy tells is the means by which he comes into his new likeness, but at the same time we are invited to consider the difficult relationship between an actual thing and a rendition of it in language. This is what the play of the *Playboy* plays with. All the time the audience is being invited to consider the relationship between Synge's 'likeness' of Ireland and its own likeness of it, that one in its head. How good is our capacity for story telling? How good is our capacity for the life it can unfold? How good is our capacity to entertain the second nature art can being forth?

Christy is reborn Christus Rex. But Old Mahon, St. Paul's old man, comes back. Formally, this is the most daring of all the play's devices. The story Christy tells is revealed as a story. What is to happen? In the end Christy tries to make his story good. He stretches his father with a loy a second time to find that the people who were enthralled by the tale are disgusted by the fact. The second felling takes place off stage, at which there is 'dead silence'. Pegeen says '... there's a great gap between a gallous story and a dirty deed', and Christy is bound and tortured. Again the Old Man arises, unvanquished, and comes in on all fours. Christy is himself on the floor and father and son confront each other on their knees. 'Are you coming to be killed a third time?' asks Christy. The son takes command and the two head off together. Christy, in his last speech, says to the Mayo people, 'you've turned me a *likely* gaffer in the end of all'. The likeness he has discovered for himself has not been annulled; it stays. The likeness to ourselves we see in the play's formal arrangements and reversals also stays. The likeness of the play is a likeness for our life, as it was for the people of Dublin in 1907. Too good a likeness, too formally confident and serene as it made its challenges and demands. So strongly integrated is the thing, so alive to its own motives and reverberations, so satisfyingly coherent in its arrangement of events, that we acknowledge it as something with its own life. The life that pervades it is like the life that arises in us, that cannot find expression but in the strange translation of art and drama. Again, we return to Yeats's 'First Principles' essay of 1904:

A feeling for the form of life, for the graciousness of life, for the moving limbs of life, for the nobleness of life, for all that cannot be written in codes, has always been greatest among the gifts of literature to mankind.

This is the kind of gift Synge made to Ireland in *The Playboy of the Western World*. In this play the Anglo-Irish drama has fully emerged.

SCENIC IMAGERY IN THE PLAYS OF YEATS AND BECKETT

KATHARINE WORTH

Not the least remarkable thing about the plays of these two great Irish poets is the brilliance of visual imagination displayed in them. Brilliant and memorable language we expect from poets, but the special kind of vision that relates words to pictures, fusing them into compelling dramatic images, is more rare, has indeed sometimes been denied to poets who have ventured into the theatre. There has been no doubt about Beckett's possession of this vision: from the abruptly leafing tree of *Godot* and the grey room of *Endgame* to the spectacular stage picture of the disembodied mouth in *Not I* or the strange look-alikes of *Ohio Impromptu*, his scenic images have been overwhelmingly effective, having power to haunt us almost without aid of words. Yeats's stage scenes may not have had quite that consistent memorability but certain plays have created images of similarly haunting force — *Purgatory*, for instance, or *At the Hawk's Well* — and the great diversity and originality of his scenic imagery has been a fertile source of inspiration for theatre directors and designers, as well as stimulating to the minds of audience and readers. Yeats's experiments with scene opened up new vistas for the theatre: in this context as in others, Beckett was able to begin several steps further on because Yeats had been before him.

Given the limitations, scenic and otherwise, of the embryonic theatre for which Yeats wrote his earliest plays, it is remarkable how clearly patterns of scenic imagery emerge in them. Obviously a good deal of struggle was involved. Yeats had to feel his way, acquiring practical experience by seeing his plays in performance (*The Land of Heart's Desire* first, in 1894) and then learning how to adapt his ideas to theatrical resources that were often pitifully inadequate. As Reg Skene says, he became adept at being 'content with what comes to hand'.[1] Sometimes he had

218

to abandon a stage picture that was too complex; 'for our stage and scenery were capable of little'.[2] The vision of an army of angels standing on a mountainside 'as if upon the air' at the close of *The Countess Cathleen* was not attainable on the 'pretty little miniature stage'[3] set up in Dublin's Antient Concert Rooms for the Irish Literary Theatre in 1899; nor could it be done in 1911 on the shallow stage of the Abbey Theatre. For that last production Yeats wrote a new version of the scene, adapted to the Craig screen set he had just acquired. But he retained the original image in the text he revised for *Collected Plays* in 1934, and one can see that he was not asking for something hopelessly impracticable. The angelic vision could surely have been realised in Yeats's own time by the Moscow Art Theatre, whose designer, Egorov, created in 1908 exquisite sets for Maeterlinck's other-worldly visions in *L'Oiseau bleu*, while in a technically well equipped modern theatre the challenge would scarcely be considered over-formidable by an imaginative lighting designer.

I want now to illustrate Yeats's innovative handling of scenic imagery by considering three types of image that recur consistently, even obsessively in his plays, looking out to Beckett at the close to see how he uses these types of Yeatsian imagery.

The first type occurs in the early plays and shows Yeats taking over for his own purposes a standard set of the theatre of his day; the domestic interior with window or door giving on to an outside view. Yeats took this mundane scenic arrangement and turned it into an image that expressed complex spiritual longings for another dimension of experience. His version of the quintessential interior scene of the fashionable theatre was to speak subliminally to the audience, as he believed any well chosen visual detail could be made to speak: '. . . a fragment of gold braid or a flower in the wallpaper may be an originating impulse to revolution or to philosophy'.[4]

Contrast is the basis of this image; a comfortable domestic interior, usually firelit, with food and drink in view, is set against a more romantic, impressionist scene glimpsed through open door or window, as the blue sea mist is glimpsed in *On Baile's Strand*. The image can be seen taking firmer shape as Yeats learned more about theatrical stylisation. In *The Countess Cathleen*, for instance, the setting for the opening scene was in some early versions of the much-revised play hardly to be distinguished from the standard theatrical interior of the period. The first text of 1892 describes the room in Shemus Rua's house in close prosaic detail:

The door is in the centre of the wall at the back. The window is at the right side of it, and a little catholic shrine hangs at the other. To the right is a pantry door and to the left a dim fire of bogwood.

The view through the window is similarly naturalistic — 'a wood of oak, hazel and quicken trees'. The description of the fire as 'dim' and the wood as 'half hidden in vapour and twilight' suggests an attempt to create an atmospheric effect: later, however, a much bolder stylisation was tried out. In the version revised for the 1934 collected edition, the wood seen through the door, 'painted in flat colour upon a gold or diapered sky' has become pure image, expressing the visionary dimension in which Cathleen has her being.

A similar movement from more or less conventional use of a standard set to the full stylisation which creates images can be seen in *The Land of Heart's Desire* (1894). Here the contrast between homely interior and remote, dream-like other world is sustained and central, in fact, the whole meaning of the play. Originally the scene in the Bruin kitchen where the action is set was entirely naturalistic; turf fire, dresser and so on: Maire (as she was first called) sat on a settle 'reading a yellow manuscript'. After the revisions inspired by production experiments, especially those with Craig's screens in 1911,[5] this scene was transformed into a highly expressive space which functions as a scenic image from the moment the curtain goes up. On one side of the stage we see an alcove (with table, eating utensils and crucifix on the wall) where the Bruins and the priest, Father Hart, are gathered. It is highlighted, literally, by a warm, red glow from the hearth fire. In strong contrast the forest seen through the open door is under a very different, colder light: 'The moon or a late sunset glimmers through the trees and carries the eye far off into a vague, mysterious world'. Mary now stands by the open door to read her 'old book' about the faery world: if she looks up from the books, says Yeats, she can see the wood; her orientation from the start is to the wood in the evening light, not to the homely glow of the hearth fire.

Karen Dorn has pointed out how new scenic arrangements in this play, as in the other two re-written for performance with Craig's screens in mind (*The Countess Cathleen* and *The Hour Glass*), create a language 'which not only acts with the stage space, but grows from movement'.[6] I want here to emphasise how the scene itself is handled so as to create not just an expressive picture, but a dynamic scenic image.

The simple change in Mary's position at the opening is one of the ways in which Yeats focuses attention on the door as a threshold between two worlds, one familiar, the other remote, dream-like, full of dangerous glamour. The separation of the young wife from husband and family under the 'other' light hints at the beginning what the end will be: but still there are moments of pain and difficulty: she is never unequivocally committed to either world. The door acquires a supernatural aura. Hung with a branch of 'blessed quicken wood', it becomes a shield between the young wife and the mystery beyond. When the branch is removed by the child out of the wood and an arm comes round the door, clearly visible 'in the silvery light', the shield has been destroyed under our eyes: the door is now the wide-open entrace for the forces of the unknown.

Everything is related to this scenic image which sets moonlight in opposition to firelight, the dream world beyond the door to the solid, homey room this side of it. 'Ah, but you love this firelight', says the faery child mockingly to Maurteen Bruin, showing that she knows the limits of her power over him. So Mary compares her husband with the 'great door-post' of the house, longs sadly to be the branch of blessed quicken wood hanging there. The humdrum interior was meant to suggest an 'interior' of another kind in which deep psychic impulses cross and collide: when Mary puts her foot across the threshold, she is going a long way in her mind. Her husband brings her back that time, and she never actually goes out through the door but collapses and dies in the room. Yeats designed a strange, near-expressionistic scenic effect for the moment when the faery child goes out alone. The moonlit wood was to come more alive than ever before, with 'distant dancing figures, and it may be a white bird, and many voices singing'. Deliberately equivocal, it suggests the continuing lure of the alien dimension, the extent of the power it gained over a character that could not commit herself: her last words are, 'I think that I would stay — and yet — and yet ... And yet'.

A more complex and ironic version of the contrast between interior and world beyond the door occurs in *Deirdre* (first produced in 1906, then in 1907 with Stella Patrick Campbell as Deirdre). By that time Yeats had acquired a designer capable of carrying through his ideas. The 'beautiful scene'[7] designed by Robert Gregory 'for Mrs. Patrick Campbell to play in' seems to have created in real stage terms the image Yeats conjures up in his stage directions.

As in *The Land of Heart's Desire* a strong contrast is established at the start between the warmth of the interior, here a room in Conchubar's guest house, and a colder though lovely world outside. The interior is lit by a warm glow from the brazier where the two women Musicians are crouching as the curtain goes up; later one of them lights torches from the brazier, a movement of 'dramatic value', as Yeats rightly said, for it is the last kind light on the lovers before Conchubar's trap is sprung.

Inside, warmth, light, domestic friendliness (stressed in an early version by objects like the wine flagon and loaf of bread, which Yeats cut from the 1907 production). Outside, seen through doors and windows, a wood with great spaces, a lonely, empty place. Even the 'thick-leaved coppice' framed in one window was to suggest 'silence and loneliness'. It is a wood for hunting in: Yeats wanted above all to convey the sense of Deirdre as a bird in a trap. He planned to bring out the trapped feeling in the scenic image by careful placing of the numerous doors and side-windows to allow a view of anyone approaching the door 'a moment before he enters'. These views are mostly sinister, threatening: Conchubar spying on the lovers, the dark-faced men who drag in Naoise, entangled in a net, and who stand in a group round Conchubar as he proclaims at the end that he has done right in 'letting no boy lover take the sway'.

But the contrast is not a simple one between safe interior and menacing world beyond. The room is indeed an oasis of human warmth in the darkening world that waits to engulf Deirdre and Naoise: such a feeling has come over strongly in any performance I have seen. Yet it is not a world they could live in. The great spaces outside, so beautiful as well as dangerous, are their true space, as we are reminded at the start of the play when the first Musician mentions Deirdre's name and the other asks her if she is speaking of 'That famous queen/who has been wandering with her lover Naoise/Somewhere beyond the edges of the world?'

'Were we not meant to wander?' Deirdre's question receives a silent answer from the scene beyond the window; a 'clear evening light' reveals its beauty but increases 'the sense of solitude and loneliness'. Yeats was tempted to abandon this view in favour of a striking new 'shadow' effect tried out with Craig's screens. But in his latest revision he retained the original image, understandably, for it captures exactly the austere isolation of the lovers which is most clearly felt as their destiny when they are looking out from the deceitful warmth of the interior.

In two other plays of this time Yeats rings a change on the image by having the sea rather than a wooded landscape represent the mysterious spaces outside. The off-stage sea is felt in both *On Baile's Strand* (1904) and *The Green Helmet* (1910) to be a force of sinister energy. In *The Green Helmet* the treatment of the image is high-spirited, near-surrealist, a style appropriate to the 'heroic farce' with its dream-like threats and resolutions.

Every detail of the scenic arrangement heightens the effect of an unfathomable outside force overwhelming the interior. Low rocks beyond the open door raise the ground outside, giving the 'other' world the commanding position and adding height and dominance to the figure of the Red Man when he appears outside the window. Through the windows 'one can see nothing but the sea'. Misty and moon-lit, it seems to encircle and threaten the room from the moment when the warriors assert that they 'have nothing to fear that has not come up from the tide'. But everything comes up from the tide; such is the counter-assertion made by the scenic image.

The final sequence is played in spectral green light after three black hands come through the window (a spectacular version of the 'arm round the door' in *The Land of Heart's Desire*) and put out all the lights. The ordinary light of the interior gives way to sea green which is reflected everywhere, even in the eyes of the black men: the subterranean life of the mind has taken over the scene.

The elaborate scenic image could hardly have been fully achieved in the first production at the Abbey Theatre: James Flannery shows that this and many kindred effects could not have been. [8] Certainly Yeats's ideas on scene were well ahead of the resources at his command even in 1910 (the shallow stage of the Abbey was only one impediment). In the earlier days when he wrote *On Baile's Strand*, he had scarcely any stage at all: the play was written, he said, for a 'large platform with a door at the back and exit through the audience at the side'. [9] In so restrictive a situation little in the way of scenic imagery could have been expected.

Yet Yeats not only found a practical solution to the problems raised by the lack of a curtain (Fool and Blind Man walk on to an empty stage at the start and leave it at the end); he drew out of the practicality a fine scenic image focused (as so often) on the door, the threshold between interior and world beyond. This door at the back of the stage is a focal point from the moment when the Fool flings it wide open, telling the Blind Man that he should not have shut out the 'witches' that follow him, begging for kisses: 'Boann herself out of the river and Fand out of the deep sea'. That deep sea lies beyond the door; distant and obscure in this play, a 'blue sea mist'. Yeats was cutting his coat according to this cloth: even the most sparsely furnished theatre could be expected to produce a blue lighting effect for the sea mist. But again, necessity bred invention: the obscurity of the sea, its intermittent disappearance from view when the door is shut, becomes the pivot on which the whole action turns. When Conchubar and company enter for the oath-taking ceremony they deliberately shut out the sea and set up a rival image. The red light of fire leaping in the ritual bowl changes the colour of the stage and the climate of feeling as the kings thrust their swords into the flames and take an oath which binds them to the values of the 'threshold and hearthstone'. A vivid, compelling image — till it is shattered by a sound which brings attention back to the door: a hammering and a shout of 'Open! Open!'.

Yeats's favourite contrast between domestic hearthfire and mysterious space beyond takes a poignant turn in this play. The figure revealed against the blue sea mist when the door is opened has nothing inhuman about him. The red-haired boy who challenges Cuchulain to single combat is appealing in his naive youthful ardour. Appealing too is Cuchulain's instant sense of rapport with him: he hardly needs to bring the boy into the light to see the likeness to his Amazonian love of long ago. The opening of the door functions like the opening of a barrier holding back memory and deep instinct.

But the depths cannot be acknowledged: when Cuchulain goes out through the open door to the sea, it is to fight against the boy he would rather fight with. The second time he goes out, learning too late that he has killed his son, it should seem inevitable that he makes for the sea (by-passing the human enemy, Conchubar) to release his misery and rage in the wild absurdity of fighting the waves. Yeats brings the focus back to the door then, placing the Fool on the threshold to look out into the blue mist and tell the Blind Man what he sees; a striking image of the obscure, roundabout way in which messages from the sea-depths are received in the interior. Cuchulain turned away from those misty depths, and now 'the waves have mastered him'.

The pattern of scenic imagery just considered is reversed in a second type which recurs persistently in Yeats's theatre. Instead of looking outwards to a remote but always visible world beyond, we now look inward through curtains to a world not normally visible at all. This is metatheatrical imagery, giving an overt dramatic role to stage machinery, especially to one standard piece of equipment, the stage curtain.

In the prologue written (though not used)[10] for *The King's Threshold* in 1903, the stage furnishing is drawn to the audience's attention when an old man professing to be one of the actors appears in front of the curtain, tells about the play and explains when he is interrupted: 'Well, it's time for me to be going. That trumpet means that the curtain is going to rise ...'. Inside the play proper a curtain figures again, in a different way. The curtained door at the head of the flight of steps to the King's palace blocks off the interior and seems meant to hint that the right to eat at the King's table (a somewhat curious demand) is, in fact, a mystery worth dying for, as Seanchan is about to do.

No more than tentative in *The King's Threshold*, both ideas — the curtain as a device of metatheatre and the curtain as a symbolic veil concealing a mystery — were taken up in the revised version of *The Hour Glass* written for performance in Craig's 'place' in 1912. Craig's screens might have allowed Yeats to abandon the traditional stage curtain altogether, as he was to do in the dance plays. Instead he took advantage of the opportunity offered by a stage built out over the orchestra to have Pupils and Fool perform a significant curtain raiser. The audience is drawn into complicity with them as they choose a text for study, getting the Fool to 'act' the lectern for their heavy book: an effect at once absurd and sinister as the whole scene should be. The text and the message given in a dream to one of the Pupils all seem part of a mysteriously stage-managed performance which threatens the Wise Man, seemingly so safe behind the curtain that hides all this from him.

The scenic image cunningly hints to us, before the Wise Man is forced to learn the unpalatable news, that there is a world beyond his vision. At the same time, Yeats preserves a degree of openness, even scepticism, by returning us after the Wise Man's death to our position outside the curtain, a position of ignorance where our only guide is the Fool who can see what we cannot see (the soul of the dead man as a white butterfly) but can explain nothing:

> ... all that I know, I know.
> But I cannot speak, I will run away.

Shortly after this, Yeats moved on to the more radical

experiment of the dance plays, breaking altogether from the proscenium convention. But his fascination with curtains remained: in 1935 it gave birth to striking new scenic images in the companion plays, *The King of the Great Clock Tower* and *A Full Moon in March*.

Curtains provide a means of producing the deeply recessive effect Yeats aims at in these plays. The stage curtain is drawn back to reveal yet another curtain and that is drawn back to reveal characters still kept at a distance from us by a mask or a veil. The scenic image speaks of unveiling, of movement further and further into the heart of a mystery. It is also an image of intense theatricality. The Attendants who stand with drum and gong on each side of the curtain are, among other things, stage managers who open and close the inner curtains on amazing tableaux — a king and queen seated on cubes for thrones, a queen dancing for a severed head. They are a continual presence, sometimes detached from the action, sometimes entering it, as when they supply music or a voice for dumb queen or severed head.

As always, Yeats economically turns practicalities to dramatic advantage. In *A Full Moon in March* the Queen is faced with a potentially awkward stage situation. The severed head must be presented to her before she can perform her sexual dance, but there would be no small risk of bathos if she had to go off stage to collect it — and in this version there was no King to do it for her (he was cut from the stripped-down version). Yeats deals with the problem by having the Attendants close the inner curtains twice (something that does not occur in the twin play), the second time at the point where the Queen dismisses the Swineherd to his death and drops her veil — with her back to the audience so that we still do not see her face. When the curtains are re-drawn she is found standing in the same position as before, dropped veil at her side, but holding high above her head the severed head.

A scenic image has been created which suspends time and suggests that the subterranean process leading to the song of the severed head and the Queen's dance has occurred in some remote dimension of the consciousness, that 'dark portion of the mind' behind the veil. The curtains are thus a way of showing that the erotic mystery must always remain obscure, while the emphasis on the Attendants' theatrical functions hints at the necessary theatricality of the unconscious. The chief characters must fall silent without the aid of these stage-managers. *The King of the Great Clock Tower* closes with an expressive silent image, the Queen standing framed in the half-closed inner curtains, the Attendants by the outer curtains. We are invited to realise that we have had a glimpse only into the mystery embodied in the enigmatic theatrical ritual.

Yeats was evidently fond of the curtain and its association with hidden things: he incorporated it into his dance play machinery (as the cloth unfolded and folded by the Musicians) though the open space formula did away with the need for curtains and there was no precedent for the cloth in his Nó model. It is a measure of his increased theatrical assurance that he was able to assimilate such a convention into the austere scenic imagery which constitutes the third major type in his theatre. This imagery is based on the idea of open space — empty except for one or two significant objects and the performers who work subtle magic on us, transforming the sparse details we see with the physical eye into the inner landscape they intend us to see. Yeats became so skilled at these evocations (far surpassing, one imagines, anything that happened in his Golden Dawn days!) that he could achieve them within theatrical conventions as different as those he employed in *At the Hawk's Well* (1916) and *Purgatory* (1938).

Yeats said of the former when it was first played in London drawing rooms (of the Ladies Cunard and Islington) that the audience's task was to imagine 'a mountain covered with thorn-trees in a drawing room'. An easier task now perhaps, when audiences are used to 'in the round' performance, but still it is not easy to see the invisible: the performers need many skills not just to draw the scene for us but to make us feel it.

The powerful rhythm of the Musicians' opening lines assures us at the start that we are in the hands of true theatre magicians who will be able to achieve this:

> I call to the eye of the mind
> A well long choked up and dry
> And boughs long stripped by the wind ...

The lonely mountainside comes before the mind's eye even as we note the intense theatricality of what is before the physical eye; the masked actors coming in through the audience, close enough to touch, the square of blue cloth which represents the well, the one scenic property apart from the patterned screen which Yeats envisaged as background (it is not strictly necessary). Very soon the blue cloth ceases to seem a theatrical property: Yeats amuses himself by testing our state of mind: it is the audience as well as the Young Man whom the Old Man challenges to look round the empty space and see what he sees:

> And are there not before your eyes at the instant
> Grey boulders and a solitary girl
> And three stripped hazels?

'Yes', we have to say, and yes, we see with the Musicians the water bubbling in the well after a spell-binding dance has been performed; and yes, we see with the Old Man the stones dark with the water he and the Young Man will never taste.

Yeats had found an image to satisfy both the dreamer and the sceptic in himself; so it can be for an audience. The bare scene, the square of blue cloth are a mocking reminder that it is all an illusion. But if the play works and the audience is won by the illusion (I have never seen it fail) our awareness that the landscape was drawn from empty air becomes part of the play's meaning; a mystery of creativity has been revealed.

Returning to the proscenium convention in *Purgatory* (1938), Yeats drew on the experience of the dance plays to create a scenic image that brings his theatre very close to Beckett's. The scene inside the proscenium frame is no longer the elaborate picture of earlier plays, foreground interior carefully contrasted with distant vista. Now the stage is an undefined space dominated by two objects which become ominous focal points for an act of mesmerism. Never were Yeats's stage directions more sparse: 'Scene. — A ruined house and a bare tree'. This is a play, like the dance plays, that can be set up anywhere: I last saw it performed in a café space at Sligo without any scenery: no ruin, no tree; they had to be deduced from the reactions of the actors.

The play can work in this way, as it did on that occasion, but it was not what Yeats intended. He wanted his audience to see for themselves the fatal objects; first in a normal light and then as they appear when transfigured by the obsessive imagination of the Old Man. Light was to be the theatrical agent of the transfiguration. Yeats had long been aware of the potentiality of theatre lighting and by the 1930s more sophisticated equipment was available to him than in earlier years.

In *Purgatory* he used it to create one of his most haunting scenic images. Three times the stage lights up in a way which takes us out of the bare external scene into the Old Man's startlingly peopled inner landscape. A window comes alight in the ruin to show a young girl standing in a room that cannot be there, lights again to show a man pouring whiskey into a glass; finally the tree is flooded with white light and stands out, a brilliant object, against the dark that descends on the stage with the murder of the Boy.

Directors have had difficulty in dealing with the ghostly figures: they are a hazard, liable to tip the play to melodrama. Perhaps they are expendable: what we must have, however, is the light — a theatrical ray of moonlight, appropriate to the histrionic Old Man — falling on objects which for him exist in some mysterious other dimension. Yeats induces us to see them in that way too: before the Boy does, we see the ghostly tableau behind the window we know does not really exist. Seeing is believing: it is hard to escape the mesmeric power that has conjured up the past in the vivid image. The Boy must seem imperceptive to us: how can he not see what is so clear (an effect lost, of course, if there is no lighted house). [11] Finally when the light falls on the bare tree, it might be hard not to feel, if only for a moment and against our will, that the glistening white object does represent, as the Old Man claims, some kind of spiritual release:

> Dear mother, the window is dark again,
> But you are in the light . . .

The murder of his own son is madness, we cannot doubt it — yet neither perhaps can we doubt that he is in touch with some awful truth beyond himself, distorted though it may have become in its passage through his mind.

Purgatory points the way to *Waiting for Godot* (1952, in French). Beckett's first play proclaims its Yeatsian affinities in scene as in other ways: his opening stage direction, equally sparse as that for *Purgatory*, calls for 'A country road. A tree. Evening'. *Endgame* (1957, in French) shows still more clearly Beckett beginning at a point where Yeats left off.

That image of the windowed interior which Yeats worked on for so many years takes instant form in Beckett's play, totally stylised, startlingly distinctive and in a way un-Yeatsian; yet recognisably the same image, the domestic interior with its distant view of a mysterious space beyond.

The view is very distant in *Endgame*. It is much harder to see out of this grey interior with its door that gives only on to another room and its small, curtained windows set so high that

Clov has to climb a ladder to reach them. Even then he needs a telescope to see anything — and Hamm, who is most avid for the view, is blind. From the audience too the view beyond the room is shut off. Shut off from the physical eye, that is. Despite the difficulty of 'seeing', or perhaps because of it (we are dependent on Clov's comic labours for a report on the unseen world) the space beyond the 'familiar chamber' (Beckett's wry word for his interior sets) acquires extraordinary reality. It contains both landscape (seen through the right-hand window) and sea scape (seen through the left one) and though it seems empty and lifeless — 'Zero . . . zero . . . and zero', Clov reports — by the end of the play something stirs in it. Astonishingly the figure of a small boy is seen through the 'earth' window.

The visitation, if such it is, is not welcomed. Hamm's feelings about the world beyond the window are ambivalent. He longs to drag himself down to the sea 'and the tide would come'. At the same time he is totally attached to the interior: 'Outside of here it's death'. Just such an ambivalence characterises the attitude to the other world in the Yeatsian interior. And Beckett's closeness to Yeats continued to show itself when he moved to another kind of scenic imagery, the metatheatrical type that gives an overt dramatic role to items of stage machinery.

For Beckett light is the crucial agent. The image of purgatory created in *Play* (1964) depends on the brilliantly simple notion of taking the spotlight from its usual humble background role to make it an actor in the piece. Really an actor: Beckett wanted built-in variations of speed and intensity in the intricate lighting plot to suggest that the spotlight was not altogether outside the purgatorial experience but was to some extent a 'victim of his own inquiry': it was to 'act the part'. It was also performing a dual role as ordinary theatre spotlight, focusing on each of three actors in turn, and as 'unique inquisitor', terrorising with light and drawing responses as if to a sentient being: ' . . . Get off me (*vehement*). Get off me! . . .'.

As Yeats manipulated the stage curtains, so Beckett uses the spotlight to probe into what is hidden, revealing deep psychic patterns behind the superficial sexual drama of his adulterous trio: they too are severed heads in a way, faces stuck in urns, cut off from their bodies. The open theatricality of a scenic image based on spotlight and black-out has the same sort of appropriateness to these beings (they have a garishly histrionic view of themselves) as the flamboyant handling of the stage curtain had to Yeats's King and Queen, performing their well-rehearsed rituals.

The scenic image of *Play* also shows how Beckett seized on the Yeatsian concept of the bare stage as a means of suggesting inner space. A characteristic setting in his later plays is a dark space where light falls on one or two strange objects. The object might be a rocking chair that gleams hypnotically as it rocks and catches the light, or a human head, or, stranger still, a Mouth babbling away on its own, '... whole body like gone ...'.

Emptiness and darkness acquire forceful dramatic life in these extraordinary scenic images. Anything that is lit becomes an object of concentration, of a sort unusual in the theatre (or perhaps out of it). In *That Time* we have nothing at all to look at except the face of the old man listening to his own voices, an 'old white face, long flaring white hair as if seen from above, outspread'. What the Listener makes us see, however, is the whole landscape of his life, its 'times' and places — and the state of mind in which he is ending it. For in this starved scene we notice everything, from the opening and closing of eyes to the smile 'toothless for preference' on which the old man's reverie concludes. So in *Not I*: the awkward orientation of the floating, luridly lit Mouth to the dimly lit Auditor on the high podium is an image of unease and dissociation; it tells us silently what Mouth tells volubly, and at the same time hints that what she tells could be seen differently — if only the Auditor's presence could be taken into her account of her wretched life.

Yeats would surely have recognised behind such images dramatic purposes very similar to his own. The treatment of stage space in his plays and in Beckett's is part of an evocation which can make us see (if only fleetingly) a bare tree as a 'purified soul', the 'rounded inward curving arms' of a rocking chair as the embrace of a force that moves human souls through life. Small wonder that the writer of *Rockaby* and *Play* should have chosen to pay tribute to Yeats in an image drawn from that most influential of plays, *At the Hawk's Well*;[12] he would give the whole of Shaw, he said (sharing Yeats's prejudice on that subject!) for a 'sup of the Hawk's well'. The two playwrights who are linked in so many ways are alike above all in this: they are painters and sculptors of the theatre, as well as its poets.

NOTES

1   R. Skene, *The Cuchulain Plays of W.B. Yeats.* London: Macmillan, 1974.

2   Preface to *Poems* (rev. ed.). London: 1901.
3   See R. Hogan and M. O'Neill, *Joseph Holloway's Abbey Theatre*. Carbondale: Southern Illinois Press, 1967.
4   In W.B. Yeats, *Autobiographies*. London: Macmillan, 1955, p.263.
5   See especially J.W. Flannery, *Yeats and the Idea of a Theatre*. New Haven and London: Yale University Press, 1976.
6   K. Dorn, 'Dialogue into Movement', in R. O'Driscoll and L. Reynolds, *Yeats and the Theatre*. Toronto: Macmillan Company of Canada, 1975, p.119.
7   Dedication to *Deirdre* (1907 edition onwards).
8   J.W. Flannery, *op.cit*, p.256.
9   Preface to *Plays in Prose and Verse*. London: Macmillan, 1922.
10   The prologue was printed in *The United Irishman*, 9 September 1903.
11   I have seen a strong effect achieved in a Departmental student production at Royal Holloway College by light falling on a piece of stage machinery (a telescope) which represented the house.
12   In Shaw Centenary programme, Gaiety Theatre, Dublin, 1956.

NOTES ON CONTRIBUTORS

Eugene Benson, Professor of English at the University of Guelph, is a novelist, playwright and librettist whose operas have been performed by the Stratford Festival (Ontario), the Canadian Opera Company, and the Guelph Spring Festival. He is the editor of the anthology *Encounter: Canadian Drama in Four Media* and of the journal *Canadian Drama/L'Art dramatique canadien*. His most recent publication is *J.M. Synge*, Macmillan (1982). His work in progress includes co-editing a forthcoming *Oxford Companion to Canadian Drama and Theatre*. He is a former Chairman of The Writers' Union of Canada and is presently Co-President of P.E.N. (Canada).

Richard Allen Cave, formerly a Scholar of St. Catharine's College, Cambridge, is Reader in Drama at Royal Holloway and Bedford New College in the University of London. His publications include *A Critical Study of the Novels of George Moore* and editions of Moore's *Hail and Farewell* and *The Lake; Terence Gray and the Festival Theatre Cambridge; The Dublin Gate Theatre: 1928–1978* (with Richard Pine); and a range of essays on the modern theatre and on Anglo-Irish drama. He is Honorary Secretary of the Consortium for Drama and Media in Higher Education; the Accredited Representative for the United Kingdom in IASAIL; and General Editor of the series of monographs on theatre history, *Theatre in Focus*.

Emelie FitzGibbon read for degrees in English and Music at University College, Cork, where she has held a part-time teaching post in English Literature and Drama since 1976. She is a regular reviewer of books on drama and theatre studies for the journal *Books Ireland*, and is a regional editor of *Theatre Ireland*. She has written York Notes on Emily Dickinson's poems and Shaw's *The Devil's Disciple*. She is a member of the board of directors of the Cork Theatre Company and has directed

233

several productions for that company. In 1985 she founded the Munster theatre-in-education company, GRAFFITI, of which she is Artistic Director.

Nicholas Grene was born in Chicago but grew up in Ireland. A graduate of Trinity College Dublin, he took his doctorate at the University of Cambridge and lectured for several years at the University of Liverpool before returning to Trinity where he is now Fellow and Director of Studies in Modern English. He is the author of three books, *Synge: a Critical Study of the Plays* (1975), *Shakespeare, Jonson, Molière: the Comic Contract* (1980) and *Bernard Shaw: a Critical View* (1984), and he has edited Synge's *The Well of the Saints*. He is currently working on Shakespearean tragedy.

Heinz Kosok studied at the universities of Marburg and Bristol. He obtained his Dr. phil. in 1960 for a dissertation on the influence of the Gothic Novel on the fiction of Herman Melville, and his *Habilitation* in 1970 for a book on the plays of Sean O'Casey. In 1972, he was appointed to the Chair of English and American Literature in the new University of Wuppertal. From 1982 to 1985, he served as Chairman of the International Association for the Study of Anglo-Irish Literature. Prof. Kosok has published widely, both in English and German, on a variety of subjects from eighteenth, nineteenth, and twentieth-century English, American and Anglo-Irish Literature.

D.E.S. Maxwell, born in Derry in 1925, was educated at Foyle College and Trinity College, Dublin. He has been a Lecturer in English at the University of Ghana (1956–61), then worked in the Civil Service Commission, London (1961–3). He was Professor of English at the University of Ibadan (1963–7) before taking up his present post as Professor of English, York University, Toronto in 1967. He was Master of Winters College 1969–79. His publications include *The Poetry of T.S. Eliot* (1952), *American Fiction* (1963), *Yeats Centenary Essays* (ed. with S.B. Bushrui 1965), *Poets of the Thirties* (1969), *Brian Friel* (1973), and *Modern Irish Drama* (1984).

Vivian Mercier, born in Dublin in 1919, grew up in Clara, Offaly. Educated at Portora and Trinity (Ph.D. 1945), he has taught in the U.S.A. for almost forty years, at Bennington, City University of New York, University of Colorado, and, since

1974, at the University of California, Santa Barbara. As well as hundreds of articles and reviews, his books include *The Irish Comic Tradition* (1962), *The New Novel: From Queneau to Pinget* (1971, including a chapter on Claude Simon, the new Nobel winner), and *Beckett/Beckett* (1977). Since 1977 he has been writing a two volume history of Anglo-Irish literature from the beginning of the Revival to the present, for the Clarendon Press.

Christopher Murray was an undergraduate at University College, Galway, and subsequently took his Ph.D. at Yale University. He is currently a statutory lecturer in the Department of English at University College, Dublin. He has written *Robert William Elliston Manager* (1975), has edited a restoration comedy, *St. Stephen's Green*, by William Philips (1980) and was guest editor of the special issue of *Irish University Review* on Sean O'Casey in 1980. His *Selected Plays of Lennox Robinson* was published in 1982. He has written numerous articles on Irish theatre and drama and contributed to the latest edition of the *Oxford Companion to the Theatre.* He was secretary of IASAIL 1973–76, and is currently on the executive board of *Irish University Review.* He is working on a biography of the nineteenth-century Irish playwright James Sheridan Knowles.

Andrew Parkin was educated at Pembroke College, Cambridge, where he was an Open Exhibitioner in English; he earned his doctorate from the Drama Department of Bristol University. He has taught English and Irish Literature and Drama in England, Hong Kong, and Canada, where he now lectures at the University of British Columbia. Author of *The Dramatic Imagination of W.B. Yeats* (1978) and Editor of *The Canadian Journal of Irish Studies*, his latest work is *Selected Plays of Dion Boucicault* to be published this year by Colin Smythe.

Masaru Sekine, a trained Noh actor, is a graduate of Waseda University, Tokyo. As a British Council scholar, he studied at the Universities of Manchester and Stirling. He was a Research Curator at Waseda University's Theatre Museum and Lecturer in English and Drama, before becoming an Associate Professor at Waseda University. He has written on various aspects of modern drama; his translation of *Pippin* was produced at the Imperial Theatre, Tokyo in 1976. He is the International Representative of IASAIL-Japan. He has written *Ze-Ami and His Theories of Noh Drama* (1985) and has edited *Irish Writers and Society at Large* (1985), both published by Colin Smythe Ltd. He is currently Japan Foundation visiting Professor at University College, Dublin.

James Simmons was born in Londonderry in 1933 and educated at the University of Leeds. He lectured at the University of Ulster until 1983. His eighth volume of poetry, *From the Irish* was published by Blackstaff Press in 1985, a critical book on O'Casey was published by Macmillan in 1983, and an L.P. of his songs *Love in the Post* sung by himself, was issued by Poor Genius Records in 1974. He was the founding editor of *The Honest Ulsterman* (1968).

Sumiko Sugiyama was educated at Kwansei Gakuin University, Japan, and at the University of Leicester where she worked on Yeats for the degree of M.Phil. under the supervision of the late G.S. Fraser and Professor J.S. Cunningham. She is now teaching English at Shinshu University, Matsumoto, Japan. *Yeats: Fatherland and Song*, the direct result of her research work at Leicester, was published in 1985; it surveys the development of Yeats's poetry in terms of its relation to that most exciting period in Irish history in which he lived.

Robert Welch is a graduate of University College Cork and the University of Leeds. He has been a Lecturer at the University of Ife, Nigeria, and at the University of Leeds, and is Professor of English and Head of the Department of English, Media and Theatre Studies at the University of Ulster. He is the author of *Irish Poetry from Moore to Yeats* (1980), *The Way Back* (1982) and *A History of Verse Translation from the Irish: 1789–1897* (1986). He is at work on a *Companion to Irish Literature*.

Katharine Worth holds the Chair of Drama and Theatre Studies in the University of London and is Head of the Department of Drama and Theatre Studies at Royal Holloway College. Her published works include *Oscar Wilde* (1983); *The Irish Drama of Europe* (1978); *Revolutions in Modern English Drama* (1973); chapters in *Eliot in Perspective* (edited by Graham Martin), on Edward Bond in *Contemporary English Drama* and on Edward Albee in *Contemporary American Drama*. She edited the symposium *Beckett the Shape Changer* (1975), and has made new productions with the University of London Audio-Visual Centre of Beckett's *Eh Joe*, *Words and Music*, *Embers* and *Cascando*. Her

Maeterlinck's Plays in Performance, a slide-set with critical monograph, was published by Chadwick-Healey in 1985.

INDEX

Note. In the listing of titles under individual writers the words 'A' and 'The' have been disregarded so far as alphabetical arrangement is concerned.